CHILTON'S
REPAIR & TUNE-UP GUIDE
CHRYSLER K- and E-CARS 1981-85

All U.S. and Canadian models of DODGE Aries, DODGE 400, DODGE 600 • PLYMOUTH Caravelle, PLYMOUTH Reliant • CHRYSLER E-Class, New Yorker, LeBaron, Town & Country, Executive Sedan

President LAWRENCE A. FORNASIERI
Vice President and General Manager JOHN P. KUSHNERICK
Executive Editor KERRY A. FREEMAN, S.A.E.
Senior Editor RICHARD J. RIVELE, S.A.E.
Editor JOHN M. BAXTER

CHILTON BOOK COMPANY
Radnor, Pennsylvania
19089

SAFETY NOTICE

Proper service and repair procedures are vital to the safe, reliable operation of all motor vehicles, as well as the personal safety of those performing repairs. This book outlines procedures for servicing and repairing vehicles using safe, effective methods. The procedures contain many NOTES, CAUTIONS and WARNINGS which should be followed along with standard safety procedures to eliminate the possibility of personal injury or improper service which could damage the vehicle or compromise its safety.

It is important to note that repair procedures and techniques, tools and parts for servicing motor vehicles, as well as the skill and experience of the individual performing the work vary widely. It is not possible to anticipate all of the conceivable ways or conditions under which vehicles may be serviced, or to provide cautions as to all of the possible hazards that may result. Standard and accepted safety precautions and equipment should be used when handling toxic or flammable fluids, and safety goggles or other protection should be used during cutting, grinding, chiseling, prying, or any other process that can cause material removal or projectiles.

Some procedures require the use of tools specially designed for a specific purpose. Before substituting another tool or procedure, you must be completely satisfied that neither your personal safety, nor the performance of the vehicle will be endangered.

Although information in this guide is based on industry sources and is as complete as possible at the time of publication, the possibility exists that the manufacturer made later changes which could not be included here. While striving for total accuracy, Chilton Book Company cannot assume responsibility for any errors, changes, or omissions that may occur in the compilation of this data.

PART NUMBERS

Part numbers listed in this reference are not recommendations by Chilton for any product by brand name. They are references that can be used with interchange manuals and aftermarket supplier catalogs to locate each brand supplier's discrete part number.

SPECIAL TOOLS

Special tools are recommended by many vehicle manufacturers to perform specific jobs. Use has been kept to a minimum in this guide, but, where absolutely necessary, special tools are referred to in the text by the part number of the tool manufacturer. These tools can be purchased, under the appropriate part number from Miller Special Tools, Division of Utica Tool Company, Inc., 32615 Park Lane, Garden City, Michigan 48135 or an equivalent tool can be purchased locally from a tool supplier or parts outlet. Before substituting any tool for the one recommended, read the SAFETY NOTICE at the top of this page.

ACKNOWLEDGMENTS

Chilton Book Company wishes to express appreciation to the Chrysler Motor Corporation, Detroit, Michigan, for their generous assistance in the preparation of this book.

Copyright © 1985 by Chilton Book Company
All Rights Reserved
Published in Radnor, Pennsylvania 19089, by Chilton Book Company

Manufactured in the United States of America
1234567890 7890123456

Chilton's Repair & Tune-Up Guide: Chrysler K– and E–Cars 1981–85
ISBN 0-8019-7562-X pbk.
Library of Congress Catalog Card No. 84-45488

CONTENTS

1 General Information and Maintenance
- 1 How to Use this Book
- 1 Tools and Equipment
- 6 Routine Maintenance and Lubrication

2 Tune-Up and Performance Maintenance
- 24 Tune-Up Procedures
- 27 Tune-Up Specifications

3 Engine and Engine Rebuilding
- 32 Engine Electrical System
- 35 Engine Service and Specifications

4 Emission Controls and Fuel System
- 61 Emission Control System and Service
- 66 Fuel System Service

5 Chassis Electrical
- 76 Accessory Service
- 81 Instrument Panel Service
- 82 Lights, Fuses and Flashers

58 Chilton's Fuel Economy and Tune-Up Tips

6 Clutch and Transaxle
- 83 Manual Transaxle
- 87 Clutch
- 88 Automatic Transaxle

7 Suspension and Steering
- 92 Front Suspension
- 95 Rear Suspension
- 97 Steering

8 Brakes
- 104 Front Brakes
- 107 Rear Brakes
- 111 Brake Specifications

9 Troubleshooting
- 113 Problem Diagnosis

- 146 Mechanic's Data
- 148 Index

122 Chilton's Body Repair Tips

Quick Reference Specifications For Your Vehicle

Fill in this chart with the most commonly used specifications for your vehicle. Specifications can be found in Chapters 1 through 3 or on the tune-up decal under the hood of the vehicle.

Tune-Up

Firing Order_____

Spark Plugs:

    Type_____

    Gap (in.)_____

Point Gap (in.)_____

Dwell Angle (°)_____

Ignition Timing (°)_____

    Vacuum (Connected/Disconnected)_____

Valve Clearance (in.)

    Intake_____ Exhaust_____

Capacities

Engine Oil (qts)

    With Filter Change_____

    Without Filter Change_____

Cooling System (qts)_____

Manual Transmission (pts)_____

    Type_____

Automatic Transmission (pts)_____

    Type_____

Front Differential (pts)_____

    Type_____

Rear Differential (pts)_____

    Type_____

Transfer Case (pts)_____

    Type_____

FREQUENTLY REPLACED PARTS

Use these spaces to record the part numbers of frequently replaced parts.

PCV VALVE

Manufacturer_____

Part No._____

OIL FILTER

Manufacturer_____

Part No._____

AIR FILTER

Manufacturer_____

Part No._____

General Information and Maintenance

HOW TO USE THIS BOOK

This book is written to help the Chrysler K- and E-car owner in performing maintenance, tune-ups and repairs on his vehicle. It will be helpful to both the amateur and experienced mechanic. Information on simple operations and more complex ones is given, allowing the user to try procedures which he or she feels confident in doing and graduating to the more difficult task as more experience is gained.

In addition to this book, a willingness to do your own work, and the time to do it right, there are a few other items you have to be aware that you will need. A basic but complete set of metric and SAE hand tools is a must. For many repair operations the factory recommends special tools be used. A conventional tool can be substituted for the special tool in a lot of cases. For those operations requiring a special tool for which no substitution can be made, this fact is called to your attention in the text. Remember that whenever the left-side of the vehicle is referred to, it is the driver's side of the car and vice versa. Also, most screws and bolts are removed by turning them counterclockwise and tightened by turning them clockwise. Left-handed threads (the opposite of above) will be brought to your attention in the text.

Before you start any project, read the entire section in the book that deals with the particular job you wish to perform. Many times a description of the system and its operation is given. This will enable you to understand the function of the system you will be working on and what must be done to fix it. Reading the procedures beforehand will help you avoid problems and to learn about your Aries/Reliant while you are working on it.

TOOLS AND EQUIPMENT

It would be impossible to catalog each and every tool that you may need to perform all the operations included in this book. It would also not be wise for the amateur to rush out and buy an expensive set of tools on the theory that he may need one of them at some time. The best approach is to proceed slowly, gathering together a good quality set of those tools that are used most frequently. Don't be misled by the low cost of bargain tools. It is far better to spend a little more for quality, name brand tools. Forged wrenches, 10 or 12 point sockets and fine-tooth ratchets are by far preferable to their less expensive counterparts. As any good mechanic can tell you, there are a few worse experiences than trying to work on a car or truck with bad tools. Your monetary savings will be far outweighed by frustration and mangled knuckles.

Begin accumulating those tools that are used most frequently; those associated with routine maintenance and tune-up. In addition to the normal assortment of screwdrivers and pliers, you should have the following tools for routine maintenance jobs:

1. SAE and Metric wrenches, sockets and combination open end/box end wrenches;
2. Jackstands—for support;
3. Oil filter wrench;
4. Oil filler spout or funnel;
5. Grease gun—for chassis lubrication;
6. Hydrometer—for checking the battery;
7. A low flat pan for draining oil;
8. Lots of rags for wiping up the inevitable mess.

In addition to the above items, there are several others that are not absolutely necessary,

2 GENERAL INFORMATION AND MAINTENANCE

but are handy to have around. These include oil drying compound, a transmission funnel, and the usual supply of lubricants, antifreeze and fluids, although these can be purchased as needed. This is a basic list for routine maintenance, but only your personal needs can accurately determine your list of tools.

The second list of tools is for tune-ups. While the tools involved here are slightly more sophisticated, they need not be outrageously expensive. There are several inexpensive tach/dwell meters on the market that are every bit as good for the average mechanic as a $100.00 professional model. Just be sure that it goes to at least 1200–1500 rpm on the tach scale, and that it works on 4, 6, and 8-cylinder engines. A basic list of tune-up equipment could include:

1. Tach/dwell meter;
2. Spark plug wrench;
3. Timing light (preferably a DC light that works from the battery);
4. A set of flat feeler gauges;
5. A set of round wire spark plug gauges.

In addition to these basic tools, there are several other tools and gauges you may find useful. These include:

1. A compression gauge. The screw-in type is slower to use, but eliminates the possibility of a faulty reading due to escaping pressure;
2. A manifold vacuum gauge;
3. A test light;
4. An induction meter. This is used for determinig whether or not there is current in a wire. These are handy for use if a wire is broken somewhere in a wiring harness. As a final note, you will probably find a torque wrench necessary for all but the most basic work. The beam type models are perfectly adequate, although the newer click type are more precise.

Special Tools

Normally, the use of special factory tools is avoided for repair procedures, since these are not readily available for the do-it-yourself mechanic. When it is possible to perform the job with more commonly available tools, it will be pointed out, but occasionally, a special tool was designed to perform a specific function and should be used. Before substituting another tool, you should be convinced that neither your safety nor the performance of the vehicle will be compromised.

Some special tools are available commercially from major tool manufacturers. Others for your Chrysler K-Car can be purchased from your dealer or from Utica Tool Co. (see the copyright page for the complete address).

SERVICING YOUR VEHICLE SAFELY

It is virtually impossible to anticipate all of the hazards involved with maintenance and service but care and common sense will prevent most accidents.

The rules of safety for mechanics range from "don't smoke around gasoline," to "use the proper tool for the job." The trick to avoiding injuries is to develop safe work habits and take every possible precaution.

Dos

• Do keep a fire extinguisher and first aid kit within easy reach.
• Do wear safety glasses or goggles when cutting, drilling, grinding or prying. If you wear glasses for the sake of vision, they should be made of hardened glass that can serve also as safety glasses, or wear safety goggles over your regular glasses.
• Do shield your eyes whenever you work around the battery. Batteries contain sulphuric acid. In case of contact with the eyes or skin, flush the area with water or a mixture of water and baking soda and get medical attention immediately.
• Do use jackstands for any undercar service. Jacks are for raising vehicles; jackstands are for making sure the vehicle stays raised until you want it to come down. Whenever your vehicle is raised, block the wheels remaining on the ground and set the parking brake.
• Do use adequae ventilation when working with any chemicals or hazardous materials.
• Do disconnect the negative battery cable when working on the electrical system. The secondary ignition system can contain up to 40,000 volts.
• Do follow manufacturer's directions whenever working with potentially hazardous materials. Both brake fluid and antifreeze are poisonous if taken internally.
• Do properly maintain your tools. Loose hammerheads, mushroomed punches and chisels, frayed or poorly grounded electrical cords, excessively worn screwdrivers, spread wrenches, cracked sockets, slipping ratchets, or faulty droplight sockets can cause accidents.
• Do use the proper size and type of tool for the job being done.
• Do when possible, pull on a wrench handle rather than push on it, and adjust your stance to prevent a fall.
• Do be sure that adjustable wrenches are tightly closed on the nut or bolt and pulled so that the face is on the side of the fixed jaw.

GENERAL INFORMATION AND MAINTENANCE

- Do select a wrench or socket that fits the nut or bolt. The wrench or socket should sit straight, not cocked.
- Do strike squarely with a hammer; avoid glancing blows.
- Do set the parking brake and block the drive wheels if the work requires the engine running.

Don'ts

- Don't run an engine in a garage or anywhere else without proper ventilation—EVER! Carbon monoxide is poisonous; it takes a long time to leave the human body and you can build up a deadly supply of it in your system by simply breathing in a little every day. You may not realize you are slowly poisoning yourself. Always use power vents, windows, fans or open the garage doors.
- Don't work around moving parts while wearing a necktie or other loose clothing. Short sleeves are much safer than long, loose sleeves; hard-toed shoes with neoprene soles protect your toes and give a better grip on slippery surfaces. Jewelry such as watches, fancy belt buckles, beads or body adornment of any kind is not safe working around a truck. Long hair should be hidden under a hat or cap.
- Don't use pockets for toolboxes. A fall or bump can drive a screwdriver deep into your body. Even a wiping cloth hanging from the back pocket can wrap around a spinning shaft or fan.
- Don't smoke when working around gasoline, cleaning solvent or other flammable material.
- Don't smoke when working around the battery. When the battery is being charged, it gives off explosive hydrogen gas.
- Don't use gasoline to wash your hands; there are excellent soaps available. Gasoline may contain lead, and lead can enter the body through a cut, accumulating in the body until you are very ill. Gasoline also removes all the natural oils from the skin so that bone dry hands will absorb oil and grease.
- Don't service the air conditioning system unless you are equipped with the necessary tools and training. The refrigerant, R-12, is extremely cold when compressed, and when released into the air will instantly freeze any surface it contacts, including your eyes. Although the refrigerant is normally non-toxic R-12 becomes a deadly poisonous gas in the presence of an open flame. One good whiff of the vapors from burning refrigerant can be fatal.

SERIAL NUMBER IDENTIFICATION

Vehicle

The vehicle serial number is located on a plate on the top left side of the instrument panel and is visible through the windshield. The VIN consists of 17 elements embossed on a gray colored plate. The chart below interprets each letter or number according to its position in the sequence for each model year.

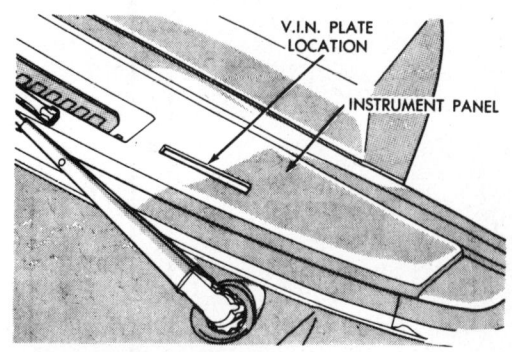

Location of V.I.N. plate

Engine Identification Number

All engine assemblies carry an engine identification number. The 135 cu. in. (2.2 Liter) engine identification number is located on the left rear face of the block directly under the head. The 156 cu. in. (2.6 Liter) identification number is located on the left side of the block between the core plug and the rear of the block.

Engine Serial Number

In addition to the EIN, each number has a serial number, which must be referred to when ordering engine replacement parts. The serial number on the 135 cu. in. (2.2 Liter) engine is located on the rear face of the block directly below the head. On the 156 cu. in. (2.6 Liter) engine it is located on the right front side of the engine block, adjacent to the exhaust manifold.

Transaxle Identification Number and Transaxle Serial Number

The Transaxle Identification Number is stamped on a boss located on the upper part of the transaxle housing. Every transaxle also carries an assembly part number, which is also required for parts ordering purposes. On the A-412 manual transaxle, it is located on the top of

GENERAL INFORMATION AND MAINTENANCE

VIN Code Chart

Position	1981	1982	1983	1984	1985
1 Country of Origin	1—US	1—US	1—US	1—US 2—Canada 3—Mexico 4—Japan	1—US 2—Canada 3—Mexico 4—Japan
2 Make	B—Dodge P—Plymouth	B—Dodge C—Chrysler P—Plymouth	B—Dodge C—Chrysler P—Plymouth	B—Dodge C—Chrysler P—Plymouth	B—Dodge C—Chrysler P—Plymouth
3 Gen'l Vehicle Type	3—Pass. Car	3—Pass. Car	3—Pass. Car	3—Pass. Car	3—Pass. Car
4 Passenger Safety System	B—Man. Seat Belts	B—Man. Seat Belts D—3000 lbs. GVW	B—Man. Seat Belts D—3000 lbs. GVW	B—Man. Seat Belts D—3000 lbs. GVW	B—Man. Seat Belts D—3000 lbs. GVW
5 Car Line	K—Aries & Reliant	C—Le Baron D—Aires P—Reliant V—400	C—Le Baron D—Aries E—600 D—Reliant T—New Yorker V—400	C—Le Baron D—Aries E—600 M—Horizon P—Reliant T—New Yorker/E Class V—600	C—Le Baron/ET5 D—Aries E—600 T—New Yorker P—Reliant V—600
6 Series	1—Economy 2—Low 3—High 5—Premium	1—Economy 2—Low 4—High 5—Premium 6—Special	1—Economy 2—Low 4—High 5—Premium 6—Special	1—Economy 2—Low 4—High 5—Premium 6—Special	1—Economy 2—Low 4—High 5—Premium 6—Special

GENERAL INFORMATION AND MAINTENANCE 5

7 Body Style	1—2 Dr. Sedan 4—2+2 Hatchback 5—2 Dr. Convertible 6—4 Dr. Sedan 8—4 Dr. Hatchback 9—4 Dr. Wagon	1—2 Dr. Sedan 2—2 Dr. Specialty Hardtop 4—2+2 Hatchback 5—2 Dr. Convertible 6—4 Dr. Sedan 8—4 Dr. Hatchback 9—4 Dr. Wagon	1—2 Dr. Sedan 2—2 Dr. Specialty Hardtop 3—2 Dr. Hardtop 4—2 Dr. Hatchback 5—2 Dr. Convertible 6—4 Dr. Sedan 8—4 Dr. Hatchback 9—4 Dr. Wagon	1—2 Dr. Sedan 2—2 Dr. Specialty Hardtop 3—2 Dr. Hardtop 4—2 Dr. Hatchback 5—2 Dr. Convertible 6—4 Dr. Sedan 8—4 Dr. Hatchback 9—4 Dr. Wagon	1—2 Dr. Sedan 2—2 Dr. Specialty Hardtop 3—2 Dr. Hardtop 4—2 Dr. Hatchback 5—2 Dr. Convertible 6—4 Dr. Sedan 8—4 Dr. Hatchback 9—4 Dr. Wagon
8 Engine	B—2.2L D—2.6L	B—2.2L C—2.2L Turbocharged D—2.6L	C—2.2L G—2.6L	C—2.2L D—2.2L EFI E—2.2L Turbocharged G—2.6L	C—2.2L D—2.2L EFI E—2.2L Turbocharged G—2.6L
9 Check Digit	The digit in position 9 is used for VIN verification. "1–9", "0", or "X"				
10 Model Year	B—'81	C—'82	D—'83	E—'84	F—'85
11 Assembly Plant	C—Jefferson D—Belvidere F—Newark	C—Jefferson D—Belvidere F—Newark G—St. Louis	C—Jefferson D—Belvidere F—Newark G—St. Louis	C—Jefferson D—Belvidere F—Newark G—St. Louis X—Missouri	C—Jefferson D—Belvidere F—Newark G—St. Louis 1 K—Pillette Road N—Sterling R—Windsor T—Toluca W—Clairpointe X—St. Louis 2
12–17 Sequence Number	These digits identify your particular car				

6 GENERAL INFORMATION AND MAINTENANCE

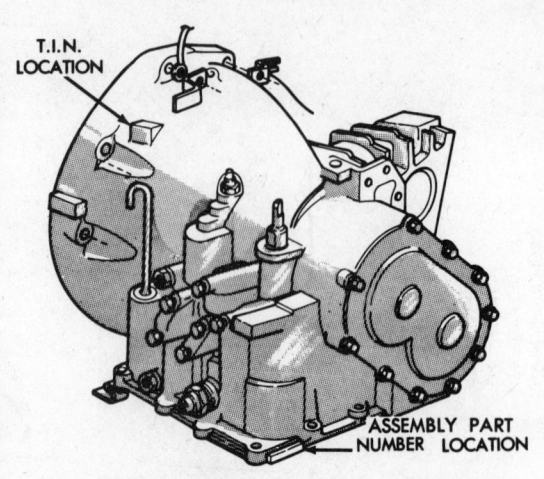

Location of the transaxle identification number (T.I.N.) on all transaxles, and the assembly part number for automatic transaxles

the housing, between the timing window and the differential.

On the A-460 and A-465 manual transaxles, this number is located on a metal tag attached to the front of the transaxle. On automatic models, it is stamped on a pad located just above the oil pan at the rear of the unit.

ROUTINE MAINTENANCE

Air Cleaner

On the 2.2 liter engine, replace the air cleaner element every 52,500 miles. Under dusty driving conditions, inspect the element frequently (about every 15,000 miles) and replace it as frequently as necessary. Generally, if you hold the element up to a strong light and you cannot see through it at all, it is clogged.

On the 2.6 liter engine, replace the element every 30,000 miles under ordinary driving conditions. If you drive under extremely dusty conditions, inspect the filter every 15,000 miles and replace it as necessary.

A dirty air cleaner will decrease fuel mileage, may overheat your catalytic converter, and could even shorten engine life by permitting dust to enter the air intake. Taking good care of it is important.

Also, in replacing the air cleaner filter, be careful to wipe dust out of the air cleaner and to prevent the entry of dirt, dust, or foreign objects. Also, make sure the air cleaner is properly installed and sealed tightly. A vacuum leak here could allow dust to enter the engine and cause severely accelerated wear.

2.2 LITER CARBURETED ENGINES

On the 2.2 liter carbureted engine, replace the air cleaner element by removing the three wing nuts retaining the air cleaner-crossover cover to the carburetor and bracket. Lift the cover, pull the element out, and replace it, making sure you install it with the screen upward. Position the cover on top, aligning the three clips and making sure the element seals all around. Let the three studs stick upward through the whole for each in the cover. Then, install the plastic wing nuts on the two studs on the carburetor and tighten each just finger tight (14 in. lbs.). Then, install the other wingnut—the one that fastens the air cleaner to the support bracket—and tighten it in a similar manner. Then, close the three hold-down clips. Make sure you perform the steps in exactly this sequence, or the air cleaner may leak.

2.2 LITER ELECTRONIC FUEL INJECTION ENGINE

To remove the air cleaner, remove the clamp fastening the air hose at the throttle body and unclip the five chips that fasten the top of the air cleaner to the lower housing. Pull the air hose off the throttle body and then lift the cover and hose off the bottom of the air cleaner. Now remove the filter.

To install the filter, drop it screen side up into the plastic bottom section of the lower housing. Install the clamp loosely onto the throttle body hose and connect the hose onto the throttle body. Slide the top of the air cleaner squarely down over the seal of the filter element, making sure it is not pinching the seal anywhere but lies flat all around. Clip the five hold-down clips and then tighten the clamp around the hose at the throttle body until it is just snug—25 in. lbs.

2.6 LITER ENGINE

To replace the air cleaner cartridge, simply unclip the four clips fastening the top in place, lift

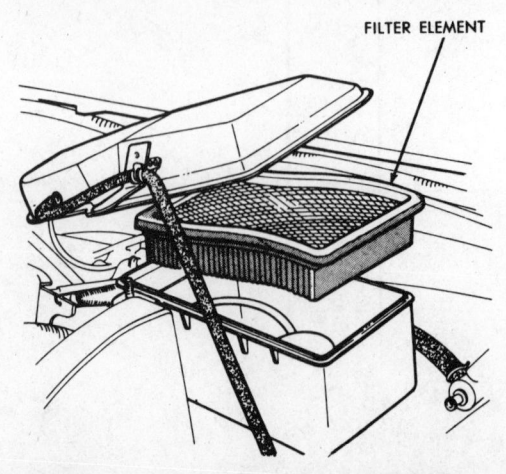

Air cleaner installation—2.2 carbureted engine

GENERAL INFORMATION AND MAINTENANCE

2.6L engine air cleaner filter

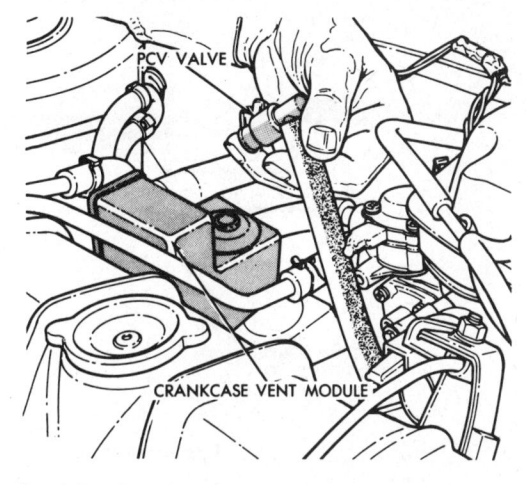

Servicing the PCV valve—2.2 liter engine shown

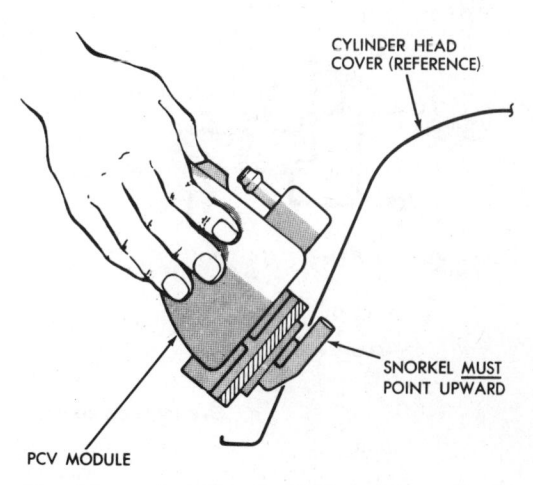

Removing or installing the PCV module on the 2.2 liter engine

the top off the lower housing (the intake hose is flexible enough to permit this) and remove the filter. Install in reverse order, making sure all parts are positioned correctly to prevent leaks. Clean the inside of the air cleaner housing before installing the air filter.

PCV Valve

The PCV system draws a small amount of air through the engine crankcase in order to remove and reburn a small amount of incompletely burned fuel that accumulates there. A vehicle run on unleaded fuel and receiving good care will rarely require maintenance of this system. Because a clogged PCV system not only increases emissions but can contribute to engine wear, or may cause rough idle or stalling, it should be inspected regularly. In addition, all cars require cleaning of the crankcase vent module at 50,000 miles.

To inspect the system pull the PCV valve out of the crankcase vent module and shake it. If the valve rattles, this is a partial indication that it is okay; if there is no sound, it must be replaced and the PCV hose cleaned by spraying solvent through it.

If the valve rattles, you should still check the PCV valve with the engine idling. Pull it out of the vent module and place your finger or thumb over the end to stop air flow. You should feel some suction, and the engine speed should drop slightly. If there is no suction, or if the engine idle speeds up and smooths out considerably, replace the valve. Inspect the PCV hose and clean it by spraying solvent through it, if the inside is coated with gum and varnish.

If the car has 50,000 miles on it or a multiple of that figure, clean the PCV module. First, remove the PCV valve and vent hose from the module. Then, depress the retaining clip and turn the module counterclockwise to remove it. Use kerosene or a similar cleaning solvent (not gasoline!) to flush the filter inside the module. Allow to dry. Then, invert the module and fill it with SAE 30 engine oil. Turn it right side up and permit the oil to drain through the vent located on top of the air cleaner. Then, carefully depress the retaining clip, insert the module and turn it clockwise until it reaches its normal position to install it. Do not force the module in or to turn. Note that the snorkel must end up pointing upward and must not be free to rotate. Reconnect the vent hose and PCV valve.

Evaporative Control System

The function of the Evaporative Control System is to prevent gasoline vapors from the fuel

8 GENERAL INFORMATION AND MAINTENANCE

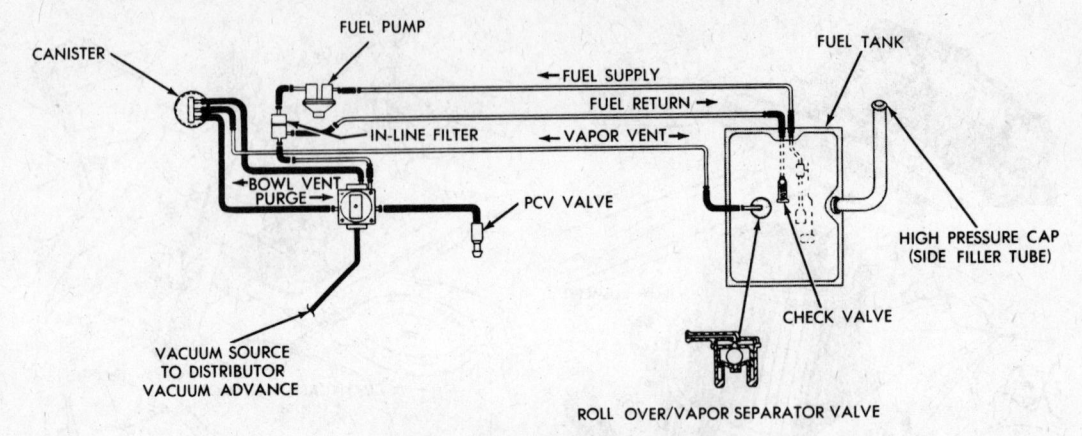

Evaporation control system—2.2L engine

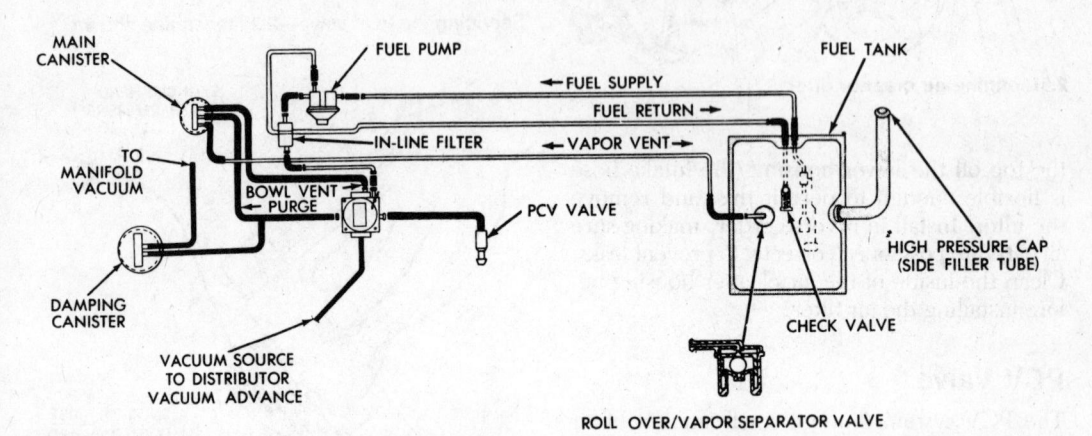

Evaporation control system—2.6L engine

tank to escape into the atmosphere. Periodic maintenance is required only on 1981–82 models. The fiberglass filter on the bottom of the canister must be replaced on these models, but only if the vehicle is driven under dusty conditions.

To replace the filter, note locations of the hoses going to the canister, and then disconnect them. Unclamp the canister, pull the filter out as shown, and replace it in reverse order.

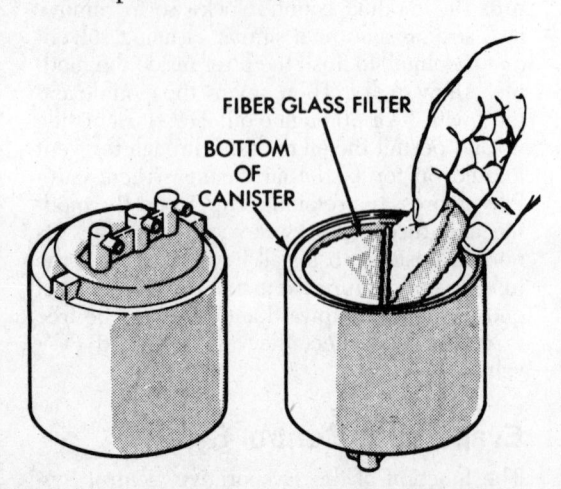

Replacing evaporative canister filter (1981–82 models)

Drive Belts

Check the drive belts every 15,000 miles for evidence of wear such as cracking, fraying, and incorrect tension.

Determine the belt tension at a point halfway between the pulleys by pressing on the belt with moderate thumb pressure. The belt should deflect about ¼–½ in. at this point. If the deflection is found to be too much or too little, loosen the accessory's slotted adjusting bracket bolt. If the hinge bolt is very tight, it too may have to be loosened. Use a wooden hammer handle or a broomstick to lever the accessory closer to or farther away from the engine to provide the correct tension. Do not use a metal prybar, which may damage the component. When the belt adjustment is correct, tighten the bolts and recheck the adjustment. Although it is better to have the belt too loose

GENERAL INFORMATION AND MAINTENANCE

HOW TO SPOT WORN V-BELTS

V-Belts are vital to efficient engine operation—they drive the fan, water pump and other accessories. They require little maintenance (occasional tightening) but they will not last forever. Slipping or failure of the V-belt will lead to overheating. If your V-belt looks like any of these, it should be replaced.

This belt has deep cracks, which cause it to flex. Too much flexing leads to heat build-up and premature failure. These cracks can be caused by using the belt on a pulley that is too small. Notched belts are available for small diameter pulleys.

Cracking or weathering

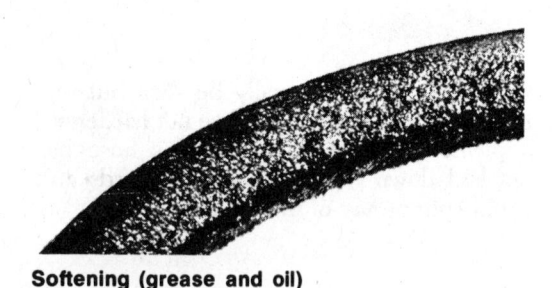

Oil and grease on a belt can cause the belt's rubber compounds to soften and separate from the reinforcing cords that hold the belt together. The belt will first slip, then finally fail altogether.

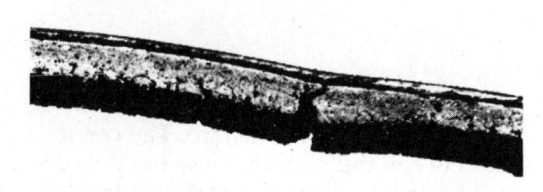

Softening (grease and oil)

Glazing is caused by a belt that is slipping. A slipping belt can cause a run-down battery, erratic power steering, overheating or poor accessory performance. The more the belt slips, the more glazing will be built up on the surface of the belt. The more the belt is glazed, the more it will slip. If the glazing is light, tighten the belt.

Glazing

The cover of this belt is worn off and is peeling away. The reinforcing cords will begin to wear and the belt will shortly break. When the belt cover wears in spots or has a rough jagged appearance, check the pulley grooves for roughness.

Worn cover

This belt is on the verge of breaking and leaving you stranded. The layers of the belt are separating and the reinforcing cords are exposed. It's just a matter of time before it breaks completely.

Separation

GENERAL INFORMATION AND MAINTENANCE

HOW TO SPOT BAD HOSES

Both the upper and lower radiator hoses are called upon to perform difficult jobs in an inhospitable environment. They are subject to nearly 18 psi at under hood temperatures often over 280°F., and must circulate nearly 7500 gallons of coolant an hour—3 good reasons to have good hoses.

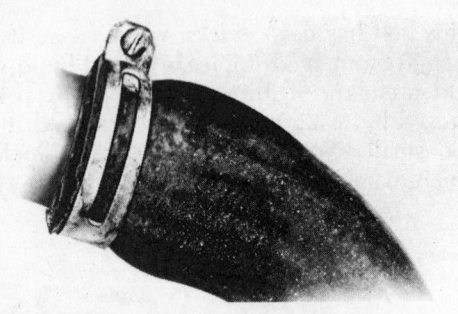

A good test for any hose is to feel it for soft or spongy spots. Frequently these will appear as swollen areas of the hose. The most likely cause is oil soaking. This hose could burst at any time, when hot or under pressure.

Swollen hose

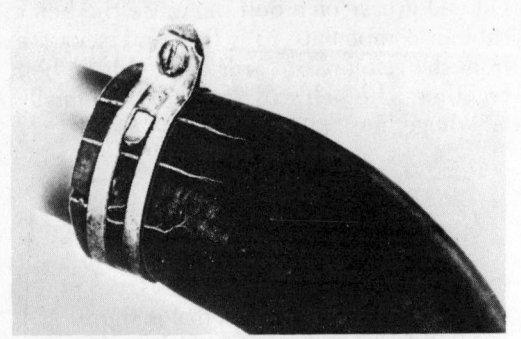

Cracked hoses can usually be seen but feel the hoses to be sure they have not hardened; a prime cause of cracking. This hose has cracked down to the reinforcing cords and could split at any of the cracks.

Cracked hose

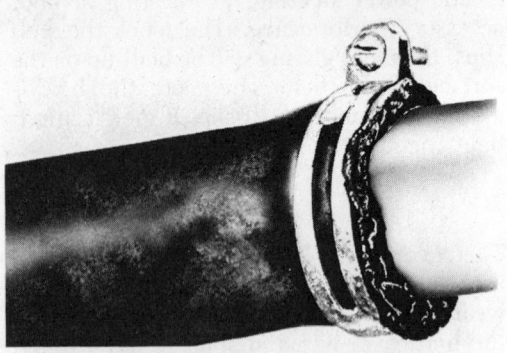

Weakened clamps frequently are the cause of hose and cooling system failure. The connection between the pipe and hose has deteriorated enough to allow coolant to escape when the engine is hot.

Frayed hose end (due to weak clamp)

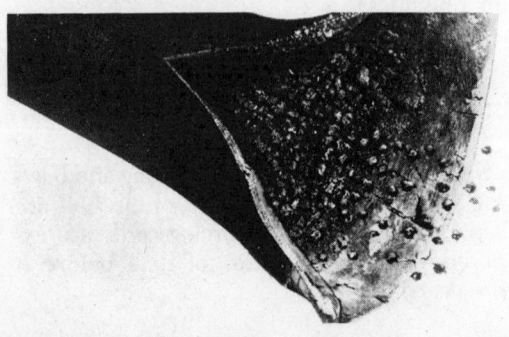

Debris, rust and scale in the cooling system can cause the inside of a hose to weaken. This can usually be felt on the outside of the hose as soft or thinner areas.

Debris in cooling system

GENERAL INFORMATION AND MAINTENANCE 11

than too tight, a loose belt may place a high impact load on a bearing due to the whipping or snapping action of the belt.

CAUTION: *Be careful not to overtighten the drive belts, as this will damage the driven component's bearings.*

Hose Replacement
ALL MODELS

CAUTION: *Do not perform this procedure on a hot or warm engine, otherwise serious injury could result.*
1. Drain the cooling system.
2. Remove the top hose from the radiator neck and the thermostat housing.
3. Remove the bottom hose from the water pump and the bottom of the radiator.
4. Check the hoses for damage. Replace them as necessary.
5. Installation is the reverse of removal.

Air Conditioning

This book contains no repair or maintenance procedures for the air conditioning system. It is recommended that any such repairs be left to the experts, whose personnel are well aware of the hazards and who have the proper equipment.

CAUTION: *The compressed refrigerant used in the air conditioning system expands into the atmosphere at a temperature of −21.7°F or lower. This will freeze any surface, including your eyes, that it contacts. In addition, the refrigerant decomposes into a poisonous gas in the presence of flame. Do not open or disconnect any part of the air conditioning system.*

NOTE: *Run the air conditioner for a few minutes, every two weeks or so, during the cold months. This avoids the possibility of the compressor seals drying out from lack of lubrication.*

You can safely determine if your car's air conditioning system needs service. The following system checks apply only to the factory-installed units. If your car has an after-market air conditioner, you will have to consult the manufacturer of the unit for the correct procedure to use.

To check the refrigerant level, first locate the sight glass. It is on top of the receiver-drier (or filter-drier), a small black, cylindrical device located right near the joint of the engine compartment hood and right (passenger's side) fender. Wipe the sightglass, located flush with the top of the drier, with a clean rag so you'll be able to see clearly what is happening inside. Temperature must be over 70 degrees F.

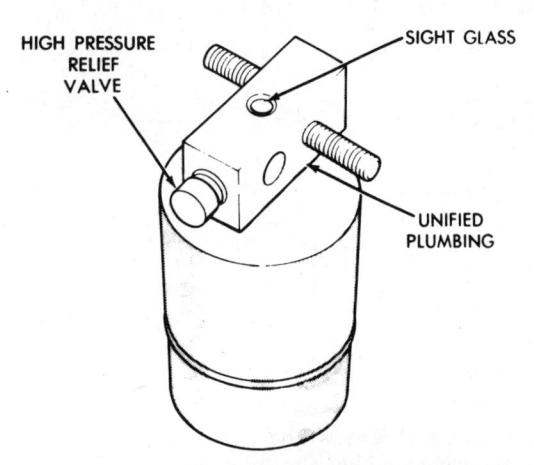

The refrigerant sightglass on air conditioned vehicles is located in the top of the receiver-drier

Start the engine and allow it to idle. Turn the air conditioner on with the temperature lever adjusted to the lowest possible setting. Put the fan on the highest speed. Operate the system for about five minutes.

Now, look at the sight glass, and cautiously feel the temperatures of the lines going into and going out of the compressor (the discharge line—going to the condenser in front of the radiator—may be hot). If the sight glass remains clear almost 100 percent of the time and there is a considerable temperature difference between the compressor inlet and outlet lines, the system is okay—it has a full charge of refrigerant. If the sight glass is clear but there is practically no difference in the temperatures of the two lines, all the refrigerant has leaked out and the system should be shut down until it can be repaired and recharged. If there are a great many bubbles in the sight glass, the system has a small leak which should be repaired, following which the system should be recharged.

If the compressor does not start running (the front surface of the clutch on the compressor will be stationary) the system may have an electrical or clutch problem, which should be repaired.

Fluid Level Checks
ENGINE OIL

The engine oil level is checked with the dipstick which is located on the radiator side of the engine.

NOTE: *The oil should be checked before the engine is started or five minutes after the engine has shut off. This gives the oil time to drain back to the oil pan and prevents an inaccurate oil level reading.*

Remove the dipstick from the tube, wipe it clean, and insert it back into the tube. Remove

12 GENERAL INFORMATION AND MAINTENANCE

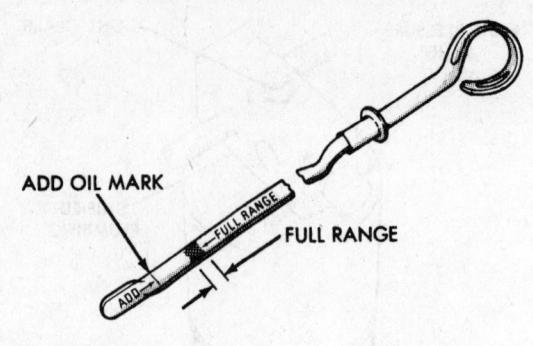

Oil dipstick

it again and observe the oil level. It should be maintained within the full range on the dipstick.

CAUTION: *Do not overfill the crankcase. This will cause oil aeration and loss of oil pressure.*

Be sure to use only oil with an SE rating.

TRANSMISSION

Some early vehicles may be equipped with the A-412 manual transaxle. This unit can be identified by locating the position of the starter which is found on the radiator side of the engine compartment. If it becomes necessary to add fluid to this unit, SAE 80W-90 gear lube is recommended.

If your vehicle has the A-460 or A-465 (four and five speed transaxles respectively) manual transaxle, the starter will be next to the firewall. When it becomes necessary to add fluid to this unit, Dexron® II is recommended.

The automatic transaxle fluid level should be checked when the engine is at normal operating temperature. It is checked in the following manner:

(1) With the parking brake engaged and the engine idling shift the transmission through the shift pattern and return it to the Park position.

(2) Remove the dipstick. The fluid level

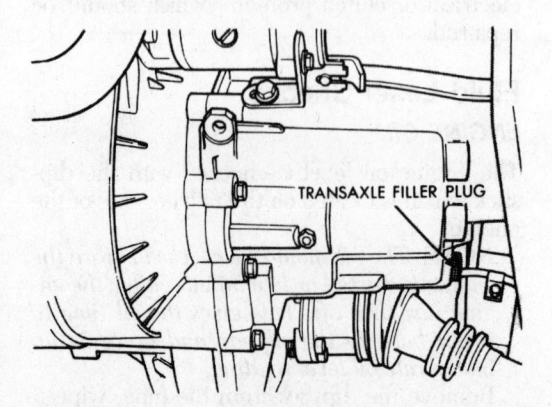

A-412 manual transaxle filler plug

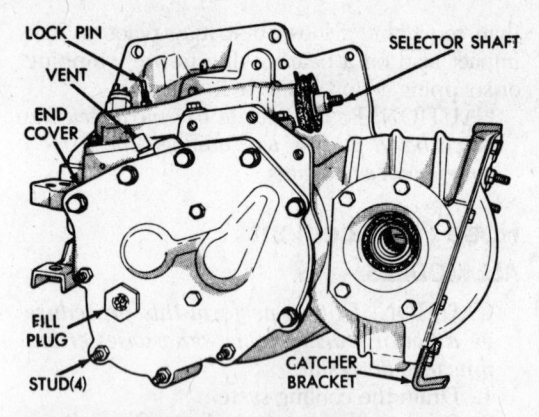

A-460 manual transaxle filler plug

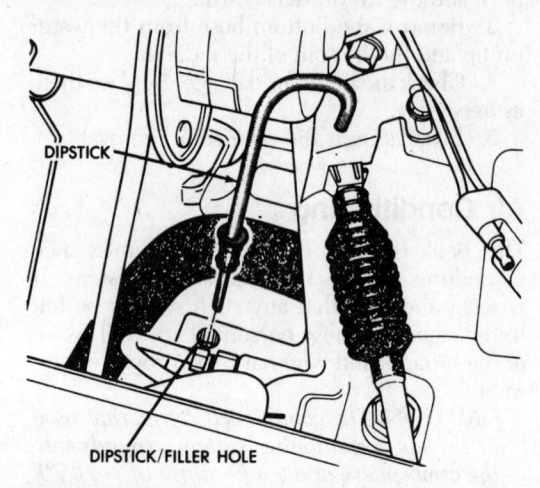

Dipstick filler hole

should be between the ADD and Full mark, but never above the Full mark.

BRAKE MASTER CYLINDER

Once every 7500 miles or 12 months check the brake fluid level in the master cylinder. The master cylinder is mounted either on the fire-

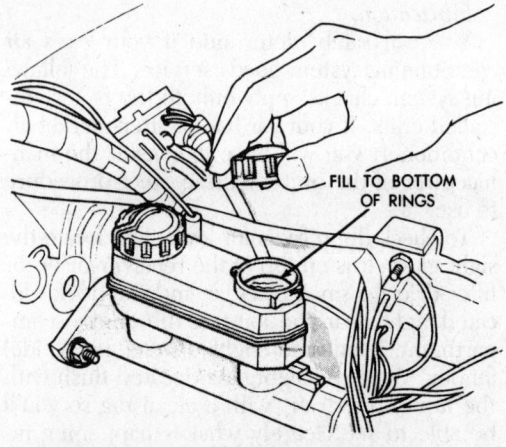

Checking the master cylinder fluid level

GENERAL INFORMATION AND MAINTENANCE

wall or the brake booster, and is divided into two reservoirs. The fluid must be maintained at the bottom of the split ring.

Remove the two master cylinder caps and fill to the bottom of the split rings using DOT 3 brake fluid. If the brake fluid is chronically low there may be a leak in the system which should be investigated immediately.

NOTE: *Brake fluid absorbs moisture from the air, which reduces its effectiveness and causes corrosion. Never leave the brake fluid can or master cylinder uncovered any longer than necessary. Brake fluid also damages paint. If any is spilled, it should be washed off immediately with clear, cold water.*

COOLANT

The coolant should be checked at each fuel stop, to prevent the possibility of overheating and serious engine damage. If not, it should at least be checked once each month.

The cooling system was filled at the factory with a high quality coolant solution that is good for year around operation and protects the system from freezing. To check the coolant level simply look into the expansion tank.

CAUTION: *The radiator coolant is under pressure when hot. To avoid the danger of physical injury, coolant level should be checked or replenished only when cool. To remove the cap, slowly rotate it counterclockwise to the stop, but do not press down. Wait until all pressure is released (indicated when the hissing sound stops) then press down on the cap while continuing to rotate it counterclockwise. War a gloeor use a thick rag for protection.*

If coolant is needed, a 50/50 mix of ethylene glycol antifreeze and water should be used. Alcohol or methanol base coolants are specifically not recommended. Antifreeze solution should be used all year, even in summer, to prevent rust and to take advantage of the solution's higher boiling point compared to plain water. This is imperative on air conditioned models; the heater core can freeze if it isn't protected.

CAUTION: *Never add large quantities of cold coolant to a hot engine. A cracked engine block may result. If it is absolutely necessary to add coolant to a hot engine do so only with the engine idling and add only small quantities at a time.*

Each year the cooling system should be serviced as follows:

1. Wash the radiator cap and filler neck with clean water.
2. Check the coolant for proper level and freeze protection.
3. Have the system pressure tested. If a replacement cap is installed, be sure that it conforms to the original specifications.
4. Tighten the hose clamps and inspect all hoses. Replace hoses that are swollen, cracked or otherwise deteriorated.
5. Clean the frontal area of the radiator core and the air conditioning condenser, if so equipped.
6. Run the engine with the cap removed and the heater on until operating temperature is reached (indicated by heat in the upper radiator hose).
7. With the engine stopped, open the radiator drain cock located at the bottom of the radiator, and (to speed the draining) the engine block drains, if any.
8. Completely drain the coolant, and close and drain cocks.
9. Add sufficient clean water to fill the system. Run the engine and drain and refill the system as often as necessary until the drain water is nearly colorless.
10. Add sufficient ethylene glycol coolant to provide the required freezing and corrosion protection (at least a 44% solution protecting to $-20°F$). Fill the radiator to the cold level. Run the engine with the cap removed until normal operating temperature is reached.
11. Check the hot level.
12. Install the cap.

DIFFERENTIAL FLUID CHECK—AUTOMATIC TRANSAXLE

1981–82 Models

Under normal operating conditions, lubricant changes are not required for this unit. However, fluid level checks are required every 7500 miles or 12 months whichever comes first. The fluid level should be within 3/8 in. of the bottom of the fill plug.

NOTE: *A rod with a U bend at the end can be made to check the fluid level.*

If it becomes necessary to add or replace the fluid use only Dexron® II automatic transmission fluid.

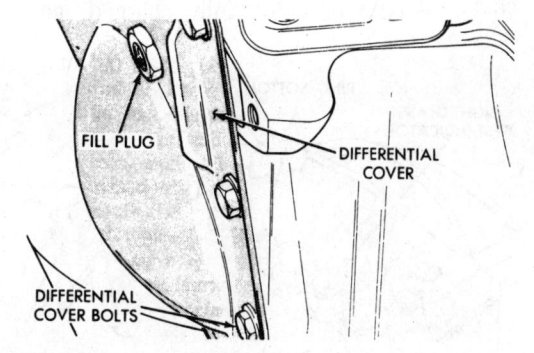

Differential (cover) fill plug location

14 GENERAL INFORMATION AND MAINTENANCE

STEERING GEAR

The manual steering gear is permanently lubricated at the factory and periodic lubrication si not needed.

POWER STEERING RESERVOIR

Maintain the proper fluid level as indicated on the cap of the reservoir. Check the level with the engine off and at normal ambient temperature. The dipstick should indicate "FULL COLD". If the reservoir needs fluid refill with power steering fluid, Part No. 2084329 or its equivalent.

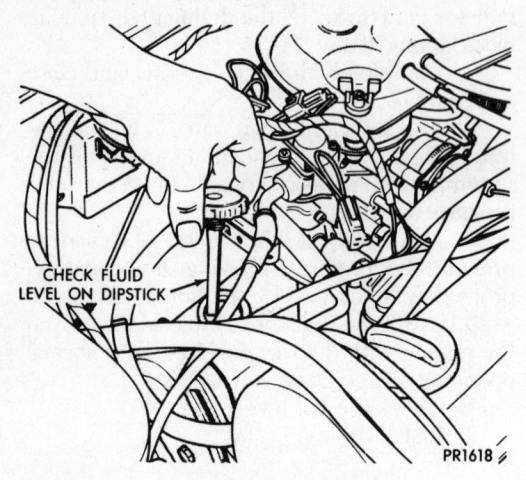

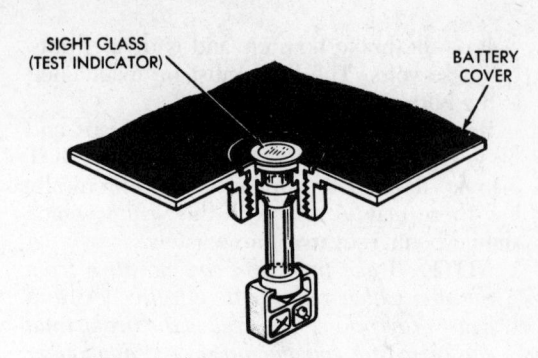

Test indicator—maintenance free battery

"Dark" if it needs charging. A light yellow means the battery requires water or may need replacing.

For Standard batteries, check the fluid level in each cell every 2 months (more often in hot weather or on long trips). If the water is low, fill it to the bottom of the filler well with distilled water.

Checking the power steering fluid level

BATTERY

Two types of batteries are used, Standard and Maintenance Free.

Both batteries are equipped with a "Test Charge Indicator". This indicator is a built in hydrometer, which replaces one of the battery filler caps in the Standard battery and is permanently installed in the cover on the Maintenance Free battery.

Visual inspection of the indicator sight glass will aid in determining battery condition. The indicator shows green if the battery is above 76–80 percent of being fully charged, and

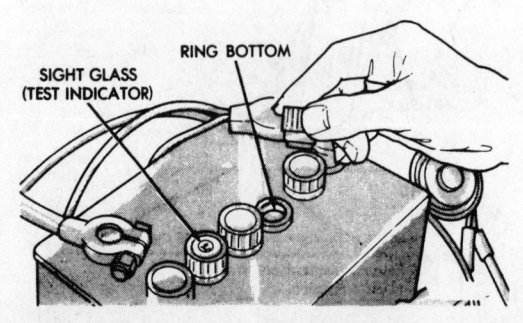

Tires

Check the air pressure in your car's tires every few weeks. Make sure that the tires cool, as you will get a false reading when the tires are heated because air pressure increases with temperature. A decal located on the glovebox door will tell you the proper tire pressure for the standard equipemnt tires. Naturally, when you replace tires you will want to get the correct tire pressures for the new ones from the dealer or manufacturer. It pays to buy a tire pressure gauge to keep in the car, since those at service stations are often inaccurate or broken.

While you are checking the tire pressure, take a look at the tread. The tread should be wearing evenly across the tire. Excessive wear in the center of the tread indicates overinflation. Excessive wear on the outer edges indicates underinflation. An irregular wear pattern is usually a sign of incorrect front wheel alignment or wheel balance. A front end that is out of alignment will usually pull the car to one side of a flat road when the steering wheel is released. Incorrect wheel balance is usually accompanied by high speed vibration. Front wheels which are out of balance will produce

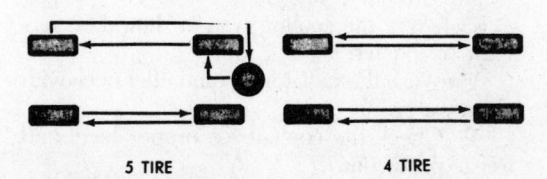

Check the fluid level—standard battery

Radial ply tire rotation

5 TIRE   4 TIRE

GENERAL INFORMATION AND MAINTENANCE

Capacities

Year	Engine Displacement Cu In.	Engine Crankcase (qts) With Filter	Engine Crankcase (qts) Without Filter	Transaxle (pts) Manual	Transaxle (pts) Automatic	Differential (pts)	Gasoline Tank (gals)	Cooling System (qts) W/ AC	Cooling System (qts) W/O AC
1981	135	4	4	4	15	2	13	7	7
	156	5	4½	4	17	2	13	8½	8½
1982	135	4	4	4	15	2	13	7	7
	156	5	4½	4	15	2	13	8½	8½
1983	135	4	4	4①	17.8	②	13③	9	9
	156	5	4½	4①	17.8	②	13③	9	9
1984–85	135	4④	4④	4①	17.8	②	14	9	9
	156	5	4½	4①	17.8	②	14	9	9

① With the 412 transaxle—1.5 qts.
  With the 465 5 speed—2.3 qts.
② The differential is combined with the transmission sump on 1983 and later models
③ Models with Electronic Fuel Injection—14
④ For 1985 only, the 135 cu. in. engine with turbo charging holds 5 qts. with or without filter change

vibration in the steering wheel, while unbalanced rear wheels will result in floor or truck vibration.

Rotating the tires every 6000 miles or so will result in increased thread life. Use the correct pattern for your tire switching. Most automotive experts are in agreement that radial tires are better all around performers, giving prolonged wear and better handling. An added benefit which you should consider when purchasing tires is that radials have less rolling resistance and can give up to a 10% increase in fuel economy over a bias-ply tire.

Tires of different construction should never be mixed. Always replace tires in sets of four or five when switching tire types and never substitute a belted tire for a bias-ply, a radial for a belted tire, etc. An occasional pressure check and periodic rotation could make your tires last much longer than a neglected set and maintain the safety margin which was designed into them.

Fuel Filter Replacement

There are two fuel filters in the present system. One is part of the gauge unit assembly located inside the fuel tank on the suction end of the tube. This filter normally does not need servicing, but may be replaced or cleaned if necessary.

The 2.2 liter engine usually uses a disposable filter-vapor separator that is located on the front side of the engine block between the fuel pump and carburetor. This filter has inlet and

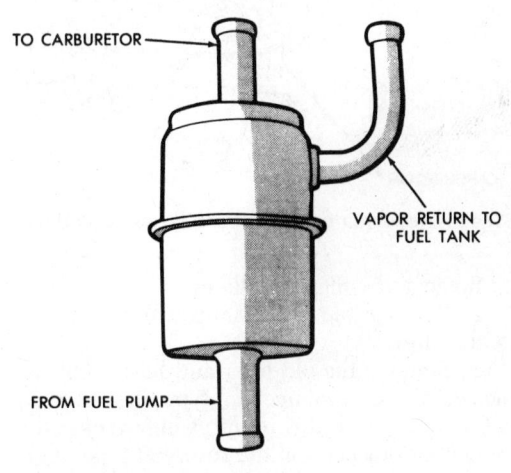

Fuel filter vapor separator 2.2L engine

outlet connections, as well as a third connection designed to permit fuel to return to the tank so that vapor that accumulates in hot weather will not interfere with carburetion.

The 2.6 liter engine uses a disposable, canister type filter in most cases. This type filter has only two connections.

A few models use a filter-reservoir assembly that attaches to the air cleaner and also has three connections, one for the elimination of vapor.

Filters do not require periodic maintenance except for those on engines with Electronic Fuel Injection. Replace these filters at least every 52,000 miles.

A plugged fuel filter can limit the speed at which a vehicle can be driven and cause hard starting.

16 GENERAL INFORMATION AND MAINTENANCE

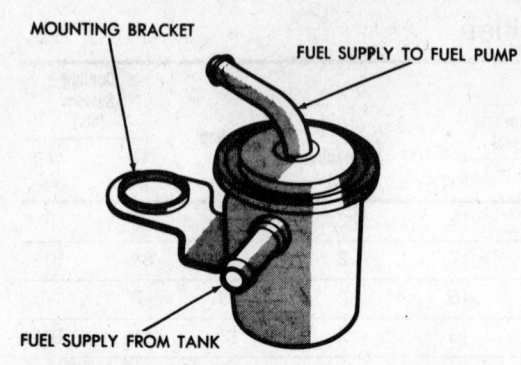

Fuel filter 2.6L engine

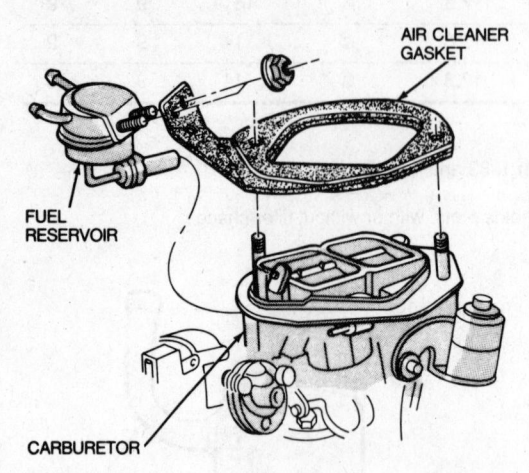

The fuel reservoir type filter used on some models

Remove the filter as follows:
1. Remove the hose clamps from each end of the filter.
2. Remove the old filter and hoses. On the non-return (two connection) type filter used on 2.6 liter engines, this requires unfastening the mounting bracket. On the reservoir type filter, remove the two mounting nuts inside the air cleaner.
3. Install the new filter, hoses, and tighten the hose clamps.
4. Start your vehicle and check for leaks.

LUBRICATION

Oil and Fuel Recommendations

Chrysler Corporation recommends the use of a high quality, heavy duty detergent oil with the proper viscosity for prevailing conditions. Oils labeled "For Service SF/CC" on the top of the can are satisfactorry for use in all engines; however, a higher quality oil, labeled "For Service SF/CD" is preferred for use in turbocharged engines.

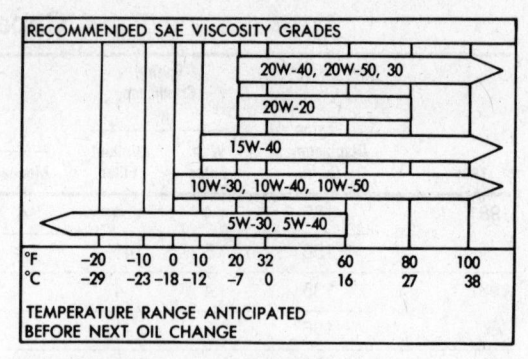

Oil viscosity chart for all models

It's important to recognize the distinctions between these oil types and the additional stresses required of oil used in turbocharged engines. Since the turbocharger bearings receive heat conducted directly from the unit's turbine, which may reach a cherry-red heat, oil passing through these bearings may reach temperatures high enough to cause chemical breakdown. This problem is especially severe right when the engine is shut down. Also, the additional power a turbocharged engine produces translates to higher mechanical loads and oil temperatures within the rest of the engine.

The CD designated oil has chemical additives capable of resisting this breakdown and countering its effects. If your car is turbocharged, it will almost surely pay you to use the better designation.

Oil must also meet viscosity standards. Follow the chart below precisely. Make sure the oil you buy is clearly labeled so as to confirm to both these basic standards.

Fuel should be selected for the brand and octane which performs without pinging. Find your exact engine model in the "General Engine Specifications" chart in Chapter 3.

Fuels of the same octane rating have varying anti-knock qualities. Thus, if your engine knocks or pings, try switching brands of gasoline before trying a more expensive higher octane fuel.

Your engine's fuel requirements can change with time, due to carbon buildup which changes the compression ratio. If switching brands or grades of gas doesn't work, check the ignition timing. If it is necessary to retard timing from specifications, don't change it more than about four degrees. Retarded timing will reduce power output and fuel mileage and increase engine temperature.

Basic engine octane requirements, to be used in your initial choice of fuel, are 87 octane, unleaded. This rating is an average of Research and Motor methods of determination (R plus M)/2). For increased vehicle performance and gas mileage, turbocharged engines, use a premium unleaded fuel—that is, one with a rating

GENERAL INFORMATION AND MAINTENANCE

of 91 octane. More octane results in better performance and economy in these engines because the ignition system will compensate for their characteristics by advancing the timing.

Gashohol consisting of 10% ethanol and gasoline may be used in your car, but gasolines containing methanol (wood alcohol) are not approved. They can damage fuel system parts and cause operating problems.

Fluid Changes

OIL CHANGES

The recommended mileage figures for Chrysler oil and filter changes are 7,500 miles or 12 months whichever comes first, assuming normal driving conditions. If your vehicle is being used under dusty conditions, frequent trailer pulling, excessive idling, or stop and go driving, it is recommended to change the oil and filter at 3,000 miles.

Always drain the oil after the engine has been running long enough to bring it to operating temperature. Hot oil will flow easier and more contaminants will be removed along with the oil than if it were drained cold. You will need a large capacity drain pan, which you can purchase at any store which sells automotive parts. Another necessity is containers for the used oil. You will find that plastic bottles, such as those used for bleach or fabric softener, make excellent storage jugs. One ecologically desirable solution to the used oil disposal problem is to find a cooperative gas station owner who will allow you to dump your used oil into his tank. Another is to keep the oil for use around the house as a preservative on fences, railroad tie borders, etc.

Chrysler recommends changing both the oil and filter during the first oil change and the filter every other oil change thereafter. On turbocharged engines, Chrysler recommends replacing the oil filter at every oil change. For the small price of an oil filter, it's cheap insurance to replace the filter at every oil change. One of the larger filter manufacturers points out in its advertisements that not changing the filter leaves one quart of dirty oil in the engine. This claim is true and should be kept in mind when changing your oil.

1. Run the engine until it reaches normal operating temperature.
2. Jack up the front of the car and support it on jack stands.
3. Slide a drain pan of at least 6 quarts capacity under the oil pan.
4. Loosen the drain plug. It is located in the lowest point of the oil pan. Turn the plug out by hand. By keeping an inward pressure on the plug as you unscrew it, oil won't escape past the threads and you can remove it without being burned by hot oil.
5. Allow the oil to drain completely and then install the drain plug. Don't overtighten the plug, or you'll be buying a new pan or a replacement plug for stripped threads.
6. Using a strap wrench, remove the oil filter. Keep in mind that it's holding about one quart of dirty, hot oil.
7. Empty the old filter into the drain pan and dispose of the filter.
8. Using a clean rag, wipe off the filter adapter on the engine block. Be sure that the rag doesn't leave any lint whidh could clog an oil passage.
9. Coat the rubber gasket on the filter with fresh oil. Spin it onto the engine *by hand;* when the gasket touches the adapter surface gived it another ½–¾ turn. No more, or you'll squash the gasket and it will leak.
10. Refill the engine with the correct amount of fresh oil. See the "Capacities" chart.
11. Crank the engine over several times and then start it. Do not rcae the engine. If the oil pressure "idiot light" doesn't go out or the pressure gauge shows zero, shut the engine down and find out what's wrong.
12. If the oil pressure is OK and there are no leaks, shut the engine off and lower the car.
13. Wait a few minutes and check the oil level. Add oil, as necessary, to bring the level up to Fill.

TRANSMISSION
Manual

Under normal operating conditions the fluid installed at the factory will give satisfactory lubrication for the life of the vehicle. Oil changes therefore, are not necessary unless the lubricant has become contaminated with water.

If the vehicle is operated under conditions of severe usage, periodic fluid changes are required. Severe usage is defined as operation at sustained high speeds in temperatures above 90 degrees F. most of the time. The transmission fluid should be changed and the magnet attached to the inside of the differential pan should be cleaned every 15,000 miles.

The fluid is drained by placing a drain pan underneath and then removing the pan cover on the side of the differential. Clean the magnet on the inside surface of the pan cover with a clean cloth while the fluid drains fully. Coat the areas of the inside of the cover adjacent to the bolt holes with a continuous bead of Room Temperature Vulcanizing sealant. Install the cover and tighten the bolts alternately and evenly. Refill the transaxle with approved fluid

18 GENERAL INFORMATION AND MAINTENANCE

as described above under the transmission fluid level check procedure.

Automatic

No service is required under normal operating conditions. If fluid is needed use only Dexron® II automatic transmission fluid.

If the vehicle is driven more than half the time in heavy city traffic with the temperature over 90 degrees F., or is used for trailer towing, the fluid should be changed and bands adjusted every 15,000 ml.

To change the fluid, remove the transaxle oil pan bolts with a large drain pan located under the pan. Tilt the transaxle pan to drain it. Wipe the oil pan with a clean rag.

See the appropriate section of Chapter 6 for the procedure to be followed in adjusting the transmission bands. Then, put a continuous bead of Room Temperature Vulcanizing sealer around the area of the pan where the boltholes are on the top surface of the pan. Install the pan and bolts and tighten the bolts alternately and evenly to 165 in. lbs. Install fluid and check the level as described above under Fluid Level Checks.

DIFFERENTIAL

Under normal operating conditions, lubricant changes in the unit are not required. However, fluid level checks should be made at 7,500 miles or 12 months, whichever comes first.

Chassis Greasing

Chassis greasing can be performed with a pressurized grease gun or it can be performed at home using a hand-operated grease gun. Wipe the fittings clean before greasing, in order to prevent the possibility of forcing any dirt into the component.

Ball joint and steering linkage are semipermanently lubricated at the factory with a special grease. They should be regreased every 30,000 miles or 3 years whichever comes first. When regreasing is necessary, use only special long life chassis grease such as Multi-Mileage lubricant Part No. 2525035 or its equivalent.

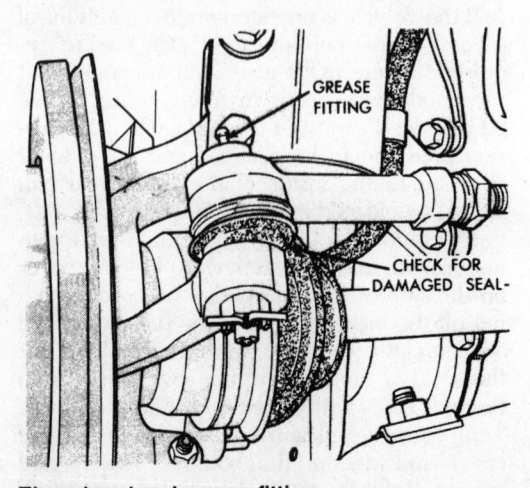

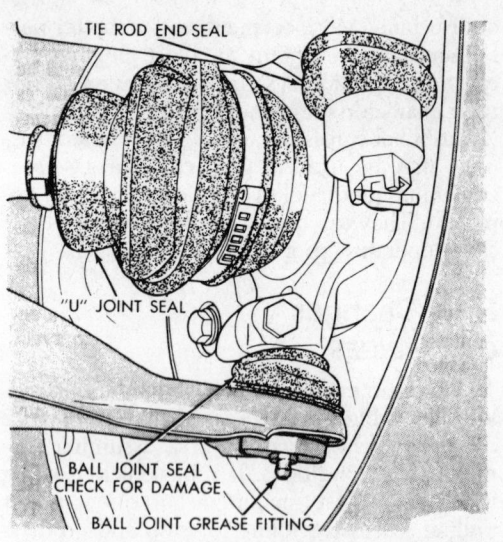

Front suspension ball joint seal and grease fitting

Front Wheel Bearings

Your Chrysler K- or E-car is equipped with permanently sealed front wheel bearings. There is no periodic adjustment for these units.

The rear wheel bearings should be inspected whenever the drums are removed to inspect or service the brakes, or at least every 22,500 miles. For lubrication procedures of these bearings refer to Chapter 8.

Towing

The vehicle can be towed from either the front or rear. If the vehicle is towed from the front for an extended distance make sure the parking brake is completely released.

Manual transmission vehicles may be towed on the front wheels at speeds up to 35 mph, for a distance not to exceed 15 miles, provided the transmission is in enutral and the driveline has not been damaged. The steering wheel must be clamped in a straight ahead position.

CAUTION: *Do not use the steering column lock to secure front wheel position for towing.*

Automatic transmission vehicles may be towed on the front wheels at speeds not to exceed 25 mph for a period of 15 miles.

CAUTION: *If this requirement cannot be met the front wheels must be placed on a dolly.*

Tie rod seal and grease fitting

GENERAL INFORMATION AND MAINTENANCE

JUMP STARTING A DEAD BATTERY

The chemical reaction in a battery produces explosive hydrogen gas. This is the safe way to jump start a dead battery, reducing the chances of an accidental spark that could cause an explosion.

Jump Starting Precautions

1. Be sure both batteries are of the same voltage.
2. Be sure both batteries are of the same polarity (have the same grounded terminal).
3. Be sure the vehicles are not touching.
4. Be sure the vent cap holes are not obstructed.
5. Do not smoke or allow sparks around the battery.
6. In cold weather, check for frozen electrolyte in the battery.
7. Do not allow electrolyte on your skin or clothing.
8. Be sure the electrolyte is not frozen.

Jump Starting Procedure

1. Determine voltages of the two batteries; they must be the same.
2. Bring the starting vehicle close (they must not touch) so that the batteries can be reached easily.
3. Turn off all accessories and both engines. Put both cars in Neutral or Park and set the handbrake.
4. Cover the cell caps with a rag—do not cover terminals.
5. If the terminals on the run-down battery are heavily corroded, clean them.
6. Identify the positive and negative posts on both batteries and connect the cables in the order shown.
7. Start the engine of the starting vehicle and run it at fast idle. Try to start the car with the dead battery. Crank it for no more than 10 seconds at a time and let it cool off for 20 seconds in between tries.
8. If it doesn't start in 3 tries, there is something else wrong.
9. Disconnect the cables in the reverse order.
10. Replace the cell covers and dispose of the rags.

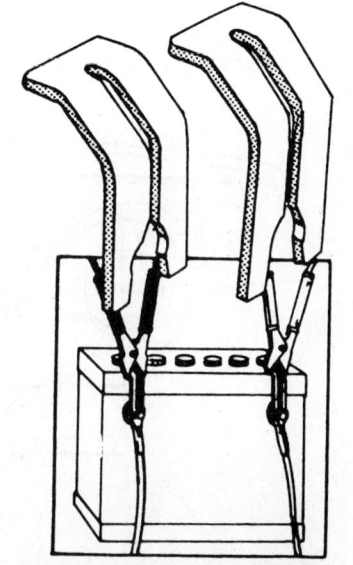

Side terminal batteries occasionally pose a problem when connecting jumper cables. There frequently isn't enough room to clamp the cables without touching sheet metal. Side terminal adaptors are available to alleviate this problem and should be removed after use.

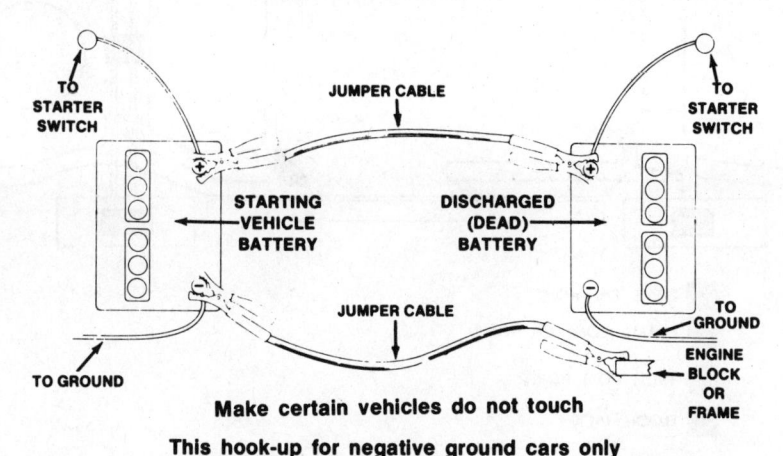

Make certain vehicles do not touch

This hook-up for negative ground cars only

GENERAL INFORMATION AND MAINTENANCE

Jacking

The standard jack utilizes special receptacles located at the body sills to accept the scissors jack supplied with the vehicle for emergency road service. The jack supplied with the car should never be used for any service operation other than tire changing. Never get under the car while it is supported by only a jack. Always block the wheels when changing tires.

The service operations in this book often require that one end or the other, or both, of the car be raised and safely supported. The ideal method, of course, would be a hydraulic hoist. Since this is beyond both the resource and requirement of the do-it-yourselfer, a small hydraulic, screw or scissors jack will suffice for the procedures in this guide. Two sturdy jackstands should be acquired if you intend to work under the car at any time. An alternate method of raising the car would be drive-on ramps. These are available commercially or can be fabricated from heavy boards or steel. Be sure to block the wheels when using ramps.

CAUTION: *Concrete blocks are not recommended for supporting the car. They are*

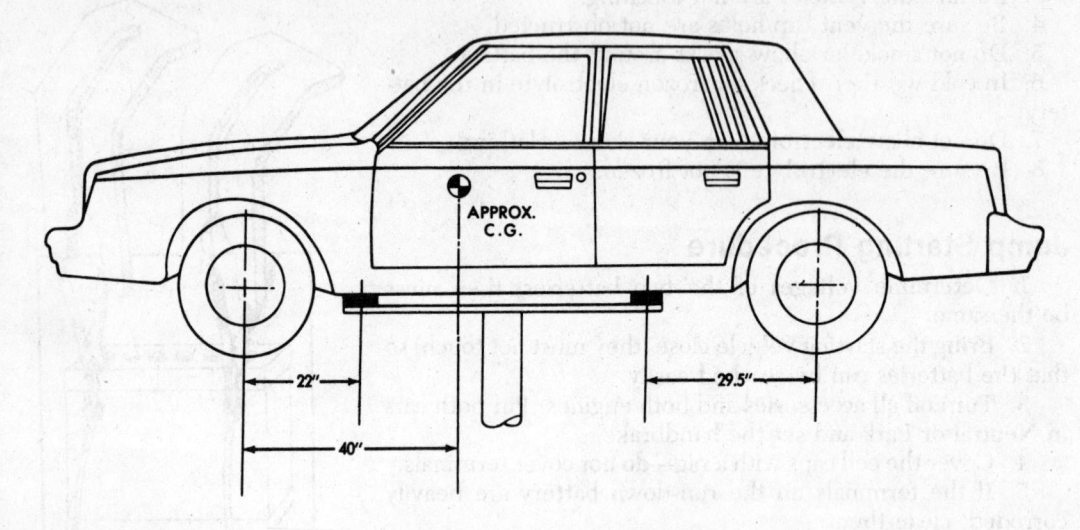

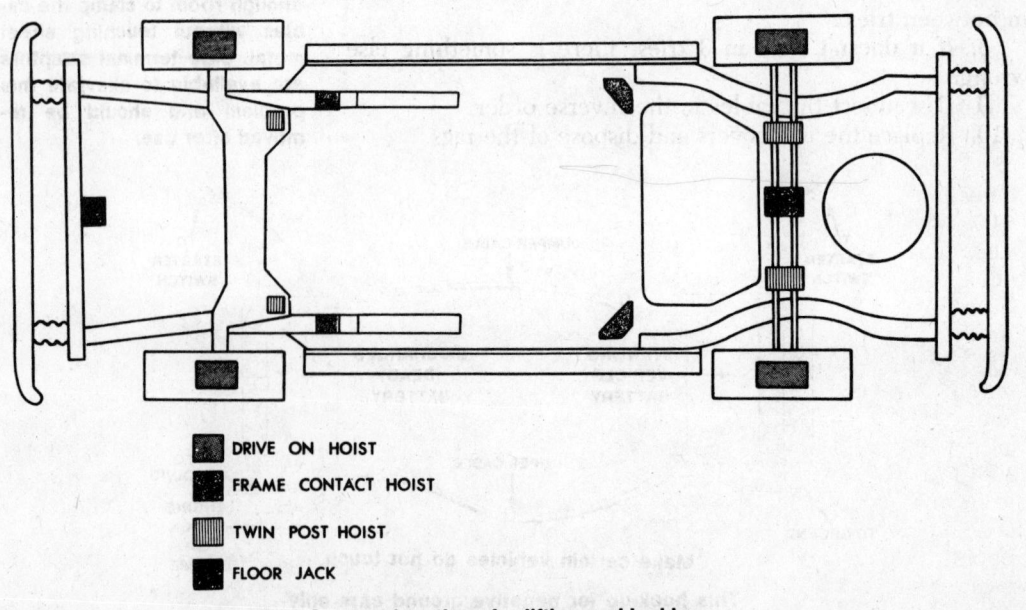

Support locations for lifting and jacking

likely to crumble if the load is not evenly distributed. Boxes and milk crates of any description must not be used to support the car!

HOW TO BUY A USED CAR

Many people believe that a two or three year old used car is a better buy than a new car. This may be true; the new car suffers the heaviest depreciation in the first two years, but is not old enough to present a lot of costly repair problems. Whatever the age of the used car you might want to buy, this section and a little patient will help you select one that should be safe and dependable.

TIPS

1. First decide what model you want, and how much you want to spend.
2. Check the used car lots and your local newspaper ads. Privately owned cars are usually less expensive, however you will not get a warranty that, in most cases, comes with a used car purchased from a lot.
3. Never shop at night. The glare of the lights make it easy to miss faults on the body caused by accident or rust repair.
4. Try to get the name and phone number of the previous owner. Contact him/her and ask about the car. If the owner of the lot refuses this information, look for a car somewhere else.

A private seller can tell you about the car and maintenance. Remember, however, there's no law requiring honesty from private citizens selling used cars. There is a law that forbids the tampering with or turning back the odometer mileage. This includes both the private citizen and the lot owner. The law also requires that the seller or anyone transferring ownership of the car must provide the buyer with a signed statement indicating the mileage on the odometer at the time of transfer.

5. Write down the year, model and serial number before you buy any used car. Then dial 1-800-424-9393, the toll free number of the National Highway Traffic Safety Administration, and ask if the car has ever been included on any manufacturer's recall list. If so, make sure the needed repairs were made.
6. Use the "Used Car Checklist" in this section and check all the items on the used car you are considering. Some items are more important than others. You know how much money you can afford for repairs, and, depending on the price of the car, may consider doing any needed work yourself. Beware, however, of trouble in areas that will affect operation, safety or emission. Problems in the "Used Car Checklist" break down as follows:

1–8: Two or more problems in these areas indicate a lack of maintenance. You should beware.
9–13: Indicates a lack of proper care, however, these can usually be corrected with a tune-up or relatively simple parts replacement.
14–17: Problems in the engine or transmission can be very expensive. Walk away from any car with problems in both of these areas.

7. If you are satisfied with the apparent condition of the car, take it to an independent diagnostic center or mechanic for a complete check. If you have a state inspection program, have it inspected immediately before purchase, or specify on the bill of sale that the sale is conditional on passing state inspection.
8. Road test the car—refer to the "Road Test Checklist" in this section. If your original evaluation and the road test agree—the rest is up to you.

USED CAR CHECKLIST

NOTE: *The numbers on the illustrations refer to the numbers on this checklist.*

1. *Mileage:* Average mileage is about 12,000 miles per year. More than average mileage may indicate hard usage. 1975 and later catalytic convertger equipped models may need converter service at 50,000 miles.
2. *Paint:* Check around the tailpipe, molding and windows for overspray indicating that the car has been repainted.
3. *Rust:* Check fenders, doors, rocker panels, window moldings, wheelwells, floorboards, under floormats, and in the trunk for signs of rust. Any rust at all will be a problem. There is no way to check the spread of rust, except to replace the part or panel.
4. *Body appearance:* Check the moldings, bumpers, grille, vinyl roof, glass, doors, trunk lid and body panels for general overall condition. Check for misalignment, loose holdown clips, ripples, scratches in glass, rips or patches in the top. Mismatched paint, welding in the trunk, severe misalignment of body panels or ripples may indicate crash work.
5. *Leaks:* Get down and look under the car. There are no normal "leaks", other than water from the air conditioning condenser.
6. *Tires:* Check the tire air pressure. A common trick is to pump the tire pressure up to make the car roll easier. Check the tread wear, open the trunk and check the spare too. Uneven wear is a clue that the front end needs alignment. See the troubleshooting chapter for clues to the causes of tire wear.
7. *Shock absorbers:* Check the shock absorbers by forcing downward sharply on each corner of the car. Good shocks will not allow

GENERAL INFORMATION AND MAINTENANCE

the car to bounce more than twice after you let go.

8. *Interior:* Check the entire interior. You're looking for an interior condition that agrees with the overall condition of the car. Reasonable wear is expected, but be suspicious of new seatcovers on sagging seats, new pedal pads, and worn armrests. These indicate an attempt to cover up hard use. Pull back the carpets and look for evidence of water leaks or flooding. Look for missing hardware, door handles, control knobs etc. Check lights and signal operations. Make sure all accessories (air conditioner, heater, radio etc.) work. Check windshield wiper operation.

9. *Belts and Hoses:* Open the hood and check all belts and hoses for wear, cracks or weak spots.

10. *Battery:* Low electrolyte level, corroded terminals and/or cracked case indicate a lack of maintenance.

11. *Radiator:* Look for corrosion or rust in the coolant indicating a lack of maintenance.

12. *Air filter:* A dirty air filter usually means a lack of maintenance.

13. *Ignition Wires:* Check the ignition wires for cracks, burned spots, or wear. Worn wires will have to be replaced.

14. *Oil level:* If the oil level is low, chances are the engine uses oil or leaks. Beware of water in the oil (cracked block), excessively thick oil (used to quiet a noisy engine), or thin, dirty oil with a distinct gasoline smell (internal engine problems).

15. *Automatic Transmission:* Pull the transmission dipstick out when the engine is running. The level should read "Full," and the fluid should be clear or bright red. Dark brown or black fluid that has distinct burnt odor, signals a transmission in need of repair or overhaul.

16. *Exhaust:* Check the color of the exhaust smoke. Blue smoke indicates, among other problems, worn rings; black smoke can indicate burnt valves or carburetor problems. Check the exhaust system for leaks; it can be expensive to replace.

17. *Spark Plugs:* Remove one of the spark plugs (the most accessible will do). An engine in good condition will show plugs with a light tan or gray deposit on the firing tip. See the color Tune-Up tips section for spark plug conditions.

ROAD TEST CHECK LIST

1. *Engine Performance:* The car should be peppy whether cold or warm, with adequate power and good pickup. It should respond smoothly through the gears.

2. *Brakes:* They should provide quick, firm stops with no noise, pulling or brake fade.

3. *Steering:* Sure control with no binding, harshness, or looseness and no shimmy in the wheel should be expected. Noise or vibration from the steering wheel when turning the car means trouble.

4. *Clutch (Manual Transmission):* Clutch action should give quick, smooth response with easy shifting. The clutch pedal should have about 1–1½ inches of free-play before it disengages the clutch. Start the engine, set the parking brake, put the transmission in first gear and slowly release the clutch pedal. The engine

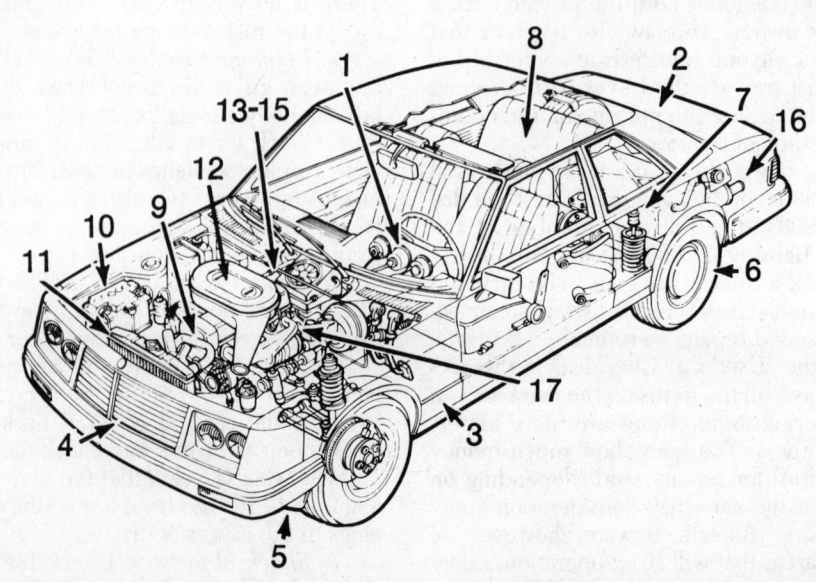

You should check these points when buying a used car. The "Used Car Checklist" gives an explanation of the numbered items

should begin to stall when the pedal is one-half to three-quarters of the way up.

5. *Automatic Transmission:* The transmission should shift rapidly and smoothly, with no noise, hesitation, or slipping.

6. *Differential:* No noise or thumps should be present. Differentials have no "normal" leaks.

7. *Driveshaft, Universal Joints:* Vibration and noise could mean driveshaft problems. Clicking at low speed or coast conditions means worn U-joints.

8. *Suspension:* Try hitting bumps at different speeds. A car that bounces has weak shock absorbers. Clunks mean worn bushings or ball joints.

9. *Frame:* Wet the tires and drive in a straight line. Tracks should show two straight lines, not four. Four tire tracks indicate a frame bent by collision damage. If the tires can't be wet for collision purpose, have a friend drive along behind you and see if the car appears to be traveling in a straight line.

Tune-Up and Performance Maintenance

TUNE-UP PROCEDURES

Neither tune-up nor troubleshooting can be considered independently since each has a direct relationship with the other.

It is advisable to follow a definite and thorough tune-up procedure. Tune-up consists of three separate steps: Analysis, the process of determining whether normal wear is responsible for performance loss, and whether parts require replacement or service and adjustment.

The manufacturer's recommended interval for tune-ups is every 30,000 miles. This interval should be shortened if the car is subjected to severe operating conditions such as trailer pulling or stop and start driving, or if starting and running problems are noticed. It is assumed that the routine maintenance described in Chapter 1 has been kept up, as this will have an effect on the results of the tune-up. All the applicable tune-up steps should be followed, as each adjustment complements the effects of the others. If the tune-up (emission control) sticker in the engine compartment disagrees with the information presented in the "Tune-up Specifications" chart in this chapter, the sticker figures must be followed. The sticker information reflects running changes made by the manufacturer during production.

Troubleshooting is a logical sequence of procedures designed to locate a particular case of trouble. The "Troubleshooting" section in Chapter 9 is general in nature (applicable to most vehicles), yet specific enough to locate the problem.

It is advisable to read the entire chapter before beginning a tune-up, although those who are more familiar with tune-up procedures may wish to go directly to the instructions.

Spark Plugs

Rough idle, hard starting, frequent engine miss at high speeds and physical deterioration are all indications that the plugs should be replaced.

The electrode end of a spark plug is a good indicator of the internal condition of your car's engine. If a spark plug is fouled, causing the engine to misfire, the problem will have to be found and corrected. Often, "reading" the plugs will lead you to the cause of the problem. Spark plug conditions and probable causes are listed in the color section.

NOTE: *A small amount of light tan or rust red colored deposits at the electrode end of the plug is normal. These plugs need not be renewed unless they are severely worn.*

Heat range is a term used to describe the cooling characteristics of spark plugs. Plugs with longer nosed insulators take a longer time to dissipate heat than plugs with shorter nosed insulators. These are termed "hot" or "cold" plugs, respectively. It is generally advisable to use the factory recommended plugs. However, in conditions of extremely hard use (cross-country driving in summer) going to the next cooler heat range may be advisable. If most driving is done in the city or over short distances, go to the next hotter heat range plug to eliminate fouling. If in doubt concerning the substitution of spark plugs, consult your Chrysler dealer.

Spark plugs should be gapped when they are checked or newly installed. Never assume that new plugs are correctly gapped.

1. Before removing the spark plugs, number the plug wires so that the correct wire goes on the plug when replaced. This can be done with pieces of adhesive tape.

2. Next, clean the area around the plugs by brushing or blowing with compressed air. You

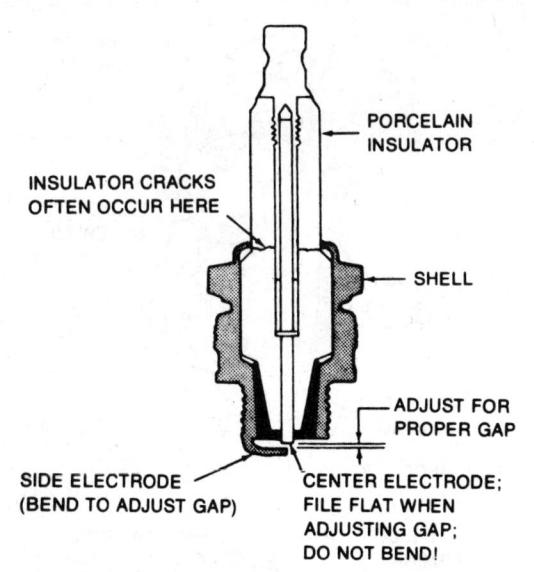

TUNE-UP AND PERFORMANCE MAINTENANCE 25

Cross section of a spark plug

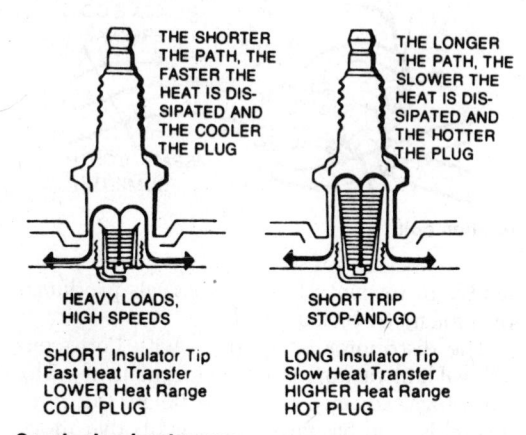

- PORCELAIN INSULATOR
- INSULATOR CRACKS OFTEN OCCUR HERE
- SHELL
- ADJUST FOR PROPER GAP
- SIDE ELECTRODE (BEND TO ADJUST GAP)
- CENTER ELECTRODE; FILE FLAT WHEN ADJUSTING GAP; DO NOT BEND!

Spark plug heat range

THE SHORTER THE PATH, THE FASTER THE HEAT IS DISSIPATED AND THE COOLER THE PLUG

THE LONGER THE PATH, THE SLOWER THE HEAT IS DISSIPATED AND THE HOTTER THE PLUG

HEAVY LOADS, HIGH SPEEDS
SHORT Insulator Tip
Fast Heat Transfer
LOWER Heat Range
COLD PLUG

SHORT TRIP STOP-AND-GO
LONG Insulator Tip
Slow Heat Transfer
HIGHER Heat Range
HOT PLUG

Pull on the rubber boot to remove the spark plug wire, not the wire itself

Keep the socket straight on the plug

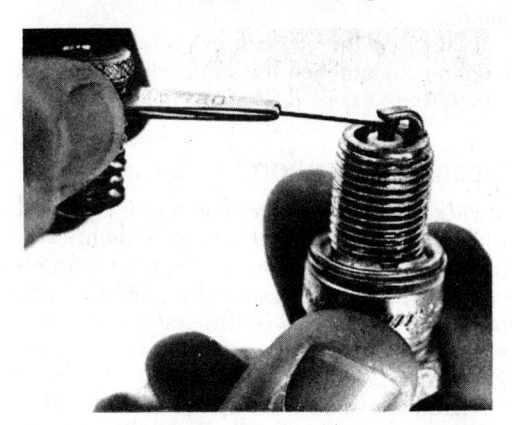

Use a wire gauge to check the electrode gap

can also loosen the plugs a few turns and crank the engine to blow the dirt away.

3. Disconnect the plug wires by twisting and pulling on the rubber cap, not on the wire.

4. Remove each plug with a rubber-insert spark plug socket. Make sure that the socket is all the way down on the plug to prevent it from slipping and cracking the porcelain insulator.

5. After removing each plug, evaluate its condition. A spark plug's useful life is approximately 30,000 miles with electronic ignition. Thus, it would make sense to replace a plug if it has been in service that long. If the plug is to be replaced, refer to the "Tune-up Specifications" chart for the proper spark plug type. The numbers indicate heat range; hotter running plugs have higher numbers.

6. If the plugs are to be reused, file the center and side electrodes flat with a fine, flat point file. Heavy or baked on deposits can be carefully scraped off with a small knife blade or the scraper tool on a combination spark plug tool. It is often suggested that plugs be tested and cleaned on a service station sandblasting machine; however, this piece of equipment is becoming rare. Check the gap between the electrodes with a round wire spark plug gapping gauge. Do not use a flat feeler gauge; it will give an inaccurate reading. If the gap is not as specified, use the bending tool on the spark plug gap gauge to bend the outside electrode. Be careful not to bend the electrode too far or too often, because excessive bending may cause

26   TUNE-UP AND PERFORMANCE MAINTENANCE

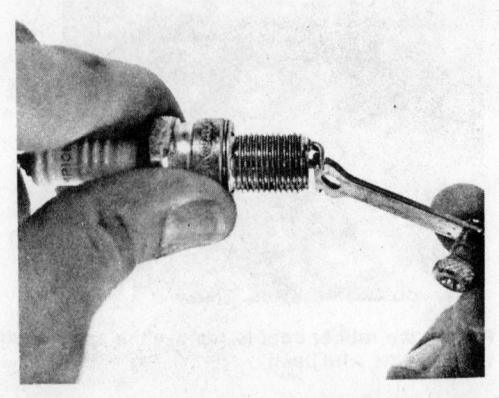

Adjust the electrode gap by bending the side electrode.

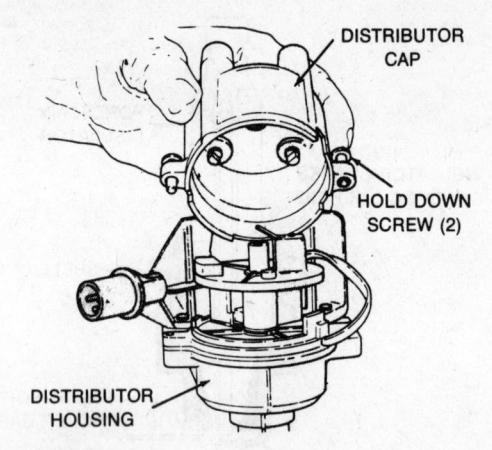

Distributor

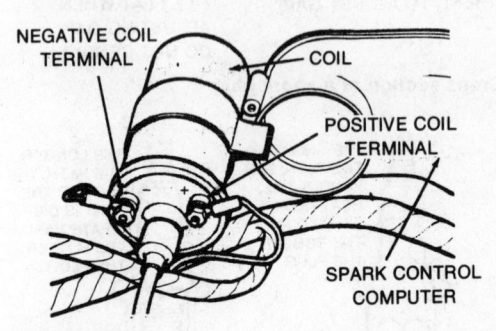

Ignition coil

the electrode to break off and fall into the combustion chamber. This would require removing the cylinder head to reach the broken piece and could also result in cylinder wall, piston ring, or valve damage.

CAUTION: *Never bend the center electrode of the spark plug. This will break the insulator and render the plug useless.*

7. Clean the threads of old plugs with a wire brush. Lubricate the threads with a drop of oil.

8. Screw the plugs in finger tight, and then tighten them with the spark plug socket. Be very careful not to overtighten them. Just snug them in.

9. Reinstall the wires. If, by chance, you have forgotten to number the plug wires, refer to the "Firing Order" illustrations in Chapter 3.

Electronic Ignition

Models using the 2.2 Liter engine are equipped with the "Electronic Fuel Control System." This consists of a Spark Control Computer, various engine sensors, and a specially calibrated carburetor. The function of this system is to provide a way for the engine to burn a correct air-fuel mixture.

The Spark Control Computer is the heart of the entire system. It has the capability of igniting the fuel mixture according to different models of engine operation by delivering an infinite amount of variable advance curves. The computer consists of one electronic printed circuit board, which simultaneously receives signals from all the sensors and within milliseconds, analyzes them to determine how the engine is operating and then advances or retards the timing.

The 2.6 Liter engine uses a system that consists of the battery, ignition switch, coil, and IC igniter (electronic control unit), built into the distributor, spark plugs and intercomponent wiring. Primary current is switched by the IC igniter in response to timing signals produced by a magnetic pickup.

The distributor is equipped with both centrifugal and vacuum advance mechanisms. The centrifugal advance is located below the rotor assembly, and has governor weights that move in and out with changes in engine speed. As speed increases the weights move outward and cause the reluctor to rotate ahead of the distributor shaft, this advances ignition timing.

The vacuum advance has a spring loaded diaphragm connected to the breaker assembly. The diaphragm is actuated against the spring pressure by carburetor vacuum pressure. When the vacuum increases, the diaphragm causes the movable breaker assembly to pivot in a direction opposite to distributor rotation, advancing the ignition timing.

Ignition Timing

Timing should be checked at each tune-up. Timing isn't likely to change very much with electronic ignition.

NOTE: *For 1985 models with Throttle Body and Multi-Point fuel injection, see the special procedure for adjusting timing at the end of Chapter 4.*

If your vehicle is equipped with the A-412

TUNE-UP AND PERFORMANCE MAINTENANCE

Tune-Up Specifications

When analyzing compression test results, look for uniformity among cylinders rather than specific pressures

Year	No. Cyl Displacement (cu. in.)	Emission ◆ Control Classification	Spark Plugs Type	Gap (in.)	Ignition Timing (deg.) ▲ Man Trans.	Ignition Timing (deg.) ▲ Auto Trans●	Valves Intake Opens ■(deg.)	Fuel Pump Pressure (psi)	Idle Speed (rpm) ▲ Man Trans.	Idle Speed (rpm) ▲ Auto Trans●
1981	4-135	All	P-65-PR4	.035	10B	10B	12	4½–6	900	900
	4-156	All	P-65-PR4	.035	—	7B	25	4½–6	—	800
1982	4-135	All	P-65-PR4	.035	12B	12B	14	4½–6	900	900
	4-156	All	RN-12Y	.035	—	7B	25	4½–6	—	800
1983	4-135	Fed-Aut	RN-12Y	.035	—	10B	16	4½–6	—	900①
	4-135	Fed-Man	RN-12Y	.035	10B	—	16	4½–6	775①	—
	4-135	Cal-Aut	RN-12Y	.035	—	10B	16	4½–6	—	900①
	4-135	Cal-Man	RN-12Y	.035	10B	—	16	4½–6	775	—
	4-135	Hi Alt.	RN-12Y	.035	6B	6B	16	4½–6	850	850
	4-156	Fed	RN-12Y	.040	7B	7B	25	4½–6	—	800
	4-156	Cal	RN-12Y	.040	7B	7B	25	4½–6	—	800
1984	4-135	Fed-Man	RN-12Y	.035	10B	—	16	4½–6	800	—
	4-135	Cal-Man	RN-12Y	.035	10B	—	16	4½–6	800	—
	4-135	Fed & Hi Alt-Aut	RN-12Y	.035	—	10B	16	4½–6	—	900
	4-135	Cal-Aut	RN-12Y	.035	—	10B	16	4½–6	—	900
	4-135	Man-EFI	RN-12Y	.035	6B	—	16	4½–6	850	—
	4-135	Auto-EFI	RN-12Y	.035	—	6B	16	4½–6	—	750
	4-135	TC	RN-12Y	.035	12B	12B	10	4½–6	990	950
	4-156	All	RN-12Y	.035–.040	—	7B	25	4½–6	—	800
1985	4-135	Man	RN-12Y	.035	10B	—	16	4½–6	800	—
	4-135	Aut	RN-12Y	.035	—	10B	16	4½–6	—	900
	4-135	Man-EFI	RN-12Y	.035	12B	—	16	4½–6	850	—
	4-135	Aut-EFI	RN-12Y	.035	—	12B	16	4½–6	—	750
	4-135	TC	RN-12Y	.035	12B	12B	10	4½–6	950	950
	4-156	All	RN-12Y	.035–.040	7B	7B	25	4½–6	800	800

▲ See text for procedure
● Figure in parentheses indicates California engine
■ All figures Before Top Dead Center
◆ Emission control classification abbreviations:
 Fed—Federal, 49 states (except California)
 CA—California cars only
 Aut—Automatic transmission
 Man—Manual transmission
 Hi. Alt—High altitude emissions package only
 EFI—Electronic Fuel Injection
 TC—Turbocharged
 Sh—Shelby
① Set idle speed with vacuum advance line connected

TUNE-UP AND PERFORMANCE MAINTENANCE

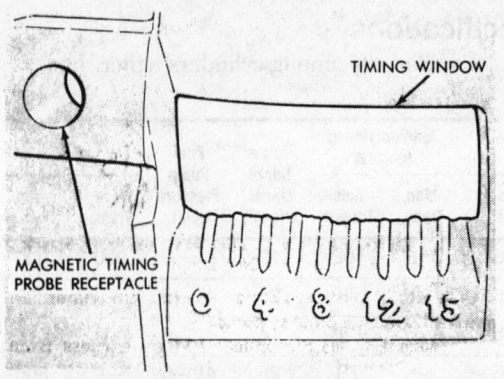

Timing mark location all manual and automatic transaxles except A-412

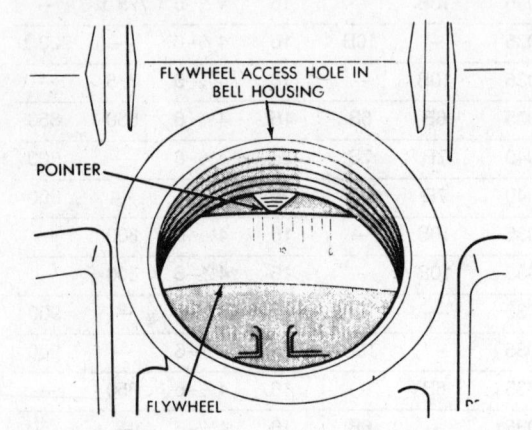

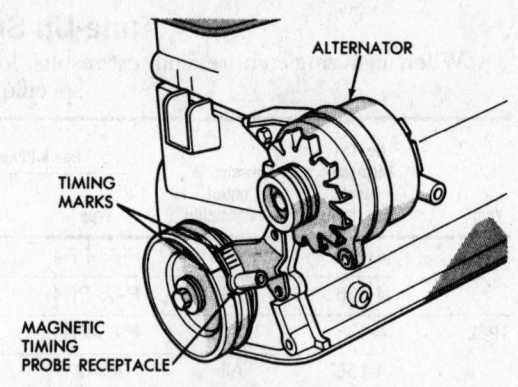

Timing marks 2.6L engine

Timing mark location A-412 transaxle

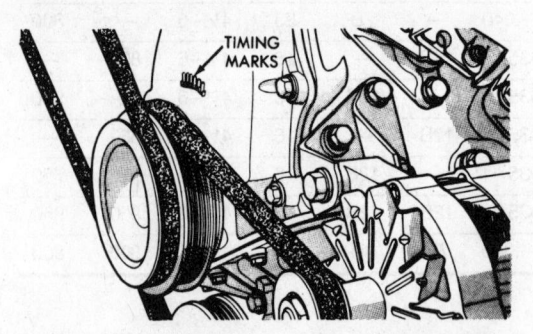

Location of timing marks on 1984 and later 2.2 liter engines. On these engines, the marks are located on the front engine timing cover, rather than on the flywheel.

transaxle, the timing marks are located on the flywheel with the pointer on the access hole. All other manual and automatic transaxles have a notch on the torque converter or flywheel, with the numerical timing marks on the bell housing. 2.2 liter engines built in 1984 and later years have the timing marks located on the front timing cover.

Models equipped with the 2.6 liter engine having the timing marks on the counter balance and the numerical pointer attached to the block.

A stroboscopic (dynamic) timing light must be used, because static lights are too inaccurate for emission controlled engines.

There are three basic types of timing light available. The first is a simple neon bulb with two wire connections. One wire connects to the spark plug terminal and the other plugs into the end of the spark plug wire for the No. 1 cylinder, thus connecting the light in series with the spark plug. This type of light is pretty dim and must be held close to the timing marks to be seen. It has the advantage of low price. The second type operates from the car's battery; two alligator clips connect to the battery terminals, while an adapter enables a third clip to be connected to the No. 1 spark plug and wire. This type provides a bright flash which can be seen even in bright sunlight. The third type replaces the battery current with 110 volt house current.

Some timing lights have other features built into them, such as dwell meters or tachometers. These are nice, in that they reduce the tangle of wires under the hood when you're working, but may duplicate the functions of tools you already have. One worthwhile feature, which is becoming more of a necessity with higher voltage ignition systems, is an inductive pickup. The inductive pickup clamps around the No. 1 spark plug wire, sensing the surges of high voltage electricity as they are sent to the plug. The advantage is that no mechanical connection is inserted between the wire and the plug, which eliminates false signals to the timing light. A timing light with an inductive pickup should be used on electronic ignition systems.

To check and adjust the timing:
1. Warm the engine to normal operating temperature. Shut off the engine and connect the timing light to the No. 1 spark plug. Do

TUNE-UP AND PERFORMANCE MAINTENANCE

not under any circumstances pierce a wire to hook up a light.

2. Clean off the timing marks and mark the pulley or damper notch and the timing scale with white chalk or paint. The timing notch on the damper or pulley can be elusive. Bump the engine around with the starter or turn the crankshaft with a wrench on the front pulley bolt to get it to an accessible position.

NOTE: *The 2.2 Liter engine has its timing marks on the flywheel and bell housing.*

3. Disconnect and plug the vacuum advance hose at the distributor or at the spark advance computer, on models that have one, to prevent any distributor advance. The vacuum line is the rubber hose connected to the metal coneshaped canister on the side of the distributor. A short screw, pencil, or a golf tee can be used to plug the hose.

4. Start the engine and adjust the idle speed to that specified in the "Tune-Up Specifications" chart. Some cars require that the timing be set with the transmission in Neutral. You can disconnect the idle solenoid, if any, to get the speed down. Otherwise, adjust the idle speed screw. This is to prevent any centrifugal advance of timing in the distributor.

5. Aim the timing light at the timing marks. Be careful not to touch the fan, which may appear to be standing still. Keep your clothes and hair, and the light's wire clear of the fan, belts, and pulleys. If the pulley or damper notch isn't aligned with the proper timing mark (see the "Tune-Up Specifications" chart), the timing will have to be adjusted.

NOTE: *TDC or Top Dead Center corresponds to 0 degrees; B, or BTDC, or Before Top Dead Center, may be shown as BEFORE; A, or ATDC, or After Top Dead Center, may be shown as AFTER.*

6. Loosen the distributor base clamp locknut. You can buy special wrenches which will make this task easy. Turn the distributor slowly to adjust the timing, holding it by the body and not the cap. Turn the distributor in the direction of rotor rotation (found in the "Firing Order" illustration in Chapter 3) to retard, and against the direction to advance.

7. Tighten the locknut. Check the timing, in case the distributor moved as you tightened it.

8. Replace the distributor vacuum hose. Correct the idle speed.

9. Shut off the engine and disconnect the light.

Valve Lash

valve adjustment determines how far the valves enter the cylinder and how long they stay open and closed.

If the valve clearance is too large, part of the lift of the camshaft will be used in removing the excessive clearance. Consequently, the valve will not be opening as far as it should. This condition has two effects: the valve train components will emit a tapping sound as they take up the excessive clearance and the engine will perform poorly because the valves don't open fully and allow the proper amount of gases to flow into and out of the engine.

If the valve clearance is too small, the intake valve and the exhaust valves will open too far and they will not fully seat on the cylinder head when they close. When a valve seats itself on the cylinder head, it does two things: it seals the combustion chamber so that none of the gases in the cylinder escape and it cools itself by transferring some of the heat it absorbs from the combustion in the cylinder to the cylinder head and to the engine's cooling system. If the valve clearance is too small, the engine will run poorly because of the gases escaping from the combustion chamber. The valves will also become overheated and will warp, since they cannot transfer heat unless they are touching the valve seat in the cylinder head.

NOTE: *While all valve adjustments must be made as accurately as possible, it is better to have the valve adjustment slightly loose then slightly tight as a burned valve may result from overly tight adjustments.*

2.2 Engine

The 2.2 liter engine uses hydraulic lash adjusters. No periodic adjustment or checking is necessary.

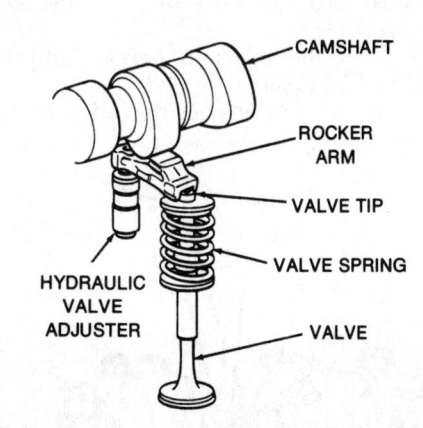

Hydraulic valve adjuster used on 2.2L engine

2.6 Engine

The 2.6 engine has a jet valve located beside the intake of each cylinder.

NOTE: *When adjusting valve clearances, the jet valve must be adjusted before the intake valve.*

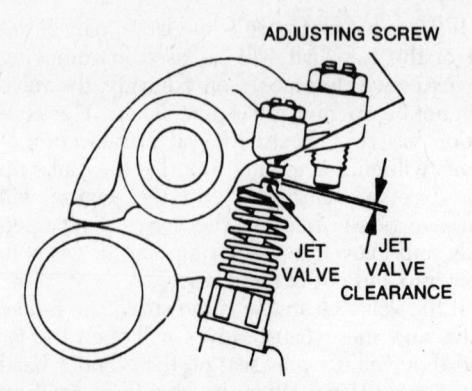

TUNE-UP AND PERFORMANCE MAINTENANCE

Adjusting the jet valve on 2.6L engines

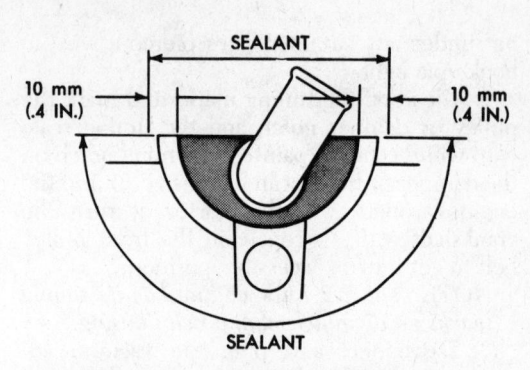

Applying sealant on the 2.6 liter valve cover

1. Start the engine and allow it to reach normal operating temperature.
2. Stop the engine and remove the air cleaner and its hoses. Remove any other cables, hoses, wires, etc., which are attached to the valve cover, and remove the valve cover.
3. Disconnect the high tension coil-to-distributor wire at the coil.
4. Watch the rocker arms for No. 1 cylinder and rotate the crankshaft until the exhaust valve is closing and the intake valve has just started to open. At this point, no. 4 cylinder will be at Top Dead Center (TDC) commencing its firing stroke.
5. Loosen the locknut on cylinder no. 4 intake valve adjusting screw 2 or more turns.
6. Loosen the locknut on the jet valve adjusting screw.
7. Turn the jet valve adjusting screw counter-clockwise and insert a 0.006 in. feeler gauge between the jet valve stem and the adjusting screw.
8. Tighten the adjusting screw until it touches the feeler gauge.
Take care not to press on the valve while adjusting because the jet valve spring is very weak.
NOTE: *If the adjusting screw is tight, special care must be taken to avoid pressing down on the jet valve when adjusting the clearance or a false reading will result.*
9. Tighten the locknut securely while holding the rocker arm adjusting screw with a screwdriver to prevent it from turning.
10. Make sure that a 0.006 in. feeler gauge can be easily inserted between the jet valve and the rocker arm.
11. Adjust no. 4 cylinder's intake valve to 0.006 in. and its exhaust value to 0.010 in. Tighten the adjusting screw locknuts and recheck each clearance.
12. Perform step 4 in conjunction with the chart below to set up the remaining three cylinders for valve adjustments.
13. Replace the valve cover and all other components. Apply sealer to the top surface of

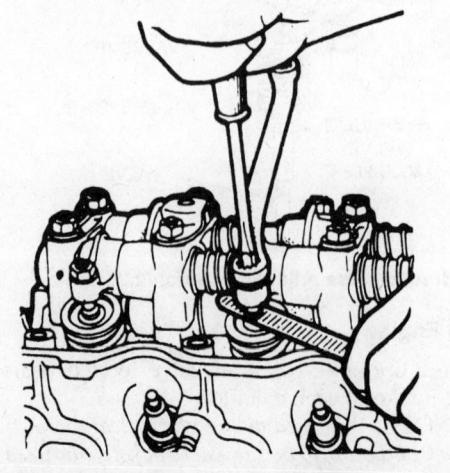

Exhaust Valve Closing	Adjust
No. 1 Cylinder	No. 4 Cylinder Valves
No. 2 Cylinder	No. 3 Cylinder Valves
No. 3 Cylinder	No. 2 Cylinder Valves
No. 4 Cylinder	No. 1 Cylinder Valves

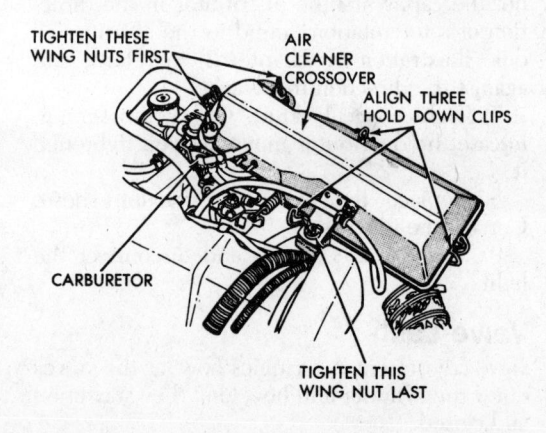

Adjusting the valve lash on 2.6L engines

TUNE-UP AND PERFORMANCE MAINTENANCE

the semi-circular packing. Run the engine and check for oil leaks at the valve cover.

Idle Speed and Mixture Adjustment

Chrysler recommends the use of propane enrichment procedure to adjust the mixture. The equipment needed for this procedure is not readily available to the general public. An alternate method recommended by Chrysler is with the use of an exhaust gas analyzer. If this equipment is not available, and a mixture adjustment must be performed, follow this procedure:

1. Run engine to normal operating temperature.
2. Place the transmission in neutral, turn off the lights and air conditioning and make certain that the electric cooling fan is operating.
3. Disconnect the EGR vacuum line, and ground the carburetor idle stop switch (if equipped) with a jumper wire.
4. Connect tachometer according to the manufacturer's instructions.

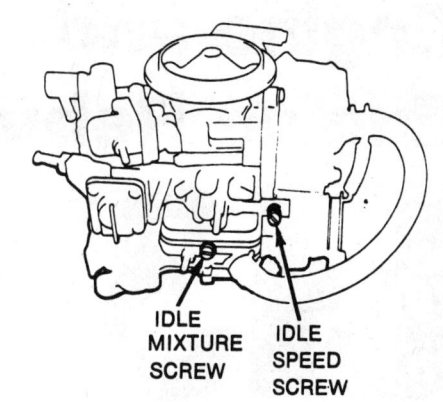

Location of idle speed and mixture adjusting screws on 2.6L engines

5. Adjust the idle screw to achieve the curb idle figure listed on the underhood sticker.
6. Back out the mixture screw to achieve the fastest possible idle.
7. Adjust the idle screw to the specified curb idle speed.

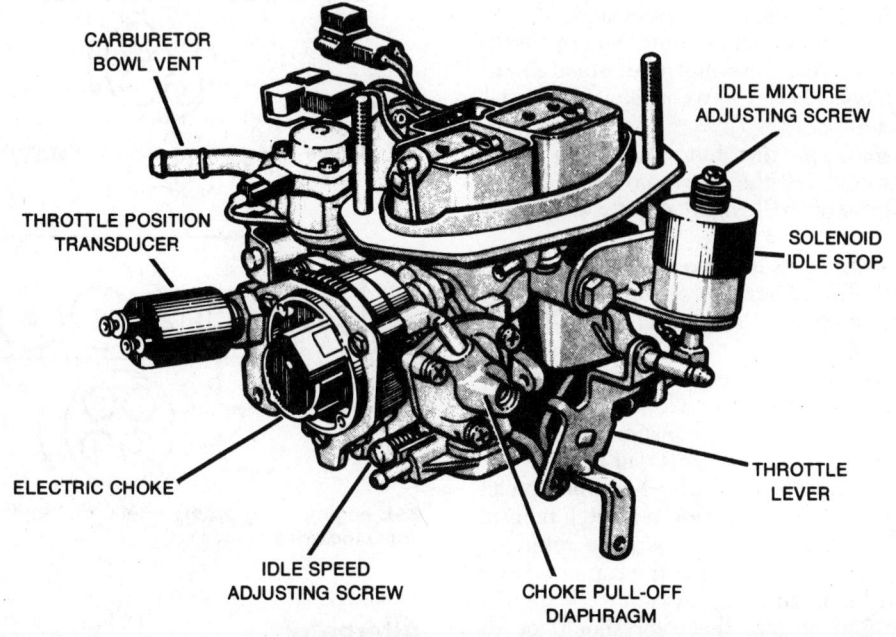

Details of the staged two-barrel carburetor

Engine and Engine Rebuilding 3

ENGINE ELECTRICAL

Distributor

REMOVAL AND INSTALLATION

1. Disconnect the distributor pickup lead wire at the harness connector.
2. Remove the distributor cap.
3. Rotate the engine crankshaft (in the direction of normal rotation) until No. 1 cylinder is at TDC on compression stroke. Make a mark on the block where the rotor points for installation reference.
4. Remove the distributor holddown bolt.
5. Carefully lift the distributor from the engine. The shaft will rotate slightly as the distributor is removed.
6. Installation is the reverse of removal.

NOTE: *The following procedure is to be used if the engine was cranked with the distributor removed.*

1. If the engine has been cranked over while the distributor was removed, rotate the crankshaft until the number one piston is at TDC on the compression stroke. This will be indicated by the O mark on the flywheel or crank pulley aligning with the pointer on the clutch housing or engine front cover. Position the rotor just ahead of the #1 terminal of the cap and lower the distributor into the engine. With the distributor fully seated, the rotor should be directly under the #1 terminal.
2. If the engine was not disturbed while the distributor was out, lower the distributor into the engine, engaging the gears and making sure that the gasket is properly seated in the block. The rotor should line up with the mark made before removal.
3. Tighten the holddown bolt and connect the wires.
4. Check and, if necessary, adjust the ignition timing.

FIRING ORDER

To avoid confusion replace the spark plug wires one at a time.

2.2L engine firing order: 1-3-4-2 distributor rotation: clockwise

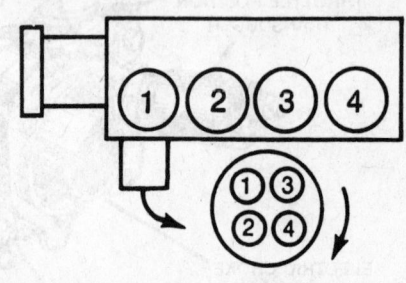

2.6L engine firing order: 1-3-4-2 distribution rotation: clockwise

Alternator

REMOVAL AND INSTALLATION

1. Disconnect the negative battery terminal.
2. Disconnect the wiring and label it for easy reinstallation.
3. Loosen the alternator adjusting bracket bolt, or adjusting nut and bolt.
4. Remove all necessary drive belts.
5. Remove the adjusting bolt or bolt and nut and the pivot bolt.

ENGINE AND ENGINE REBUILDING 33

6. Remove the alternator.
7. Installation is the reverse of removal. Adjust the belt tension to allow ½ in. of play on the longest run.

Regulator
REMOVAL AND INSTALLATION

NOTE: *The alternator on the 2.6 liter engine has an integral regulator. No adjustments are possible.*

1. Disconnect the negative battery terminal.
2. Remove the electrical connection.
3. Remove the bolts and remove the regulator.
4. This regulator is not adjustable and must be replaced as a unit if found to be defective.
5. Installation is the reverse of removal.

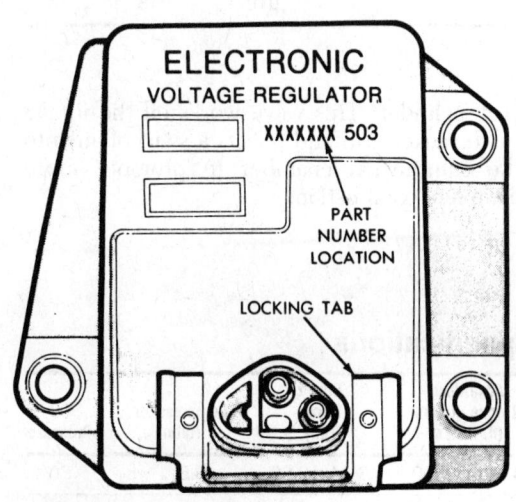

Electronic voltage regulator

Starter
REMOVAL AND INSTALLATION

1. Disconnect the negative battery terminal.
2. Remove the bolts attaching the starter to the flywheel housing and the rear bracket to the engine or transaxle.
3. On the 2.2 liter engine loosen the air pump tube at the exhaust manifold and move the tube bracket away from the starter.
4. Remove the heatshield and its clamp if so equipped.
5. Remove the electrical connections from the starter.
6. Remove the starter.
7. Installation is the reverse of removal.

SOLENOID REPLACEMENT

1. Remove the starter as previously outlined.
2. Disconnect the field coil wire from the solenoid.
3. Remove the solenoid mounting screws.
4. Remove the solenoid.
5. Installation is the reverse of removal.

Battery
REMOVAL AND INSTALLATION

1. Loosen the nuts which secure the cable ends to the battery terminals. Lift the battery cables from the terminals with a twisting motion.
2. If there is a battery cable puller available, make use of it.
3. Remove the hold-down nuts from the battery hold-down bracket and remove the bracket and the battery. Lift the battery straight up and out of the vehicle, being sure to keep the battery level to avoid spilling the battery acid.
4. Before installing the battery in the vehicle, make sure that the battery terminals are clean and free from corrosion. Use a battery terminal cleaner on the terminals and on the inside of the battery cable ends. If a cleaner is not available, use coarse grade sandpaper to remove the corrosion. A mixture of baking soda and water poured over the terminals and cable ends will help remove and neutralized any acid buildup. Before installing the cables onto the terminals, cut a piece of felt cloth, or something similar into a circle about 3 in. across. Cut a hole in the middle about the size of the battery terminals at their base. Push the cloth pieces over the terminals so that they lay flat on the top of the battery. Soak the pieces of cloth with oil. This will keep the formation of oxidized acid to a minimum. Place the battery in the vehicle. Install the cables onto the terminals. Tighten the nuts on the cable ends. Smear a light coating of grease on the cable ends and tops of the terminals. This will further prevent the buildup of oxidized acid on

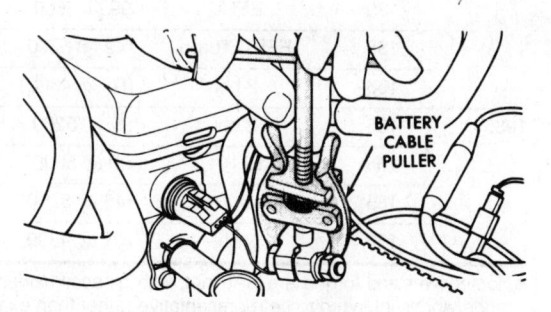

Disconnecting the battery cables

ENGINE AND ENGINE REBUILDING

the terminals and the cable ends. Install and tighten the nuts of the battery hold-down bracket.

ENGINE MECHANICAL

Design

Two engines are used in Chrysler K-Car models. A 135 cu. in. (2.2 Liter) engine is standard. The 156 cu. in. (2.6 Liter) engine is optional. Also optional on some recent models is a turbocharged version, employing dished pistons which lower the compression ratio to 8.5:1.

The 2.2 Liter engine is a four cylinder overhead camshaft power plant with a cast iron cylinder head. The crankshaft is supported by five main bearings. No vibration damper is used. A sintered iron timing belt sprocket is mounted on the crankshaft. The intake manifold and oil filter base are aluminum.

The 2.6 Liter optional engine is also a four cylinder overhead camshaft power plant with a cast iron block, aluminum head and a silent shaft system. The countershafts (silent shafts) are incorporated in the cylinder block to reduce noise and vibration. Its most distinguishing feature is a "jet valve" located beside the intake valve of each cylinder. This valve works off the intake valve rocker arm and injects a swirl of air into the combustion chamber to promote more complete combustion.

Ring Gap
All measurements are given in inches

Year	Engine No. Cyl Displacement (cu. in.)	Top Compression	Bottom Compression	Oil Control
1981	135	.011–.021	.011–.021	.015–.055
	156	.011–.018	.011–.018	.0078–.035
1982	135	.011–.021	.011–.021	.015–.055
	156	.011–.018	.011–.018	.0078–.035
1983–85	135	.011–.021	.011–.021	.015–.055
	135 Turbo	.010–.020	.009–.018	.015–.055
	156	.010–.018	.010–.018	.0078–.035

General Engine Specifications

Year	Engine Displacement Cu. In.■	Carburetor Type	Advertised Horsepower @ rpm■	Advertised Torque @ rpm (ft. lbs.)■	Bore x Stroke (in.)	Compression Ratio	Oil Pressure
1981	135	2 bbl	84 @ 4800	111 @ 2800	3.44 x 3.62	8.5:1	50
	156	2 bbl	92 @ 4500	131 @ 2500	3.59 x 3.86	8.2:1	57
1982	135	2 bbl	84 @ 4800	111 @ 2800	3.44 x 3.62	8.5:1	50
	156	2 bbl	92 @ 4500	131 @ 2500	3.59 x 3.86	8.2:1	57
1983	135	2 bbl	94 @ 4800	158 @ 2800	3.44 x 3.62	9.0:1	50
	156	2 bbl	93 @ 4500	179 @ 2500	3.59 x 3.86	8.2:1	56.5
1984	135	2 bbl	96 @ 5200	119 @ 3200	3.44 x 3.62	9.0:1	50
	135	EFI①	99 @ 5600	121 @ 3200	3.44 x 3.62	9.0:1	50
	135	EFI① Turbo	142 @ 5600	160 @ 3600	3.44 x 3.62	8.1:1	50
	156	2 bbl	101 @ 4800	140 @ 2800	3.59 x 3.86	8.7:1	85
1985	135	2 bbl	96 @ 5200	119 @ 3200	3.44 x 3.62	9.0:1	50
	135	EFI①	99 @ 5600	121 @ 3200	3.44 x 3.62	9.0:1	50
	135	EFI① Turbo	146 @ 5200	168 @ 3600	3.44 x 3.62	8.1:1	50
	156	2 bbl	101 @ 4800	140 @ 2800	3.59 x 3.86	8.7:1	85

■Horsepower and torque are SAE net, with all accessories installed and operating. Figure may vary from model-to-model and is intended to be representative rather than exact.
① EFI—Electronic Fuel Injection

ENGINE AND ENGINE REBUILDING

Valve Specifications

Year	Engine Displacement Cu. In.	Seat Angle (deg)	Face Angle (deg)	Spring Test Pressure (lbs. @ in.)	Spring Installed Height (in.)	Stem to Guide Clearance (in.) Intake	Stem to Guide Clearance (in.) Exhaust	Stem Diameter (in.) Intake	Stem Diameter (in.) Exhaust
1981	135	45	45.5	175 @ 1.22	1.65	.001–.003	.002–.004	.312–.313	.311–.312
	156	43.75	45.25	34.1 @ 1.18	1.59	.001–.002	.002–.003	.315	.315
1982	135	45	45.5	175 @ 1.22	1.65	.001–.003	.002–.004	.312–.313	.311–.312
	156	43.75	45.22	34.1 @ 1.18	1.59	.001–.002	.002–.003	.315	.315
1983–84	135	45	45	175 @ 1.22	1.65	.0009–.0026	.0030–.0047	.3124	.3103
	156	45	45	61 @ 1.59	1.59	.0012–.0024	.0020–.0035	.315	.315
1985	135	45	45	150 @ 1.22 ①	1.65	.0009–.0026	.0030–.0047	.3124	.3103
	156	45	45	61 @ 1.59	1.59	.0012–.0024	.0020–.0035	.315	.315

① 175—Turbocharged engines

Crankshaft and Connecting Rod Specifications
All measurements are given in inches

Year	Engine Displacement Cu. In.	Main Brg Journal Dia	Main Brg Oil Clearance	Shaft End-Play	Thrust on No.	Journal Diameter	Oil Clearance	Side Clearance
1981	135	2.362–2.363	.0004–.0026	.002–.007	3	1.968–1.969	.0004–.0026	.005–.013
	156	2.3622	.0008–.0028	.002–.007	3	2.0866	.0008–.0028	.004–.010
1982	135	2.362–2.363	.0004–.0026	.002–.007	3	1.968–1.969	.0004–.0026	.005–.013
	156	2.3622	.0008–.0028	.002–.007	3	2.0866	.0004–.0026	.005–.013
1983–85	135	2.362–2.363	.0003–.0031	.002–.007	3	1.968–1.969	.0008–.0034	.005–.013
	135 Turbo	2.362–2.363	.0004–.0023	.002–.007	3	1.968–1.969	.0008–.0031	.005–.013
1983–85	156	2.3622	.0008–.0028	.002–.007	3	2.0866	.0008–.0028	.004–.010

Engine Removal and Installation

Manual Transmission

NOTE: *The engine and transmission must be removed together, or the transmission should be completely removed from the car first. The following is for engine/transmission assembly removal.*

1. Disconnect the battery.
2. Mark the hood hinge outline and remove the hood.
3. Drain the cooling system.
4. Remove the radiator hoses and remove the radiator, fan and shroud assembly.
5. Remove the air cleaner and hoses.
6. The air conditioning compressor does not have to be disconnected. Remove it from its bracket and position it out of the way. Securing it with wire is the best method.

NOTE: *On A/C cars do not disconnect any hoses from the A/C system. Disconnect compressor with hoses attached. If the car has power steering, remove the power steering pump mounting bolts and set the pump aside without disconnecting any hoses.*

7. Disconnect all wiring from the engine, alternator and carburetor.
8. Disconnect the fuel line, heater hoses and accelerator linkage.
9. Disconnect the air pump lines.

36 ENGINE AND ENGINE REBUILDING

Ring Side Clearance
All measurements are given in inches

Year	Engine	Top Compression	Bottom Compression	Oil Control
1981	135	.0015–.0031	.0015–.0037	Snug
	156	.0024–.0039	.0008–.0024	Snug
1982	135	.0015–.0031	.0015–.0037	Snug
	156	.0024–.0039	.0008–.0024	Snug
1983–85	135	.0015–.0031	.0015–.0037	Snug
	156	.0024–.0039	.0008–.0024	Snug

Piston Clearance

Year	Engine No. Cyl. Displacement (cu. in.)	Piston to Bore Clearance (in.)
1981	135	.0005–.0240
	156	.0005–.0240
1982	135	.0005–.0240
	156	.0005–.0240
1983–85	135	.0005
	156	.0008–.0016

Torque Specifications
All readings in ft. lbs.

Year	Engine Displacement Cu In.	Cylinder Head Bolts	Rod Bearing Bolts	Main Bearing Bolts	Crankshaft Pulley Bolt	Flywheel-to Crankshaft Bolts	Manifolds Intake	Manifolds Exhaust	Camshaft Cap Bolts
1981	135	45 ①	40 ②	30 ②	50	NA	17	17	14
	156	69 ③	34	58	87	97	13	13	13
1982–85	135	45 ①	40 ②	30 ②	50	65	200 ④	200 ④	165 ④
	156	69 ③	34	58	87	—	150 ④	150 ④	160 ④

① Torque Sequence 30–45–45 plus ¼ turn
② Plus ¼ turn
③ Cold engine; Hot engine 76 ft. lbs.
④ Readings in inch pounds
NA—not available

10. Remove the alternator. Remove the oil filter.
11. Disconnect the clutch and speedometer cables.
12. Raise the vehicle and support it on jackstands.
13. Remove the starter.
14. Disconnect the exhaust pipe.
15. Remove the air pump. Remove the right inner splash shield.
16. Disconnect the transmission linkage.
17. Lower the vehicle.
18. Attach a lifting fixture and shop crane to the engine. Support the transmission securely. Remove the engine ground strap. Remove the bolt that passes through the insulator on the right side engine mount. Remove the bolts fastening the transmission case to the cylinder block. Remove the transmission case lower cover. Make sure the clutch cable has been disconnected. Remove the front engine mount screw and nut. Remove the front engine mount screw and nut. Remove the transmission anti roll strut on 1983 and later models. On 1984 and later models, remove the insulator through-bolt from inside the wheel house. Remove the engine from the vehicle.
19. Lower the engine into place and loosely install all the engine mounting bolts. When all are installed, torque to 40 ft. lbs. Install the transmission case to cylinder block mounting screws and torque to 70 ft. lbs.
20. Remove the lifting fixture and raise the vehicle, supporting it on jackstands.

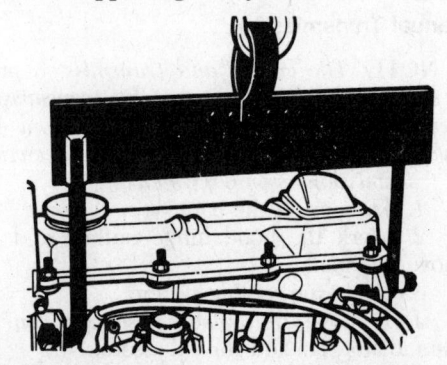

Engine lifting device

ENGINE OVERHAUL

Most engine overhaul procedures are fairly standard. In addition to specific parts replacement procedures and complete specifications for your individual engine, this chapter also is a guide to accepted rebuilding procedures. Examples of standard rebuilding practice are shown and should be used along with specific details concerning your particular engine.

Competent and accurate machine shop services will ensure maximum performance, reliability and engine life. Procedures marked with the symbol shown above should be performed by a competent machine shop, and are provided so that you will be familiar with the procedures necessary to a successful overhaul.

In most instances it is more profitable for the do-it-yourself mechanic to remove, clean and inspect the component, buy the necessary parts and deliver these to a shop for actual machine work.

On the other hand, much of the rebuilding work (crankshaft, block, bearings, pistons, rods, and other components) is well within the scope of the do-it-yourself mechanic.

Tools

The tools required for an engine overhaul or parts replacement will depend on the depth of your involvement. With a few exceptions, they will be the tools found in a mechanic's tool kit (see Chapter 1). More in-depth work will require any or all of the following:
- a dial indicator (reading in thousandths) mounted on a universal base
- micrometers and telescope gauges
- jaw and screw-type pullers
- scraper
- valve spring compressor
- ring groove cleaner
- piston ring expander and compressor
- ridge reamer
- cylinder hone or glaze breaker
- Plastigage®
- engine stand

Use of most of these tools is illustrated in this chapter. Many can be rented for a one-time use from a local parts jobber or tool supply house specializing in automotive work.

Occasionally, the use of special tools is called for. See the information on Special Tools and the Safety Notice in the front of this book before substituting another tool.

Inspection Techniques

Procedures and specifications are given in this chapter for inspecting, cleaning and assessing the wear limits of most major components. Other procedures such as Magnaflux and Zyglo can be used to locate material flaws and stress cracks. Magnaflux is a magnetic process applicable only to ferrous materials. The Zyglo process coats the material with a flourescent dye penetrant and can be used on any material. Check for suspected surface cracks can be more readily made using spot check dye. The dye is sprayed onto the suspected area, wiped off and the area sprayed with a developer. Cracks will show up brightly.

Overhaul Tips

Aluminum has become extremely popular for use in engines, due to its low weight. Observe the following precautions when handling aluminum parts:
- Never hot tank aluminum parts (the caustic hot-tank solution will eat the aluminum)
- Remove all aluminum parts (identification tag, etc.) from engine parts prior to hot-tanking.
- Always coat threads lightly with engine oil or anti-seize compounds before installation, to prevent seizure.
- Never over-torque bolts or spark plugs, especially in aluminum threads.

Stripped threads in any component can be repaired using any of several commercial repair kits (Heli-Coil, Microdot, Keenserts, etc.)

When assembling the engine, any parts that will be in frictional contact must be pre-lubed to provide lubrication at initial start-up. Any product specifically formulated for this purpose can be used, but engine oil is not recommended as a pre-lube.

When semi-permanent (locked, but removable) installation of bolts or nuts is desired, threads should be cleaned and coated with Loctite® or other similar, commercial non-hardening sealant.

Repairing Damaged Threads

Several methods of repairing damaged threads are available. Heli-Coil® (shown here), Keenserts® and Microdot® are among the most widely used. All involve basically the same principle—drilling out stripped threads, tapping the hole and installing a pre-wound insert—making welding, plugging and oversize fasteners unnecessary.

Two types of thread repair inserts are usually supplied—a standard type for most Inch Coarse, Inch Fine, Metric Coarse and Metric Fine thread sizes and a spark plug type to fit most spark plug port sizes. Consult the individual manufacturer's catalog to determine exact applications. Typical thread repair kits will contain a selection of pre-wound threaded inserts, a tap (corresponding to the outside diameter threads of the insert) and an installation tool. Spark plug inserts usually differ because they require a tap equipped with pilot threads and a combined reamer/tap section. Most manufacturers also supply blister-packed thread repair inserts separately in addition to a master kit containing a variety of taps and inserts plus installation tools.

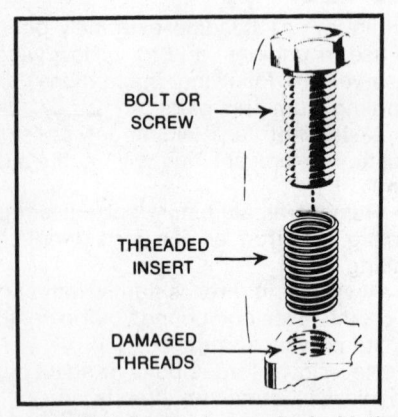

Before effecting a repair to a threaded hole, remove any snapped, broken or damaged bolts or studs. Penetrating oil can be used to free frozen threads; the offending item can be removed with locking pliers or with a screw or stud extractor. After the hole is clear, the thread can be repaired, as follows:

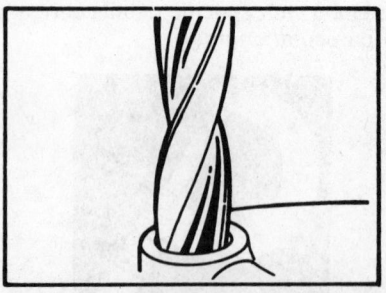

Drill out the damaged threads with specified drill. Drill completely through the hole or to the bottom of a blind hole

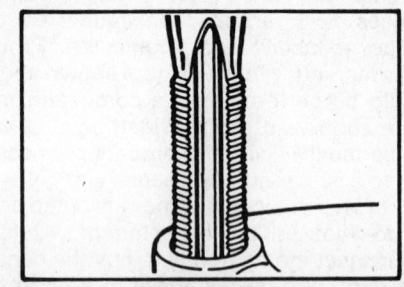

With the tap supplied, tap the hole to receive the thread insert. Keep the tap well oiled and back it out frequently to avoid clogging the threads

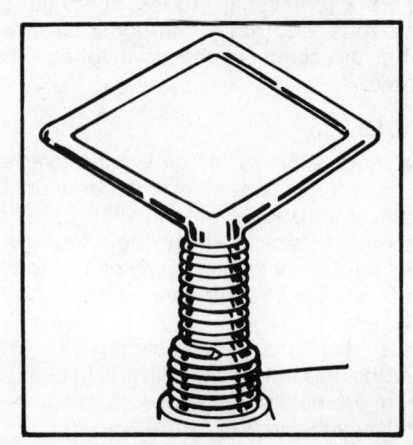

Damaged bolt holes can be repaired with thread repair inserts

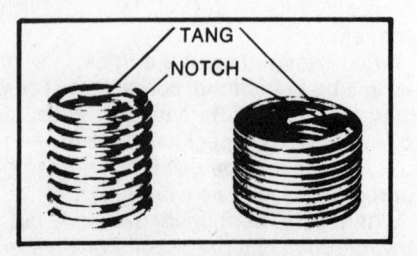

Standard thread repair insert (left) and spark plug thread insert (right)

Screw the threaded insert onto the installation tool until the tang engages the slot. Screw the insert into the tapped hole until it is ¼–½ turn below the top surface. After installation break off the tang with a hammer and punch

ENGINE AND ENGINE REBUILDING

Standard Torque Specifications and Fastener Markings

In the absence of specific torques, the following chart can be used as a guide to the maximum safe torque of a particular size/grade of fastener.
- There is no torque difference for fine or coarse threads.
- Torque values are based on clean, dry threads. Reduce the value by 10% if threads are oiled prior to assembly.
- The torque required for aluminum components or fasteners is considerably less.

U.S. Bolts

SAE Grade Number	1 or 2			5			6 or 7		
Number of lines always 2 less than the grade number.									
	Maximum Torque			Maximum Torque			Maximum Torque		
Bolt Size (Inches)—(Thread)	Ft./Lbs.	Kgm	Nm	Ft./Lbs.	Kgm	Nm	Ft./Lbs.	Kgm	Nm
¼—20	5	0.7	6.8	8	1.1	10.8	10	1.4	13.5
—28	6	0.8	8.1	10	1.4	13.6			
5/16—18	11	1.5	14.9	17	2.3	23.0	19	2.6	25.8
—24	13	1.8	17.6	19	2.6	25.7			
⅜—16	18	2.5	24.4	31	4.3	42.0	34	4.7	46.0
—24	20	2.75	27.1	35	4.8	47.5			
7/16—14	28	3.8	37.0	49	6.8	66.4	55	7.6	74.5
—20	30	4.2	40.7	55	7.6	74.5			
½—13	39	5.4	52.8	75	10.4	101.7	85	11.75	115.2
—20	41	5.7	55.6	85	11.7	115.2			
9/16—12	51	7.0	69.2	110	15.2	149.1	120	16.6	162.7
—18	55	7.6	74.5	120	16.6	162.7			
⅝—11	83	11.5	112.5	150	20.7	203.3	167	23.0	226.5
—18	95	13.1	128.8	170	23.5	230.5			
¾—10	105	14.5	142.3	270	37.3	366.0	280	38.7	379.6
—16	115	15.9	155.9	295	40.8	400.0			
⅞—9	160	22.1	216.9	395	54.6	535.5	440	60.9	596.5
—14	175	24.2	237.2	435	60.1	589.7			
1—8	236	32.5	318.6	590	81.6	799.9	660	91.3	894.8
—14	250	34.6	338.9	660	91.3	849.8			

Metric Bolts

Relative Strength Marking	4.6, 4.8			8.8		
Bolt Markings						
	Maximum Torque			Maximum Torque		
Bolt Size Thread Size x Pitch (mm)	Ft./Lbs.	Kgm	Nm	Ft./Lbs.	Kgm	Nm
6 x 1.0	2–3	.2–.4	3–4	3–6	.4–.8	5–8
8 x 1.25	6–8	.8–1	8–12	9–14	1.2–1.9	13–19
10 x 1.25	12–17	1.5–2.3	16–23	20–29	2.7–4.0	27–39
12 x 1.25	21–32	2.9–4.4	29–43	35–53	4.8–7.3	47–72
14 x 1.5	35–52	4.8–7.1	48–70	57–85	7.8–11.7	77–110
16 x 1.5	51–77	7.0–10.6	67–100	90–120	12.4–16.5	130–160
18 x 1.5	74–110	10.2–15.1	100–150	130–170	17.9–23.4	180–230
20 x 1.5	110–140	15.1–19.3	150–190	190–240	26.2–46.9	160–320
22 x 1.5	150–190	22.0–26.2	200–260	250–320	34.5–44.1	340–430
24 x 1.5	190–240	26.2–46.9	260–320	310–410	42.7–56.5	420–550

ENGINE AND ENGINE REBUILDING

CHECKING ENGINE COMPRESSION

A noticeable lack of engine power, excessive oil consumption and/or poor fuel mileage measured over an extended period are all indicators of internal engine wear. Worn piston rings, scored or worn cylinder bores, blown head gaskets, sticking or burnt valves and worn valve seats are all possible culprits here. A check of each cylinder's compression will help you locate the problems.

As mentioned in the "Tools and Equipment" section of Chapter 1, a screw-in type compression gauge is more accurate than the type you simply hold against the spark plug hole, although it takes slightly longer to use. It's worth it to obtain a more accurate reading. Follow the procedures below for gasoline and diesel-engined cars.

Gasoline Engines

1. Warm up the engine to normal operating temperature.
2. Remove all spark plugs.

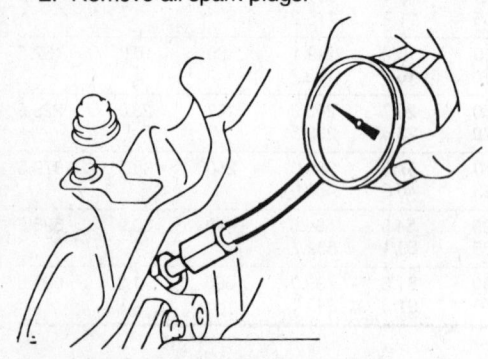

The screw-in type compression gauge is more accurate

3. Disconnect the high-tension lead from the ignition coil.
4. On carbureted cars, fully open the throttle either by operating the carburetor throttle linkage by hand or by having an assistant "floor" the accelerator pedal. On fuel-injected cars, disconnect the cold start valve and all injector connections.
5. Screw the compression gauge into the No. 1 spark plug hole until the fitting is snug.
NOTE: *Be careful not to crossthread the plug hole. On aluminum cylinder heads use extra care, as the threads in these heads are easily ruined.*
6. Ask an assistant to depress the accelerator pedal fully on both carbureted and fuel-injected cars. Then, while you read the compression gauge, ask the assistant to crank the engine two or three times in short bursts using the ignition switch.
7. Read the compression gauge at the end of each series of cranks, and record the highest of these readings. Repeat this procedure for each of the engine's cylinders. Compare the highest reading of each cylinder to the compression pressure specifications in the "Tune-Up Specifications" chart in Chapter 2. The specs in this chart are maximum values.

A cylinder's compression pressure is usually acceptable if it is not less than 80% of maximum. The difference between each cylinder should be no more than 12–14 pounds.

8. If a cylinder is unusually low, pour a tablespoon of clean engine oil into the cylinder through the spark plug hole and repeat the compression test. If the compression comes up after adding the oil, it appears that that cylinder's piston rings or bore are damaged or worn. If the pressure remains low, the valves may not be seating properly (a valve job is needed), or the head gasket may be blown near that cylinder. If compression in any two adjacent cylinders is low, and if the addition of oil doesn't help the compression, there is leakage past the head gasket. Oil and coolant water in the combustion chamber can result from this problem. There may be evidence of water droplets on the engine dipstick when a head gasket has blown.

Diesel Engines

Checking cylinder compression on diesel engines is basically the same procedure as on gasoline engines except for the following:

1. A special compression gauge adaptor suitable for diesel engines (because these engines have much greater compression pressures) must be used.
2. Remove the injector tubes and remove the injectors from each cylinder.
NOTE: *Don't forget to remove the washer underneath each injector; otherwise, it may get lost when the engine is cranked.*

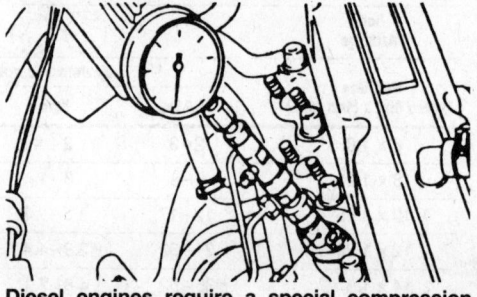

Diesel engines require a special compression gauge adaptor

3. When fitting the compression gauge adaptor to the cylinder head, make sure the bleeder of the gauge (if equipped) is closed.
4. When reinstalling the injector assemblies, install new washers underneath each injector.

ENGINE AND ENGINE REBUILDING

21. Install the right inner splash shield. Install the starter. Connect the ground strap.
22. Connect the transmission linkage, install the air pump, connect the exhaust pipe and lower the vehicle.
23. Connect the clutch and speedometer cables.
24. Install the alternator. Install the oil filter.
25. Install the air pump lines.
26. Connect the fuel line, heater hoses and accelerator linkage.
27. Connect all wiring.
28. Mount the air conditioning compressor.
29. Install the air cleaner.
30. Install the radiator and hoses.
31. Fill the cooling system.
32. Install the hood.
33. Connect the battery.
34. Start the engine and run it to normal operating temperature.
35. Check the timing and adjust if necessary. Adjust the carburetor idle speed and mixture, and the transmission linkage.

Automatic Transmission

The engine is removed without the transmission.

1. Disconnect the battery.
2. Scribe the outline of the hood hinges and remove the hood.
3. Drain the cooling system.
4. Disconnect the hoses from the radiator and engine.
5. Remove the air cleaner and hoses.
6. Disconnect the air conditioning compressor and set it aside, with refrigerant lines attached.
   CAUTION: *Do not disconnect any of the refrigerant lines.*
7. Disconnect and tag all electrical connections from the engine.
8. Disconnect the fuel line, accelerator cable and heater hoses. Plug the lines to prevent leakage.
9. Remove the diverter valve and lines from the air pump.
10. Remove the alternator.
11. Remove the upper bell housing bolts.
12. Raise and support the vehicle.
13. Remove the wheels and right and left splash shields.
14. Remove the power steering pump and set it aside. Do not disconnect the lines.
15. Remove the water pump and crankshaft pulleys.
16. Remove the front engine mounting bolt.
17. Remove the inspection cover from the transmission and remove the bolts from the flex plate. Mark the flex plate for installation in the same position. Install a C-clamp so as to hold the torque converter in position.
18. Remove the starter.
19. Remove the remaining lower bell housing bolts.
20. Lower the vehicle and support the transmission with a jack.
21. Remove the oil filter and drain the oil.
22. Attach a lifting fixture to the engine and remove the engine.
23. Installation is the reverse of removal. Be sure to connect all lines, hoses and wires. Fill the engine with oil and coolant and test for leaks.

Cylinder Head

REMOVAL AND INSTALLATION

2.2 Engines

1. Disconnect the negative battery terminal.
2. Drain the cooling system.
3. Remove the air cleaner assembly.
4. Disconnect all lines, hoses and wires from the head, manifold and carburetor.
5. Disconnect the accelerator linkage.
6. Remove the distributor cap.
7. Disconnect the exhaust pipe.
8. Remove the carburetor.
9. Remove the intake and exhaust manifolds.
10. Remove the upper portion of the front cover.
11. Turn the engine by hand until all gear timing marks are aligned.
12. Loosen the drive belt tensioner and slip the belt off the camshaft gear.
13. If equipped with air conditioning, remove the compressor from the mounting brackets and support it out of the way with wires. Remove the mounting brackets from the head.
14. Remove the valve cover, gaskets and seals.
15. Remove head bolts in reverse order of the tightening sequence.
16. Lift off the head and discard the gasket.
17. Installation is the reverse of removal. Make certain all gasket surfaces are thoroughly cleaned and are free of deep nicks or scratches. Always use new gaskets and seals. Never reuse a gasket or seal, even if it looks good. When positioning the head on the block, insert bolts 8 and 10 (see illustration) to align the head. Tighten bolts in the order shown to specifications. This is a four step procedure: first torque the bolts in the order shown to 30 ft. lbs.; then, torque them in the order shown to 45 ft. lbs.; again, in the order shown, torque them to 45 ft. lbs; then, turn each bolt ¼ turn tighter, again in the order shown. Make sure all timing marks

42 ENGINE AND ENGINE REBUILDING

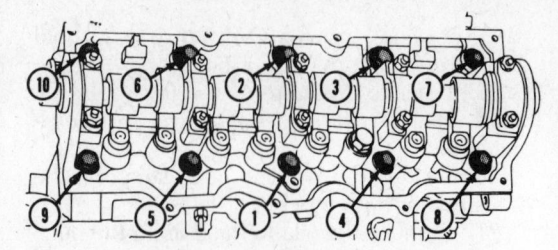

2.2L cylinder head bolt tightening sequence

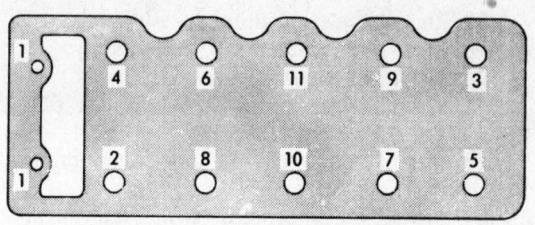

2.6.1. engine cylinder head bolt loosening sequence

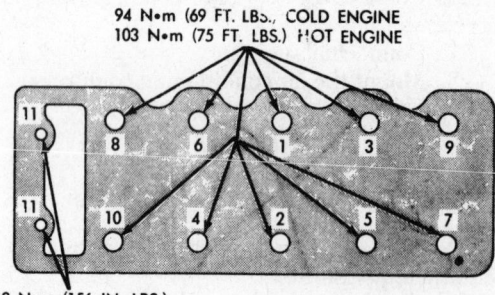

2.6L cylinder head bolt tightening sequence
94 N•m (69 FT. LBS.) COLD ENGINE
103 N•m (75 FT. LBS.) HOT ENGINE
18 N•m (156 IN. LBS.)

are aligned before installing the drive belt. The drive belt is correctly tensioned when it can be twisted 90° with the thumb and index finger midway between the camshaft and the intermediate shaft.

2.6 Engines

CAUTION: *Do not perform this operation on a warm engine. Remove the head bolts in the sequence shown in several steps. Loosen the head bolts evenly, not one at a time. Do not attempt to slide the cylinder head off the block, as it is located with dowel pins. Lift the head straight up and off the block.*

1. Disconnect the battery. Remove the air cleaner and duct. Remove the PCV hose. Remove the water pump pulley cover and remove the fuel pump and carb-to-head cover bracket. Remove the water pump drive belt.
2. Remove the two bolts that retain it and remove the cylinder head cover.
3. Drain the cooling system. Disconnect the upper radiator hose and heater hoses.
4. Turn the crankshaft until No. 1 piston is at the top of its compression stroke (both No. 1 cylinder valves closed and timing marks at Top Center). Remove the distributor cap and match mark the distributor body with the rotor and the cylinder head. Also matchmark the timing gear and chain.
5. Mark the spark plug wires and disconnect them. Remove the mounting bolt and remove the distributor.
6. Disconnect power brake and any other vacuum hoses that are in the way. Disconnect all wiring that is in the way. Disconnect the carburetor linkage.
7. Remove the camshaft sprocket bolt, sprocket, and distributor drive gear. Disconnect the air feeder hoses from underneath the vehicle.
8. If the car has power steering, unbolt the pump and move it aside without disconnecting hoses.
9. Remove the ground wire and dipstick tube. Remove the exhaust manifold heat shield and separate the exhaust manifold from the catalytic converter.
10. Remove the cylinder head bolts in several stages, using the sequence illustrated. Then, pull the cylinder head off the engine.
11. Install the new gasket without sealer and in a position that causes all bolt holes and the outer border to line up with the bolt holes and outer edge of the block. Lightly oil all the bolts and install them finger tight. Then, torque the bolts to 35 ft. lbs. in the sequence shown. Now, torque the bolts to 69 ft. lbs. in the sequence shown. Torque the cylinder head to timing chain cover bolts to 156 in. lbs. Reverse the remaining removal procedures to reassemble.

CYLINDER HEAD INSPECTION

Inspect the cylinder head with a straightedge and flat feeler gauge in all the directions illustrated. Warp limit is .004 in. for both engines. If the limit is exceeded, have the cylinder head machined flat by a competent automotive machine shop.

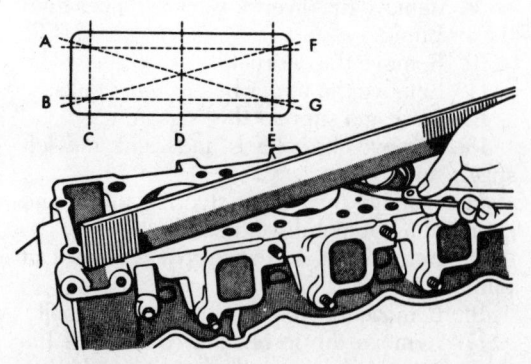

Inspect the cylinder head for flatness in every direction illustrated

ENGINE AND ENGINE REBUILDING 43

Valves and Springs

ADJUSTMENT

The 2.2 liter engine has hydraulic lash adjusters. All that is necessary is that they be replaced with some oil inside them after valve work is completed. On the 2.6 liter engine, intake, exhaust, and jet valves must be adjusted as described in Chapter 2.

REMOVAL AND INSTALLATION

2.2 Liter Engine

1. Remove the cylinder head as described above. Mark all valves and rockers for reinstallation in the same positions.

2. You'll need a valve spring compressor tool such as Chrysler No. 4682. This tool hooks around the thinnest diameter sections of the camshaft and pushes downward on either side of of each valve spring retainer. Rotate the camshaft so the first rocker arm is under the base circle of the cam. Then, depress the valve spring with the special tool just until the rocker arm can be slid out.

3. Repeat this procedure for each of the rest of the rockers.

4. Remove all the hydraulic lash adjusters, keeping them in order. Support each valve from underneath and then depress each valve spring retainer with the special tool. Remove the keepers from either side of the valve stem and then slowly release spring pressure. Remove the spring.

5. Remove the stem seal by gently prying it side-to-side with a screwdriver blade. Work the seal off the guide post and remove it. Repeat Steps 4 and 5 for each valve. Then, the valves may be removed from the head from underneath.

6. To install, first coat the valve stems with clean engine oil, and then insert each valve into the guide from the lower side of the head.

7. Install new valve seals by pushing each firmly and squarely over the guide so that the center bead of the seal lodges in the valve guide groove. The lower edge of the seal must rest on the valve guide boss. Note that if oversize valves have been installed, oversize seals must also be installed. Install the valve springs.

8. Support the valve you're working on from underneath. Install the valve spring retainer over each spring, depress the spring just enough to expose the grooves for the spring keepers. Make sure to depress the spring squarely so the spring does not touch the valve stem. Install the keepers securely and raise the retainer slowly, making sure the keepers stay in position. Repeat these steps for all eight valves.

9. Install each of the hydraulic lash ad-

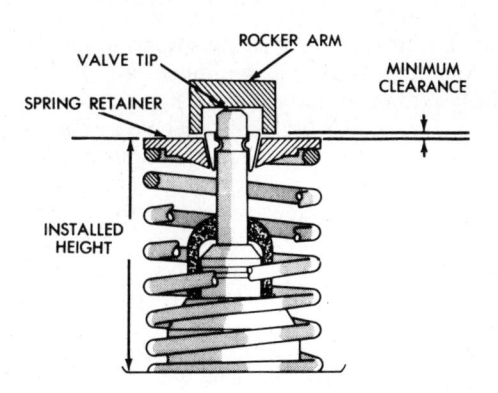

Checking clearance between the valve rocker ears and spring retainers on the 2.2 1 engine

justers in its proper position. Oil should be drained out.

10. Check the valve spring installed height. If it exceeds specifications, valve spring tension will not be adequate. If necessary, install a spring seat under each spring whose height is too great to make it meet specification.

11. Install the rockers, each in its original position, in reverse of the removal procedure. Depress the valve spring retainers *only* enough to install the rockers, and make sure the keepers stay in place. Check the clearance between the ears of the rocker arm and the spring retainer for each valve with the lash adjuster dry of oil and fully collapsed. If the minimum clearance of .020 in. is not met, the rocker will have to be machined to create it. After clearance specifications are met, remove the rockers and adjusters, immerse adjusters in clean engine oil and pump them to prime them with oil. Finally, reinstall the adjusters and rockers. Make sure, if you're working with the head on the engine, yo you don't turn the camshaft until lifters have had at least 10 minutes to leak down.

2.6 LITER ENGINE

1. Remove the cylinder head as described above. Remove the camshaft bearing caps and rocker shafts as an assembly (see the procedure for camshaft removal). Leave the bolts in the front and rear caps.

2. Using a spring compressor designed for use on overhead cam engines with inclined valves, depress each valve spring, remove keepers, and then remove each valve from underneath. Support each valve while doing this so you won't have to depress the spring unnecessarily.

3. Remove each jet valve by unscrewing it with a special socket wrench designed for this purpose. Pull out valve stems seals with a pair of pliers.

4. Valve stems should be coated with oil before each valved is installed. Assemble the

44 ENGINE AND ENGINE REBUILDING

springs, retainers, and keepers, making sure you do not depress retainers unnecessarily. Check installed height and compare it with specification. If installed height is excessive, install a thicker spring seat until specifications are met. Disassemble valves, springs, and retainers.

5. Install new valve seals onto the cylinder head by tapping them lightly via a special installer such as Chrysler part No. MD998005. Now, springs, retainers, and keepers may be installed.

6. Install jet valves by screwing them in. Torque to 168 in. lbs. The jet valves themselves have springs, retainers, keepers, and seals. You'll need a special tool No. MD998309 to compress the spring, and another, No. MD998308 to install the seal. Keep all jet valve parts together for each jet valve assembly—do not mix them up. The jet valve stem seal is installed by tapping on the special tool to gently force the seal over the jet body. Also, install a new jet valve O-ring coated with clean engine oil before installing the jet valve back into the head.

7. Make sure in final assembly to set the jet valve clearance after the head bolts are torqued and before setting intake valve clearance. Both must finally be set with the engine hot.

VALVE INSPECTION

2.2 Liter Engine

1. Clean the valves thoroughly and discard burned, warped, or cracked valves.
2. If the valve face is only lightly pitted, the valve may be refaced to an angle of 45° by a qualified machine shop.
3. Measure the valve stem for wear at various points and check it against the specifications shown in the "Valve Specifications" chart.
4. Once the valve face has been cleaned up, margin must also be checked. This is the thickness of the valve head below the face. It must be .031 in. on the intake and .0469 on the exhaust. Valves must also meet standards as to head diameter and length. These are Intake, 1.60 in. and 4.425 in.; Exhaust, 1.39 in. and 4.425 in.

2.6 LITER ENGINE

1. Check the tip of the stem for pitting (A).
2. Check stem to guide clearance (B). It must be .004 in. or less for intake and .006 in. or less for exhaust.
3. Check margin. It must be .028 in. or more for intake and .039 in. or more for exhaust. If reusable, valves should be refaced by a competent automotive machine shop.

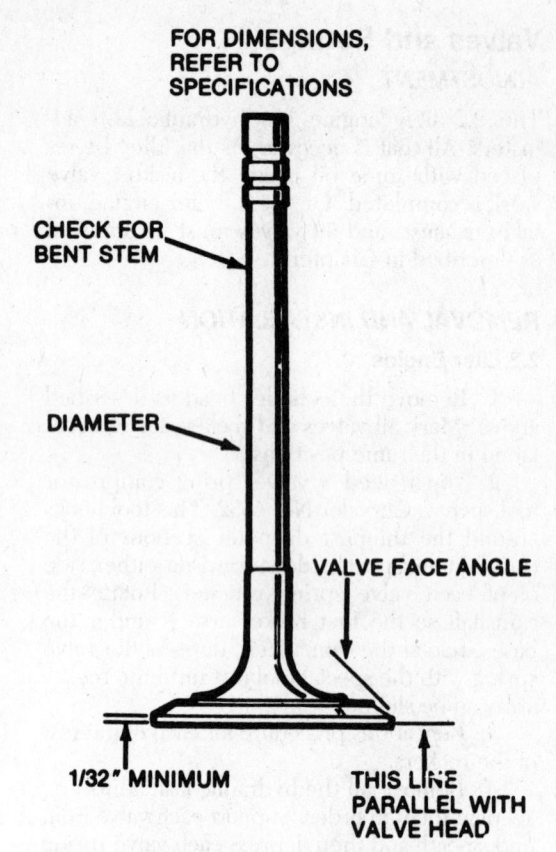

Critical valve dimensions—2.2 liter engine

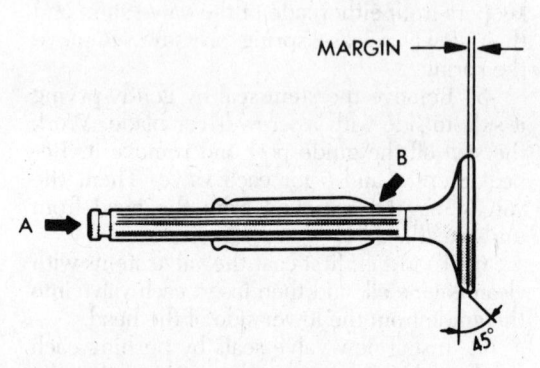

Critical valve dimensions—2.6 liter engine

SPRING INSPECTION

Springs must be inspected for squareness standing up straight against a straightedge, and for tension. The tension test requires a device which applies and measures load on the spring and at the same time meassures spring length. See the specifications chart for figures that apply to the tension test.

The spring mustr also be measured as to height at various positions. Height must be consistent within 1/16 in. on the 212 liter engine, or 3 degrees on the 2.6 liter engine.

ENGINE AND ENGINE REBUILDING 45

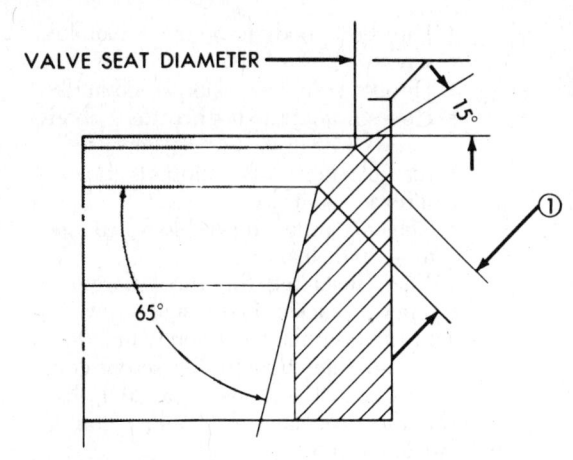

Valve seat dimensions and angles—2.2 liter engine

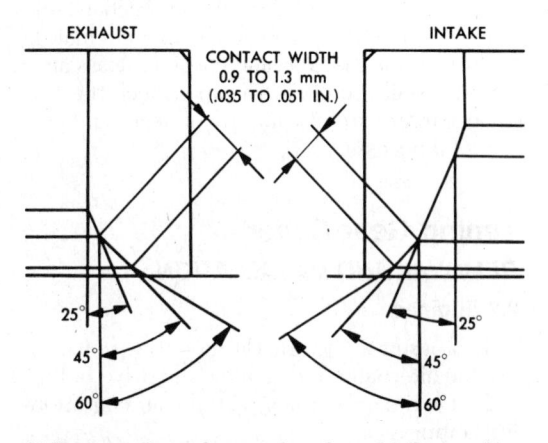

Valve seat dimensions and angles—2.6 liter engine

Valve Seats
CUTTING THE SEATS
Measuring and, if necessary, cutting the valve seat surfaces of the cylinder head are operations requiring precision instruments and machinery. In some cases, if wear is excessive, the cylinder head may have to be replaced, as seats are integral with the head.

Valve Guides
REMOVAL AND INSTALLATION
2.2 Liter Engine
Valve guides are replaceable, but they should not be replaced in a cylinder head in which the valve seats cannot be refaced.

Worn guides should be pressed out from the combustion chamber side and new guides pressed in as far as they will go.

NOTE: *Service valve guides have a shoulder. Once the guide is seated, do not use more than 1 ton pressure or the guide shoulder could break.*

Rocker Shafts
REMOVAL AND INSTALLATION
Refer to the camshaft removal and installation procedure for the 2.6 liter engine.

Intake Manifold
REMOVAL AND INSTALLATION
1. Drain the cooling system.
2. Remove the air cleaner and hoses.
3. Remove all wiring and any hoses connected to the carburetor and manifold.
4. Disconnect the accelerator linkge and shift linkage (if equipped).
5. Remove the intake-to-exhaust manifold bolts.
6. Remove the manifold-to-head bolts and lift out the intake manifold.
7. Clean all gasket surfaces and install the intake manifold using new gaskets.
8. Connect all hoses and wires and install the air cleaner.
9. Connect the accelerator linkage and shift linkage (if equipped).

Exhaust Manifold
REMOVAL AND INSTALLATION
2.2 Engine
1. Follow the intake manifold removal procedure above.
2. Disconnect the exhaust pipe.
3. Unbolt and remove the exhaust manifold.
4. Clean the gasket surfaces and use a new gasket.
5. Installation is the reverse of removal.

2.6 Engines
1. Remove air cleaner.
2. Remove the heat shield from the exhaust manifold. Remove the EGR lines and reed valve, if equipped.
3. Unbolt the exhaust flange connection.
4. Remove the nuts holding manifold to the cylinder head.
5. Remove the manifold.
6. Installation is the reverse of removal. Tighten flange connection bolts to 11–18 ft. lb. Tighten manifold bolts to 11–14 ft. lb.

Turbocharger
REMOVAL AND INSTALLATION
1. Disconnect the battery and drain coolant.
2. From under the car:
   a. Disconnect the exhaust pipe at the

46 ENGINE AND ENGINE REBUILDING

atriculated joint and disconnect the O$_2$ sensor electrical connections.

b. Remove the turbocharger-to-block support bracket.

c. Loosen the clamps for the oil drain-back tube and then move the tube downward onto the block fitting so it no longer connects with the turbocharger.

d. Disconnect the turbocharger coolant supply tube at the block outlet below the power steering pump bracket and at the tube support bracket.

3. Disconnect and remove the air cleaner complete with the throttle body adaptor, hose, and air cleaner box and support bracket.

4. Loosen the throttle body to turbocharger inlet hose clamps. Then, remove the three throttle body-to-intake manifold attaching screws and remove the throttle body.

5. Loosen the turbocharger discharge hose end clamps, leaving the center band in plate to retain the deswirler.

6. Pull the fuel rail out of the way after removing the hose retaining bracket screw, four bracket screws from the intake manifold, and two bracket-to-heat shield retaining clips. The rail, injectors, wiring harness, and fuel lines will be moved as an assembly.

7. Disconnect the oil feed line at the turbocharger bearing housing.

8. Remove the three screws attaching the heat shield to the intake manifold and remove the shield.

9. Disconnect the coolant return tube and hose assembly at the turbocharger and water box. Remove the tube support bracket from the cylinder head and remove the assembly.

10. Remove the four nuts attaching the turbocharger to the exhaust manifold. Then, remove the turbocharger by lifting it off the exhaust manifold studs, tilting it downward toward the passenger side of the car, and then pulling it up and out of the engine compartment.

11. Install the unit in reverse order, noting these important points:

a. When repositioning the turbo on the mounting studs, make sure the discharge tube goes in position so it's properly connected to both the intake manifold and turbocharger. Apply an antiseize compound such as Loctite® 771-64® or equivalent to the threads. Torque the nuts to 30 ft. lbs.

b. Observe the following torques:
- Oil feed line nuts—125 in. lbs.
- Heat shield to intake manifold screws—105 in. lbs.
- Coolant tube nuts—30 ft. lbs.
- Fuel rail bracket-to-intake manifold retaining screws—250 in. lbs.
- Discharge tube hose clamp—35 in. lbs.
- Throttle body-to-intake manifold screws—250 in. lbs.
- Throttle body hose clamps—35 in. lbs.
- Hose adapter-to-throttle body screws—55 in. lbs.
- Air cleaner box support bracket screws—40 ft. lbs.
- Coolant tube nut-to-block connector—30 ft. lbs.

c. When installing the turbocharger-to-block support bracket, first install screws finger tight. Tighten the block screw first (to 40 ft. lbs.), and then tighten the screw going into the turbocharger housing (to 20 ft. lbs.). Tighten the articulated ball joint shoulder bolts to 250 in. lbs.

d. Make sure to fill the cooling system back up before starting the engine, recheck the level after the coolant begins circulating through the radiator, and check for leaks after you install the pressure cap. Check the turbocharger carefully for any oil leaks and correct if necessary.

Timing Gear Cover
REMOVAL AND INSTALLATION
2.2 Engines

1. Loosen the alternator mounting bolts, pivot the alternator and remove the drive belt.
2. Do the same thing with the air conditioning compressor.
3. Remove the cover retaining nuts, washers and spacers.
4. Remove the cover.
5. Installation is the reverse of removal.

Timing Belt
REMOVAL AND INSTALLATION

1. Remove the timing belt cover.
2. While holding the large hex on the tension pulley, loosen the pulley nut.
3. Remove the belt from the tensioner.
4. Slide the belt off the three toothed pulleys.
5. Using the larger bolt on the crankshaft pulley, turn the engine until the #1 cylinder is at TDC of the compression stroke. At this point the valves for the #1 cylinder will be closed and the timing mark will be aligned with the pointer on the flywheel housing. Make sure that the dots on the cam sprocket and cylinder head are aligned.
6. Check that the V-notch in the crankshaft pulley aligns with the dot mark on the intermediate shaft.

CAUTION: *If the timing marks are not per-*

ENGINE AND ENGINE REBUILDING

fectly aligned, poor engine performance and probable engine damage will result!

7. Install the belt on the pulleys.

8. Adjust the tensioner by turning the large tensioner hex to the right. Tension is correct when the belt can be twisted 90° with the thumb and forefinger, midway between the camshaft and intermediate pulleys.

9. Tighten the tensioner locknut to 32 ft. lb.

10. Install the timing belt cover and check the ignition timing.

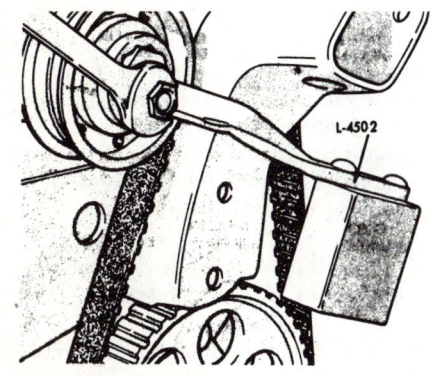

Adjusting drive belt tension on 2.2L engines

Timing Chain, Cover, "Silent Shafts" and Tensioner
REMOVAL AND INSTALLATION
2.6 Engines

NOTE: *All 2.6 engines are equipped with two "Silent Shafts" which cancel the vertical vibrating force of the engine and the secondary vibrating forces, which include the sideways rocking of the engine due to the turning direction of the crankshaft and other rolling parts. The shafts are driven by a duplex chain and are turned by the crankshaft. The silent shaft chain assembly is mounted in front of the timing chain assembly and must be removed to service the timing chain.*

1. Disconnect the negative battery terminal.

2. Drain the radiator and remove it from the vehicle.

3. Remove the cylinder head.

4. Remove the cooling fan, spacer, water pump pulley and belt.

5. Remove the alternator and water pump.

6. Raise the front of the vehicle and support it on jack stands.

7. Remove the oil pan and screen. Remove the crankshaft pulley.

8. Remove the timing case cover.

9. Remove the chain guides, side (A), top (B), bottom (C), from the "B" chain (outer).

10. Remove the locking bolts from the "B" chain sprockets.

11. Remove the crankshaft sprocket, silent shaft sprocket and the outer chain.

12. Remove the crankshaft and camshaft sprockets and the timing chain.

13. Remove the camshaft sprocket holder and the chain guides, both left and right.

14. Remove the tensioner.

15. Remove the sleeve from the oil pump. Remove the oil pump by first removing the bolt locking the oil pump driven gear and the right silent shaft, then remove the oil pump mount-

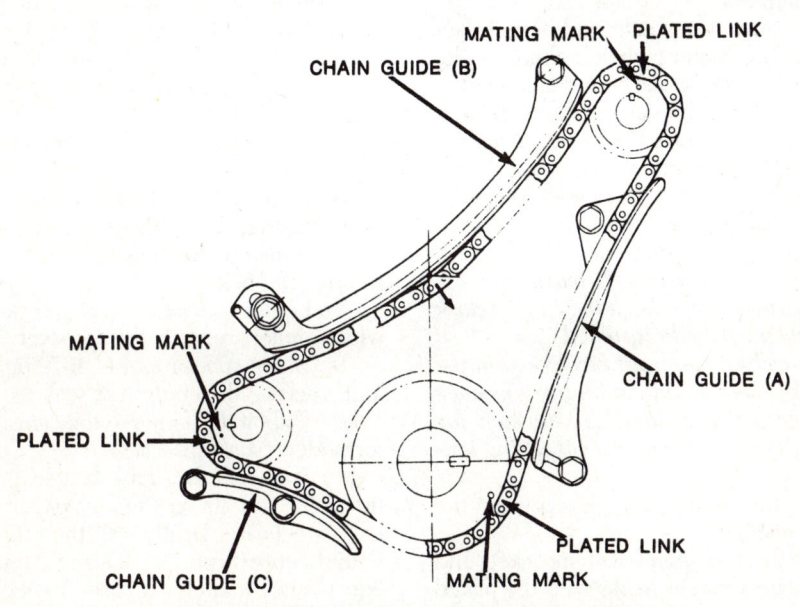

"Silent Shaft" balancing system on 2.6L engines

48 ENGINE AND ENGINE REBUILDING

ing bolts. Remove the silent shaft from the engine block.

NOTE: *If the bolt locking the oil pump and the silent shaft is hard to loosen, remove the oil pump and the shaft as a unit.*

16. Remove the left silent shaft thrust washer and take the shaft from the engine block.

Installation is performed in the following manner:

1. Install the right silent shaft into the engine block.
2. Install the oil pump assembly. Do not lose the woodruff key from the end of the silent shaft. Torque the oil pump mounting bolts from 6 to 7 ft. lbs.
3. Tighten the silent shaft and the oil pump driven gear mounting bolt.

NOTE: *The silent shaft and the oil pump can be installed as a unit, if necessary.*

4. Install the left silent shaft into the engine block.
5. Install a new "O" ring on the thrust plate and install the unit into the engine block, using a pair of bolts without heads, as alignment guides.

CAUTION: *If the thrust plate is turned to align the bolt holes, the "O" ring may be damaged.*

6. Remove the guide bolts and install the regular bolts into the thrust plate and tighten securely.
7. Rotate the crankshaft to bring No. 1 piston to TDC.
8. Install the cylinder head.
9. Install the sprocket holder and the right and left chain guides.
10. Install the tensioner spring and sleeve on the oil pump body.
11. Install the camshaft and crankshaft sprockets on the timing chain, aligning the sprocket punch marks to the plated chain links.
12. While holding the sprocket and chain as a unit, install the crankshaft sprocket over the crankshaft and align it with the keyway.
13. Keeping the dowel pin hole on the camshaft in a vertical position, install the camshaft sprocket and chain on the camshaft.

NOTE: *The sprocket timing mark and the plated chain link should be at the 2 to 3 o'clock position when correctly installed.*

CAUTION: *The chain must be aligned in the right and left chain guides with the tensioner pushing against the chain. The tension for the inner chain is determined by spring tension.*

14. Install the crankshaft sprocket for the outer or "B" chain.
15. Install the two silent shaft sprockets and align the punched mating marks with the plated links of the chain.
16. Holding the two shaft sprockets and chain, install the outer chain in alignment with the mark on the crankshaft sprocket. Install the shaft sprockets on the silent shaft and the oil pump driver gear. Install the lock bolts and recheck the alignment of the punch marks and the plated links.
17. Temporarily install the chain guides, *Side* (A), *Top* (B), and *Bottom* (C).
18. Tighten *Side* (A) chain guide securely.
19. Tighten *Bottom* (C) chain guide securely.
20. Adjust the position of the *Top* (B) chain guide, after shaking the right and left sprockets to collect any chain slack, so that when the chain is moved toward the center, the clearance between the chain guide and the chain links will be approximately 9/64 inch. Tighten the *Top* (B) chain guide bolts.
21. Install the timing chain cover using a new gasket, being careful not to damage the front seal.
22. Install the oil screen and the oil pan, using a new gasket. Torque the bolts to 4.5 to 5.5 ft. lbs.
23. Install the crankshaft pulley, alternator and accessory belts, and the distributor.
24. Install the oil pressure switch, if removed, and install the battery ground cable.
25. Install the fan blades, radiator, fill the system with coolant and start the engine.

Timing Gears

REMOVAL AND INSTALLATION

2.2 Engines

1. Raise and support the car on jackstands.
2. Remove the right inner splash shield.
3. Remove the crankshaft pulley.
4. Unbolt and remove both halves of the timing belt cover.
5. Take up the weight of the engine with a jack.
6. Remove the right engine mount bolt and raise the engine slightly.
7. Remove the timing belt tensioner and remove the belt.
8. Remove the crankshaft sprocket bolt, and with a puller, remove the sprocket.
9. Using special tool C-4679 or its equivalent, remove the crankshaft seal.
10. Unbolt and remove the camshaft and intermediate shaft sprockets.
11. To install the crankshaft seal, first polish the shaft with 400 grit emery paper. If the seal has a steel case, lightly coat the OD of the seal with Loctite Stud N' Bearing Mount® or its equivalent. If the seal case is rubber coated, generously apply a soap and water solution to

ENGINE AND ENGINE REBUILDING 49

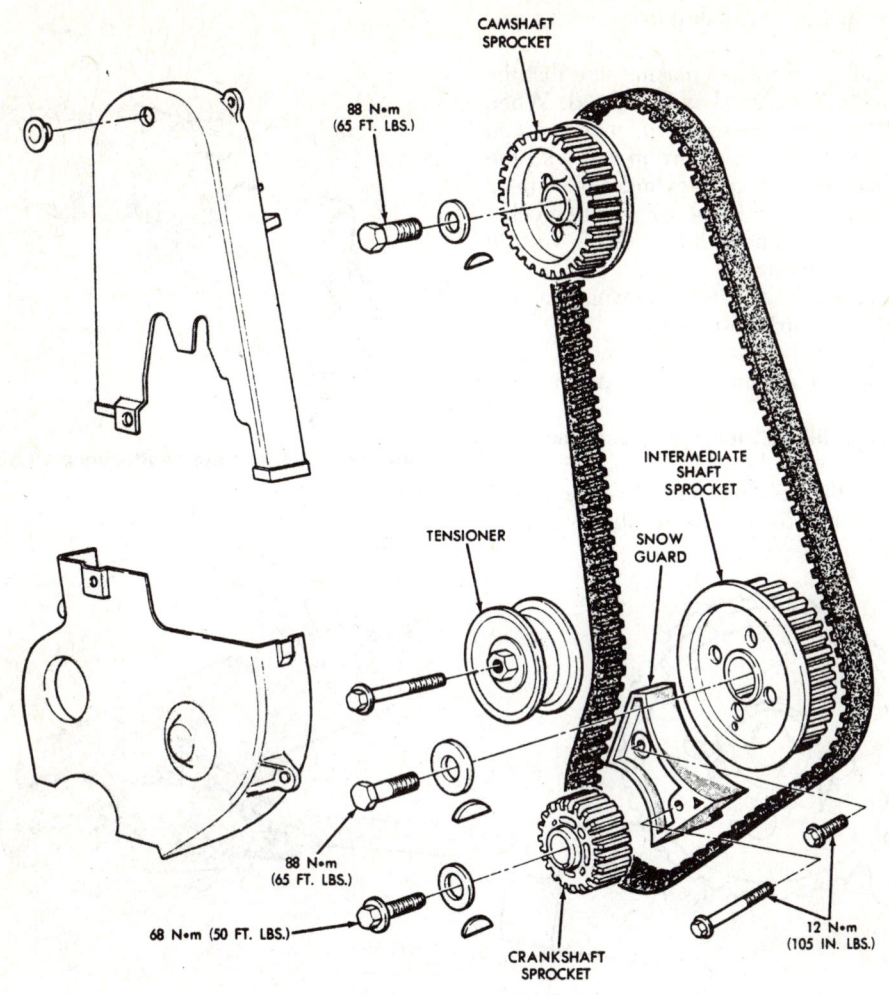

Timing sprockets and oil seals

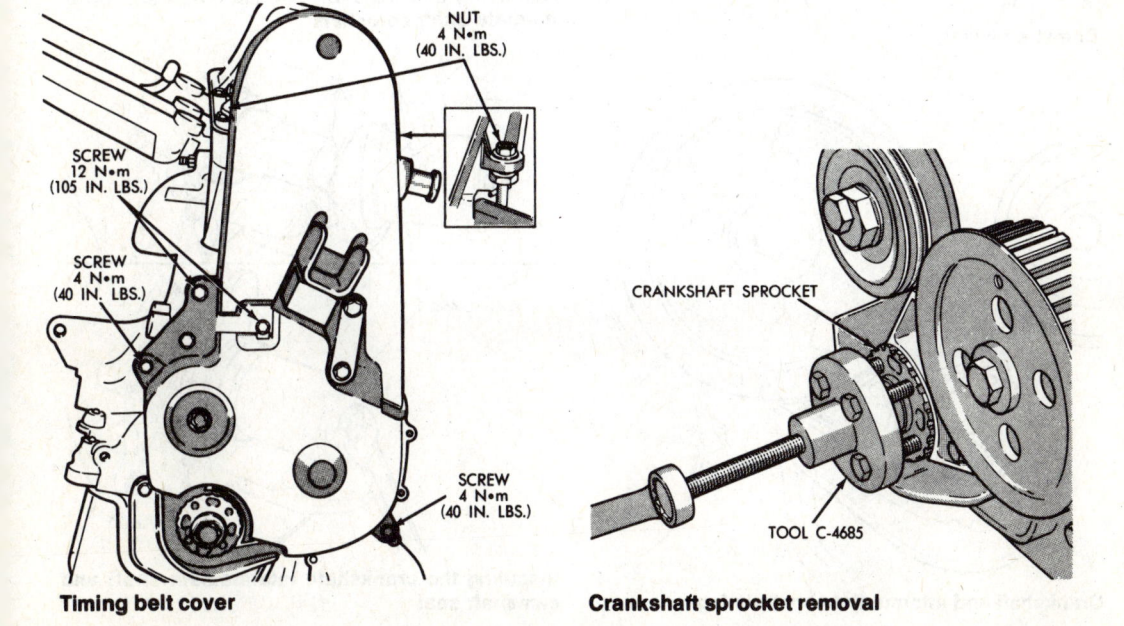

Timing belt cover

Crankshaft sprocket removal

50 ENGINE AND ENGINE REBUILDING

facilitate installation. Install the seal with a seal driver.

12. Install the sprockets making sure that the timing marks are aligned as illustrated. When installing the camshaft sprocket, make certain the arrows on the sprocket are in line with the #1 camshaft bearing cap-to-cylinder head line.

13. The small hole in the camshaft sprocket must be at the top and in line with the vertical center line of the engine.

14. Rotate the engine two full revolutions and recheck timing mark positioning.

15. Install the belt.

16. Rotate the engine to the #1 piston TDC position.

17. Install the belt tensioner and place tool C-4703 on the large hex nut.

18. Reset the belt tension so that the axis of the tool is about 15° off of horizontal.

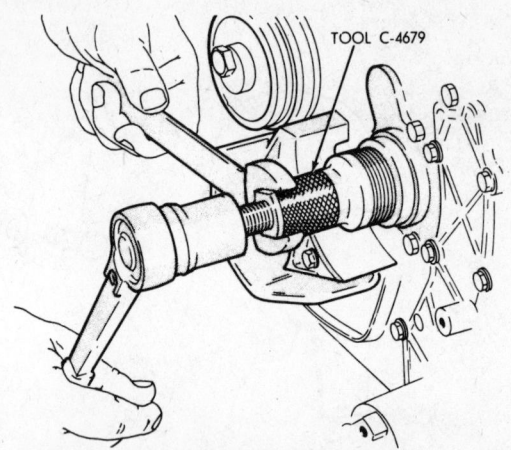

Crankshaft, intermediate shaft, camshaft oil seal removal

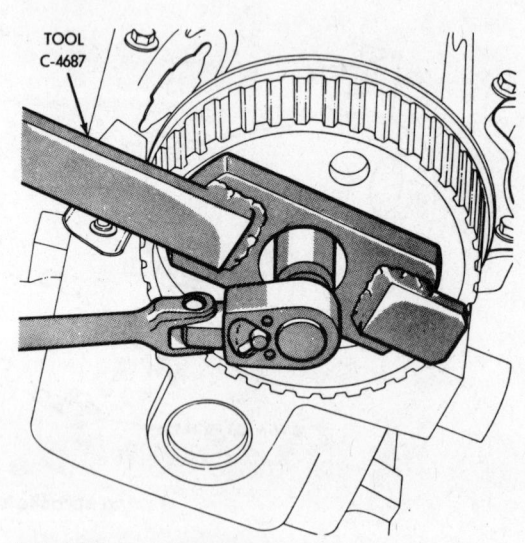

Camshaft timing

Removing and installing the camshaft and intermediate shaft sprockets

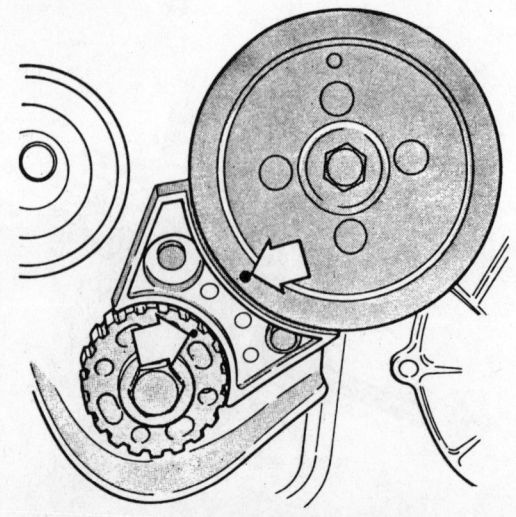

Crankshaft and intermediate shaft timing

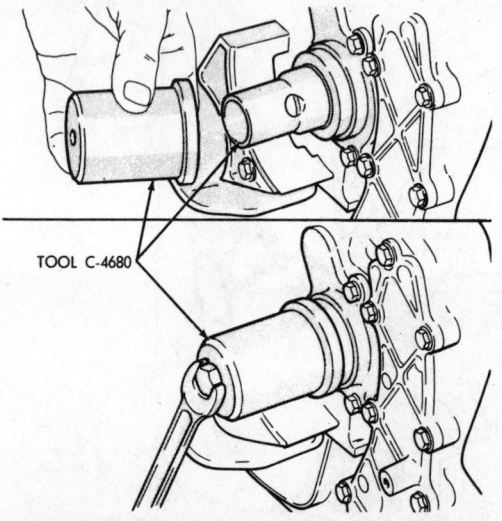

Installing the crankshaft, intermediate shaft and camshaft seal

ENGINE AND ENGINE REBUILDING

19. Turn the engine clockwise two full revolutions to #1 TDC.
20. Tighten the tensioner locknut using a weighted wrench as shown in the illustration. Torques: Timing belt cover bolts, 105 in. lb.
    Camshaft sprocket bolt, 65 ft. lb.
    Crankshaft sprocket bolt, 50 ft. lb.
    Intermediate shaft sprocket bolt, 65 ft. lb.

2.6 Engines

See the procedures under Timing Chain, Cover and Silent Shafts.

Camshaft

REMOVAL AND INSTALLATION

2.2 Engines

1. Remove the timing belt.
2. Mark the rocker arms for installation identification.
3. Loosen the camshaft bearing capnuts several turns each.
4. Using a wooden or rubber mallet, rap the rear of the camshaft a few times to break it loose.
5. Remove the capnuts and caps being very careful that the camshaft does not cock. Cocking the camshaft could cause irreparable damage to the bearings.
6. Check all oil holes for blockage.
7. Install the bearing caps with #1 at the timing belt end and #5 at the transmission end. Caps are numbered and have arrows facing forward. Capnut torque is 14 ft. lb.
8. Apply RTV silicone gasket material to the seal ends.
9. Install the bearing caps BEFORE the seals are installed.
10. The rest of the procedure is the reverse of disassembly.

CAMSHAFT ENDPLAY CHECK

1. Move the camshaft as far forward as possible.
2. Install a dial indicator on the end of the camshaft.
3. Zero the indicator, push the camshaft backward, then forward as far as possible and record the play. Maximum play should be .006 in.

2.6 Engines

1. Remove the breather hoses and purge hose.
2. Remove the air cleaner and fuel line.
3. Remove the fuel pump. Remove the distributor.
4. Disconnect the spark plug cables.
5. Remove the rocker cover.

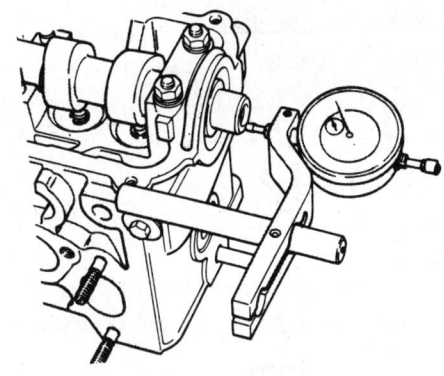

Checking camshaft end play

6. Remove the breather and semi-circular seal.
7. After slightly loosening the camshaft sprocket bolt, turn the crankshaft until No. 1 piston is at Top Dead Center on compression stroke (both valves closed).
8. Remove the camshaft sprocket bolt and distributor drive gear.
9. Remove the camshaft sprocket with chain and allow it to rest on the camshaft sprocket holder.
10. Remove the camshaft bearing cap tightening bolts. Do not remove the front and rear bearing cap bolts altogether, but keep them inserted in the bearing caps so that the rocker assembly can be removed as a unit.
11. Remove the rocker arms, rocker shafts and bearing caps as an assembly.
12. Remove the camshaft.
13. Installation is the reverse of removal. Lubricate the camshaft lobes and bearings and fit camshaft into head. Install the assembled rocker arm shaft assembly. The camshaft should be positioned so that the dowel pin on the front end of the cam is in the 12 o'clock position and in line with the notch in the top of the front bearing cap.

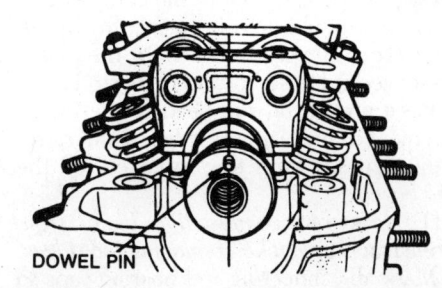

Install the camshaft on 2.6L engines by aligning the dowel pin with the notch in the top of the front bearing cap

INSPECTING THE CAMSHAFT

1. Measure cam lobe height at the nose or thickest point. Measure at the very edge of the

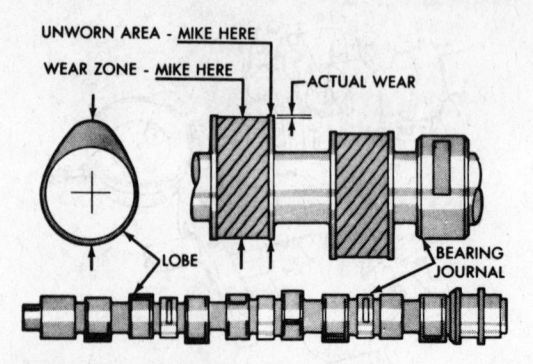

52 ENGINE AND ENGINE REBUILDING

Measuring cam lobe wear

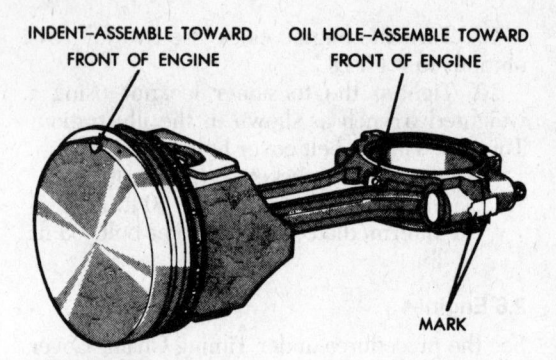

2.2L pistons

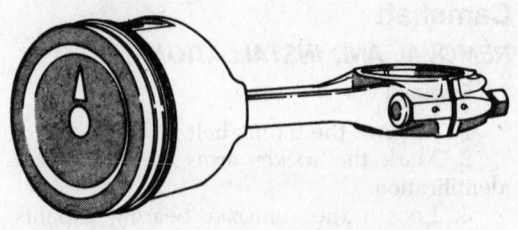

2.6L pistons with connecting rod markings

lobe, where there is no wear, and at the center, where wear is at a maximum. On the 2.2 liter engine, .010 in. wear is permitted, while on the 2.6, the figure is .020 in. Replace the camshaft if it is worn excessively.

Pistons and Connecting Rods

IDENTIFICATION

The pistons used in the 2.2 Liter engine have notches in them to indicate the proper installed position. The notch faces the front of the engine, when installed. Connecting rods have no markings.

2.6 Liter engines have arrows on the pistons. These arrows must face front when installed in the engine. The connecting rods are numbered for easy identification.

REMOVAL AND INSTALLATION

2.2 Liter Engine

1. Follow the instructions under "Cylinder Head" removal and "Timing Belt" or "Timing Chain" removal.
2. Remove the oil pan as described later in this chapter.
3. This procedure is much easier performed with the engine out of the car.
4. Pistons should be removed in the order: 1–3–4–2. Turn the crankshaft until the piston to be removed is at the bottom of its stroke.
5. Place a cloth on the head of the piston to be removed and using a ridge reamer, remove the deposits from the upper end of the cylinder bore.
   NOTE: *Never remove more than 1/22 in. from the ring travel area when removing the ridges.*
6. Mark all connecting rod bearing caps so that they may be returned to their original locations in the engine. The connecting rod caps are marked with rectangular forge marks which must be mated during assembly and be installed on the intermediate shaft side of the engine. Mark all pistons so they can be returned to their original cylinders.

CAUTION: *Don't score the cylinder walls or the crankshaft journal.*

7. Using an internal micrometer, measure the bores across the thrust faces of the cylinder and parallel to the axis of the crankshaft at a minimum of four equally spaced locations. The bore must not be out-of-round by more than 0.005 in. and it must not taper more than 0.010 in. Taper is the difference in wear between two bore measurements in any cylinder. See the "Engine Rebuilding" section for comolete details.

8. If the cylinder bore is in satisfactory condition, place each ring in the bore in turn and square it in the bore with the head of the piston. Measure the ring gap. If the ring gap is greater than the limit, get a new ring. If the ring gap is less than the limit, file the end of the ring to obtain the correct gap.

9. Check the ring side clearance by installing rings on the piston, and inserting a feeler gauge of the correct dimension between the ring and the lower land. The gauge should slide freely around the ring circumference without binding. Any wear will form a step on the lower land. Remove any pistons having high steps. Before checking the ring side clearance, be sure that the ring grooves are clean and free of carbon, sludge, or grit.

10. Piston rings should be installed so that their ends are at three equal spacings. Avoid installing the rings with their ends in line with the piston pin bosses and the thrust direction.

11. Install the pistons in their original bores, if you are reusing the same pistons. Install short

ENGINE AND ENGINE REBUILDING 53

lengths of rubber hose over the connecting rod bolts to prevent damage to the cylinder walls or rod journal.

12. Install a ring compressor over the rings on the piston. Lower the piston and rod assembly into the bore until the ring compressor contacts the block. Using a wooden hammer handle, push the piston into the bore while guiding the rod onto the journal.

NOTE: *On 2.2L engine the arrow on the piston should face toward the front (drive belt) of the engine.*

CLEANING AND INSPECTION

1. Use a piston ring expander and remove the rings from the piston.
2. Clean the ring grooves using an appropriate cleaning tool, exercise care to avoid cutting too deeply.
3. Clean all varnish and carbon from the piston with a safe solvent. Do not use a wire brush or caustic solution on the pistons.
4. Inspect the pistons for scruffing, scoring, cracks, pitting or excessive ring groove wear. If wear is evident, the piston must be replaced.

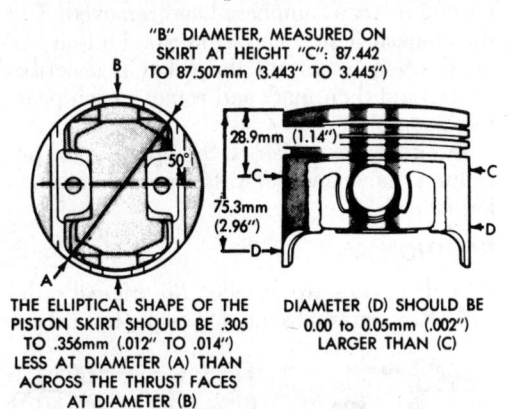

"B" DIAMETER, MEASURED ON SKIRT AT HEIGHT "C": 87.442 TO 87.507mm (3.443" TO 3.445")

28.9mm (1.14")
75.3mm (2.96")

THE ELLIPTICAL SHAPE OF THE PISTON SKIRT SHOULD BE .305 TO .356mm (.012" TO .014") LESS AT DIAMETER (A) THAN ACROSS THE THRUST FACES AT DIAMETER (B)

DIAMETER (D) SHOULD BE 0.00 to 0.05mm (.002") LARGER THAN (C)

Measuring piston wear—normally aspirated 2.2 liter engine

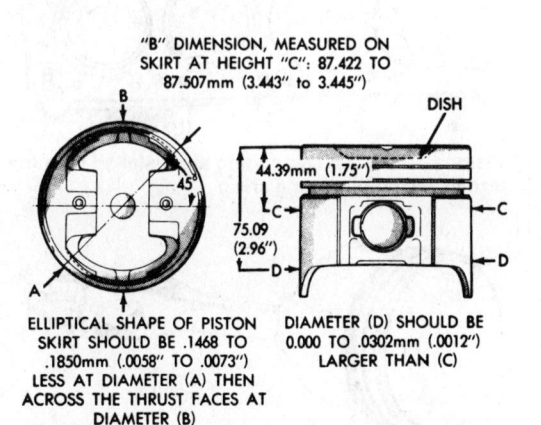

"B" DIMENSION, MEASURED ON SKIRT AT HEIGHT "C": 87.422 TO 87.507mm (3.443" to 3.445")

DISH
44.39mm (1.75")
75.09 (2.96")

ELLIPTICAL SHAPE OF PISTON SKIRT SHOULD BE .1468 TO .1850mm (.0058" TO .0073") LESS AT DIAMETER (A) THEN ACROSS THE THRUST FACES AT DIAMETER (B)

DIAMETER (D) SHOULD BE 0.000 TO .0302mm (.0012") LARGER THAN (C)

Measuring piston wear—turbocharged 2.2 liter engine

5. Have the piston and connecting rod assembly checked by a machine shop for correct alignment, piston pin wear and piston diameter. If the piston has "collapsed" it will have to be replaced or knurled to restore original diameter. Connecting rod bushing replacement, piston pin fitting and piston changing can be handled by the machine shop.

CYLINDER BORE

Check the cylinder bore for wearing using a telescope gauge and a micrometer, measure the cylinder bore diameter perpendicular to the piston pin at a point 2½ inches below the top of the engine block. Measure the piston skirt perpendicular to the piston pin. The difference between the two measurements is the piston clearance. If the clearance is within specifications, finish honing or glaze breaking is all that is required. If clearance is excessive a slightly oversize piston may be required. If greatly oversize, the engine will have to be bored and .010 inch or larger oversized pistons installed.

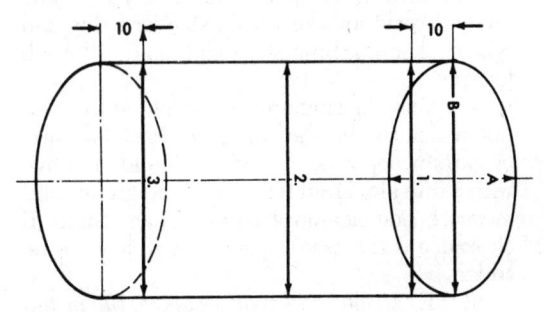

Check cylinder bore wear at these positions on the 2.2 liter engine. Measure at a point 10 mm or ⅜ in. from the top and bottom

PISTON PINS

The pin connecting the piston and connecting rod is press fitted. If too much free play develops take the piston assemblies to the machine shop and have oversize pins installed. Installing new rods or pistons requires the use of a press—have the machine shop handle the job for you.

Fitting and Positioning Piston Rings

2.2 Liter Engine

1. Take the new piston rings and compress them, one at a time into the cylinder that they will be used in. Press the ring about one inch below the top of the cylinder block using an inverted piston.
2. Use a feeler gauge and measure the distance between the ends of the ring, this is called,

54 ENGINE AND ENGINE REBUILDING

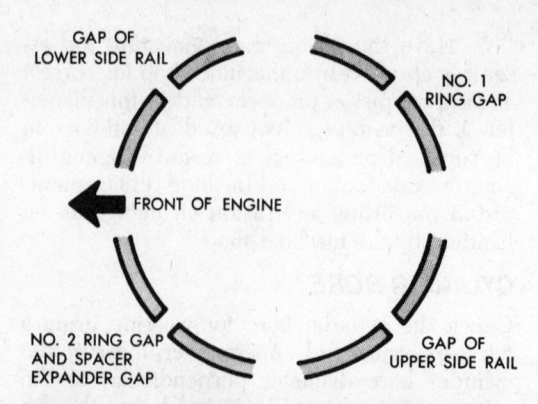

Align the piston ring gaps so they are offset as shown, to prevent ring leakage

measuring the ring end-gap. Compare the reading to the one called for in the specifications table. File the ends of the ring with a fine file to obtain necessary clearance.

NOTE: *If inadequate ring end-gap is utilized ring breakage will result*

3. Inspect the ring grooves on the piston for excessive wear or taper. If necessary have the grooves recut for use with a standard ring and spacer. The machine shop can handle the job for you.

4. Check the ring groove by rolling the new piston ring around the groove to check for burrs or carbon deposits. If any are found, remove with a fine file. Hold the ring in the groove and measure side clearance with a feeler gauge. If clearance is excessive, spacer(s) will have to be added.

NOTE: *Always add spacers above the piston ring.*

5. Install the rings on the piston, lower ring first using a ring installing tool. Consult the instruction sheet that comes with the rings to be sure they are installed with the correct side up. A mark on the ring usually faces upward.

6. When installing oil rings; first, install the ring in the groove. Hold the ends of the ring butted together (they must not overlap) and install the bottom rail (scraper) with the end about one inch away from the butted end of the control ring. Install the top rail about an inch away from the butted end of the control but on the opposite side from the lower rail.

7. Install the two compression rings.

8. Consult the illustration with piston ring set instruction sheet for ring positioning, arrange the rings as shown, install a ring compressor and insert the piston and rod assembly into the engine.

REMOVAL AND INSTALLATION
2.6 Liter Engine

Pistons and rods are usually (and most easily) removed as part of a complete engine overhaul. A complete disassembly entails removing the engine from the car and mounting it on a stand, and then removing the cylinder head and oil pan. The front cover, timing chain, and rear main seal are removed. Then, the connecting rod caps are marked and removed and kept in order. The crankshaft is supported or the engine turned upside down and the caps marked, removed, and kept in order. The crankshaft is removed.

Now, the ridge formed at the top of each cylinder by ring wear is removed with a ridge reamer. This is done to prevent damage to the rings or cylinder as the piston is removed. Protect the wear surfaces from grit formed in the reaming process by covering the piston and nearby areas of the cylinder with a clean rag that will catch all the particles. Once the ridges are reamed out, number and remove the pistons and rods.

If, for some reason the engine has suffered ring and cylinder wear but does not require an entire rebuild, you can remove the pistons and rods with the engine in the car. The cylinder head and oil pan must be removed, and connecting rod caps numbered and removed. Turn the crankshaft so each piston is at bottom center position, ream out the ridge as described above, and then mark and remove each piston rod assembly.

In either case, refer to the appropriate procedures above and below for more detailed information.

POSITIONING

All four pistons are installed (in original order) with the arrows facing forward—toward the

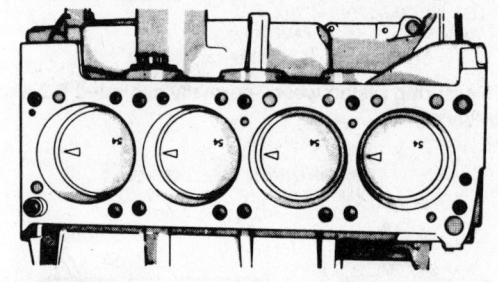

Pistons on the 2 6 liter engine are installed with the arrows facing the timing chain

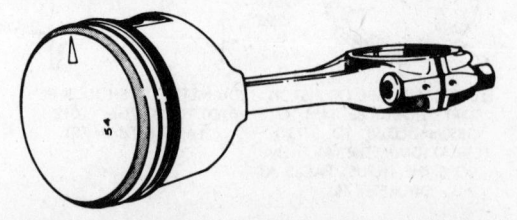

On the 2.6 liter engine, note the relationship between the arrow on the top of the piston, and numbered marks on both connecting rod and cap

ENGINE AND ENGINE REBUILDING 55

timing chain. Note the relationship between the arrow and marks on the connecting rod and cap. These marks will end up below the number on the top face of the piston.

PISTON RING REPLACEMENT

Piston rings and grooves must be thoroughly cleaned to check side clearance. Remove the rings from each piston with an expander, clean both ring grooves and rings, and reinstall (see below). Measure side clearance with a flat feeler gauge.

The cylinder bores will have to be measured for wear as described below under "Cleaning and Inspection". If the bores are satisfactory, and ring side clearance is satisfactory too, each ring must be individually installed in the bottom of its cylinder bore at least .63 in. from the bottom. Use the piston, inserted part way into the bore, to square the ring's position. Measure end gap with a flat feeler gauge. Excessive dimensions in terms of either side clearance or ring gap require replacement of rings and, if this does not cure excessive side clearance, the rings and piston.

Install the oil ring expander first, and then the upper oil ring side rail and, finally the lower oil ring side rail. When installing the side rails, do not use a ring expander, but place one end between the piston and ring groove and the ring expander. Hold the end firmly and work your way around the expander from that point to work it down and into position.

With a ring expander, install first the No. 2 ring and, finally, the No. 1 ring. Finally, stagger the ring gaps as shown in the illustration. The oil ring expander gap must be at least 45 degrees from the side rail gaps but not aligned either with the piston pin or the thrust direction.

PISTON AND BLOCK INSPECTION

Measure piston diameter with a micrometer in the thrust direction approximately .08 in. above the bottom of the skirt. Replace the piston if wear is excessive.

Measure the cylinder bores with an inside micrometer at top, just below center, and bottom and in both the thrust and piston pin installation directions. Top and bottom measurements should be .38 in. from the extreme top or bottom of the bore. The bore dimension must not exceed 3.5866 in. Out-of-round or taper must not exceed .0008 in. In other words, the highest and lowest readings must not be more than .008 in. apart. These figures must also produce piston clearance within specifications (piston diameter subtracted from bore dimension).

PISTON PINS AND CONNECTING ROD BUSHINGS

The piston pin is press fitted into the piston; the pin bushing in the rod is also press fitted into the top of the rod. You should take the piston/rod assemblies to a machine shop to have pin/bushing wear checked and corrected, if necessary. The shop should also check the connecting rods for straightness at this time, and replace them, if necessary.

ROD BEARING REPLACEMENT

The crankshaft must be miked to ensure that it meets wear specifications. See the section below on Crankshaft and Main Bearings. In addition, assuming that connecting rod bearings do not show signs of excess wear or heat (roughness, grooving, blue color from heat, etc.), the bearing clearance must be checked with Plastigage.® This is done by drying all the surfaces and then inserting a Plastigage® insert in between the crankpin and the bearing surface. Assemble the connecting rod cap to the rod and torque the bolts to 34 ft. lbs. Do not turn the crankshaft.

Then, remove the cap and read the clearance by comparing the width of the groove left on the crankpin to the width of the marks on a

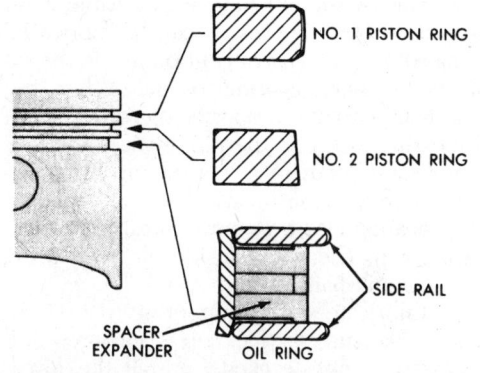

Install the rings on the 2.6 liter engine as shown. Note the difference between No. 1 and No. 2 rings. Markings on the rings should face upward.

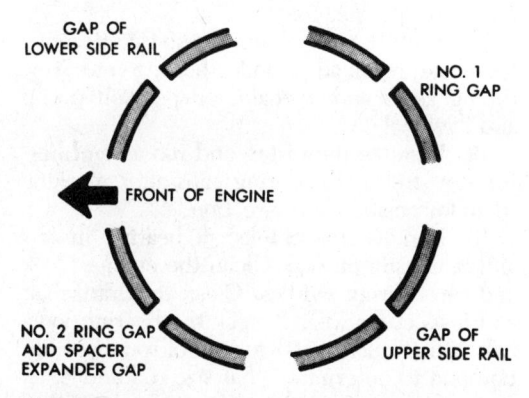

Stagger the rings gaps as shown to prevent ring leakage

56 ENGINE AND ENGINE REBUILDING

scale provided with the insert kit. If the bearing clearance meets specifications, make sure to clean the insert mark off the crankpin and thoroughly lubricate all parts with clean engine oil before final assembly.

In most cases, if wear is excessive, the crankshaft should be machined and undersize bearings installed. This work should be done by a competent machine shop.

You must also check connecting rods for excessive clearance between the side of the rod and the cheek of the crankshaft. The clearance must be .004–.010 in. Check with a flat feeler gauge. Excess clearance must be corrected by replacing the rod or possibly the rod and crankshaft.

Pistons must be installed into their original bores. All parts must be thoroughly lubricated with engine oil. Use a ring compressor to hold the rings in the compressed position as you slip the piston/rod assembly down into the cylinder. The compressor will rest right against the top of the block. If the crankshaft is still in place, make sure the crankpin is in Bottom Dead Center position. Protect the crankpin from contact with connecting rod studs, if necessary, by slipping lengths of rubber hose over the studs. Make sure the rod caps face in the right direction and torque the nuts to 34 ft. lbs.

Crankshaft and Main Bearings
REMOVAL AND INSTALLATION

1. Rod bearings can be installed when the pistons have been removed for servicing (rings etc) or, in most cases, while the engine is still in the car. Rearing replacement, however, is far easier with the engine out of the car and disassembled.

2. For in car service, remove the oil pan, spark plugs and front cover if necessary. Turn the engine until the connecting rod to be serviced is at the bottom of it's travel. Remove the bearing cap, place two pieces of rubber hose over the rod cap bolts and push the piston and rod assembly up the cylinder bore until enough room is gained for bearing insert removal. Take care not to push the rod assembly up too far or the top ring will engage the cylinder ridge or come out of the cylinder and require head removal for reinstallation.

3. Clean the rod journal, the connecting rod end and the bearing cap after removing the old bearing inserts. Install the new inserts in the rod and bearing cap, lubricate them with oil. Position the rod over the crankshaft journal and install the rod caps. Make sure the cap and rod numbers match, torque the rod nuts to specifications.

4. Main bearings may be replaced while the engine is still in the car by "rolling" them out and in.

5. Special roll-out pins are available from automotive parts houses or can be fabricated from a cotter pin. The roll out pin fits in the oil hole of the main bearing journal. When the crankshaft is rotated opposite the direction of the bearing lock tab, the pin engages the end of the bearing and "rolls" out the insert.

6. Remove main bearing cap and roll out upper bearing insert. Remove insert from main bearing cap. Clean the inside of the bearing cap and crankshaft journal.

7. Lubricate and roll upper insert into position, make sure the lock tab is anchored and the insert is not "cocked." Install the lower bearing insert into the cap; lubricate and install on the engine. Make sure the main bearing cap is installed facing in the correct direction and torque to specifications.

8. With the engine out of the car. Remove the intake manifold, cylinder head, front cover, timing gears and/or chain, oil pan, oil pump and flywheel.

9. Remove the piston and rod assemblies. Remove the main bearing caps after marking them for position and direction.

10. Remove the crankshaft bearing inserts and rear main oil seal. Clean the engine block and cap bearing saddles. Clean the crankshaft and inspect for wear. Check the bearing journals with a micrometer for out-of-round condition and to determine what size rod and main bearing inserts to install.

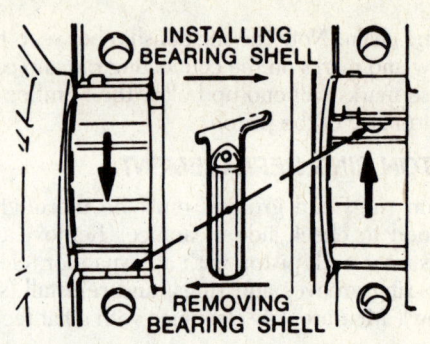

Removing/installing the upper bearing insert with a roll-out pin

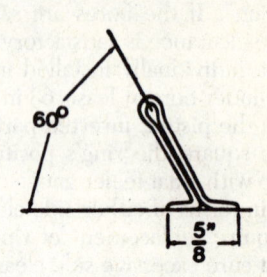

Here's how to make your own roll-out pin

ENGINE AND ENGINE REBUILDING

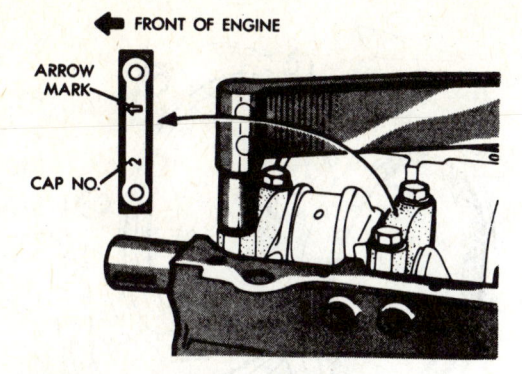

On the 2.6 liter engine, install the caps in numbered order, arrows facing forward

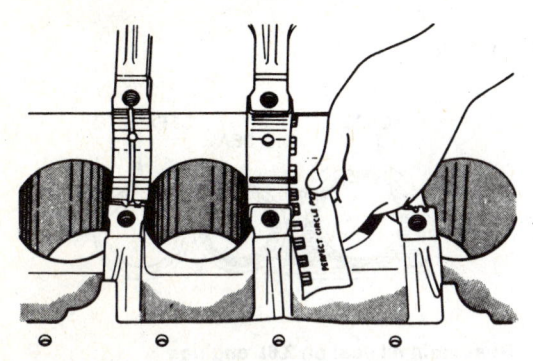

Checking main bearing clearance on the 2.6 liter engine

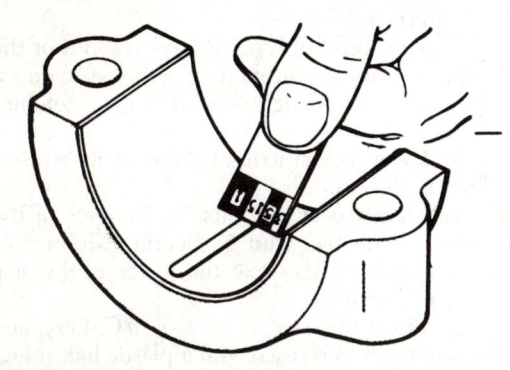

Measure Plastigage® to determine main bearing clearance

11. Install the main bearing upper inserts and rear main oil seal half (2.2 liter engine only) into the engine block.

12. Lubricate the bearing inserts and the crankshaft journals. Slowly and carefully lower the crankshaft into position.

13. On the 2.2 liter engine, install the bearing inserts and rear main seal into the bearing caps, install the caps from the middle out. Torque cap bolts to specifications in stages, rotate the crankshaft after each torque stage.

On the 2.6 liter engine, install the main caps in numbered sequence, No. 1 nearest the timing chain and No. 5 at the transmission end. Make sure the arrows on the caps point toward the timing chain end of the engine. Torque alternately and in three stages to 58 ft. lbs.

14. Remove bearing caps, one at a time and check the oil clearance with Plastigage.® Reinstall if clearance is within specifications. Check the crankshaft end-play, if within specifications install connecting rod and piston assemblies with new rod bearing inserts. Check connecting rod bearing oil clearance and rod side play, if correct and assemble the rest of the engine.

BEARING OIL CLEARANCE

Remove cap from the bearing to be checked. Using a clean, dry rag, thoroughly clean all oil from crankshaft journal and bearing insert.

NOTE: *Plastigage® is soluble in oil; therefore, oil on the journal or bearing could result in erroneous readings.*

Place a piece of Plastigage® along the full width of the insert, reinstall cap, and torque to specifications.

NOTE: *Specifications are given in the engine specifications earlier in this chapter.*

Remove bearing cap, and determine clearance by comparing width of Plastigage® to the scale on Plastigage envelope. Journal taper is determined by comparing width of the Plastigage® strip near its ends. Rotate crankshaft 90° and retest, to determine journal eccentricity.

NOTE: *Do not rotate crankshaft with Plastigage® installed. If bearing insert and journal appear intact, and are within tolerances, no further main bearing service is required. If bearing or journal appear defective, cause of failure should be determined before replacement.*

CRANKSHAFT END-PLAY/CONNECTING ROD SIDE PLAY

Place a pry bar between a main bearing cap and crankshaft casting taking care not to damage any journals. Pry backward or forward and measure the distance between the thrust bearing (center main 3) and crankshaft with a feeler gauge. Compare reading with specifications. If too great a clearance is determined, a larger thrust bearing and crank machining may be required. Check with an automotive machine shop for their advice.

Connecting rod clearance between the rod and crankthrow casting can be checked with a feeler gauge. Pry the rod carefully to one side as far as possible and measure the distance on the other side of the rod.

58   ENGINE AND ENGINE REBUILDING

CRANKSHAFT REPAIRS

If a journal is damaged on the crankshaft, repair is possible by having the crankshaft machined, after removal from engine to a standard undersize. Consult the machine shop for their advice.

ENGINE LUBRICATION

All engines have pressurized lubrication systems with full-flow oil filters.

Oil Pump
REMOVAL AND INSTALLATION

2.2 Engines

1. Remove the oil pan.
2. Remove the two pump mounting bolts.
3. Pull the pump down and out of the engine.
4. Installation is the reverse of removal. Torque the pump mounting bolts to 9 ft. lbs.

2.6 Engines

See Timing Chain, Cover, "Silent Shaft" and Tensioner removal and installation procedure.

Oil Pan
REMOVAL AND INSTALLATION

1. Drain the engine oil.
2. Support the pan and remove the attaching bolts.
3. Lower the pan and remove the gasket.
4. Clean all gasket surfaces thoroughly. Install the pan using gasket sealer and a new gasket.
   NOTE: *The 2.2 Liter engine uses a form-in-place type gasket. Chrysler Part Number 4205918 or its equivalent RTV gasket material must be used.*
5. Torque the pan bolts to 17 ft. lbs. (2.2 Liter) and 5 ft. lbs. (2.6 Liter).
6. Refill the engine with oil, start the engine, and check for leaks.

Rear Main Seal
REMOVAL AND INSTALLATION

2.2 Engines

The rear main seal is located in a housing on the rear of the block. To replace the seal it is necessary to remove the engine.

1. Remove the transmission and flywheel.
   CAUTION: *Before removing the transmission, align the dimple on the flywheel with the pointer on the flywheel housing. The transmission will not mate with the engine*

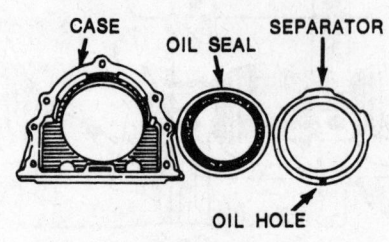

Installing rear oil seal

Rear main oil seal on 2.6L engines

during installation unless this alignment is observed.

2. Very carefully, pry the oil seal out of the support ring. Be careful not to nick or damage the crankshaft flange seal surface or retainer bore.
3. Place special tool #C-4681 or its equivalent on the crankshaft.
4. Lightly coat the outside diameter of the seal with Loctite Stud N' Bearing Mount® or its equivalent. Also coat the inside of the seal with engine oil.
5. Place the seal over tool #C-4681 and gently tap it into place with a plastic hammer.
6. Reinstall the remaining parts in the reverse order of removal.

2.6 Engines

The rear main oil seal is located in a housing on the rear of the block. To replace the seal, remove the transmission and flywheel or flex plate and do the work from underneath the vehicle or remove the engine and do the work on the bench.

1. Remove the housing from the block.
2. Remove the separator from the housing.
3. Pry out the old seal.
4. Lightly oil the replacement seal. The oil seal should be installed so that the seal plate fits into the inner contact surface of the seal

CHILTON'S
FUEL ECONOMY & TUNE-UP TIPS

Tune-up • Spark Plug Diagnosis • Emission Controls
Fuel System • Cooling System • Tires and Wheels
General Maintenance

55 WAYS TO IMPROVE FUEL ECONOMY

CHILTON'S FUEL ECONOMY & TUNE-UP TIPS

Fuel economy is important to everyone, no matter what kind of vehicle you drive. The maintenance-minded motorist can save both money and fuel using these tips and the periodic maintenance and tune-up procedures in this Repair and Tune-Up Guide.

There are more than 130,000,000 cars and trucks registered for private use in the United States. Each travels an average of 10-12,000 miles per year, and, and in total they consume close to 70 billion gallons of fuel each year. This represents nearly $2/3$ of the oil imported by the United States each year. The Federal government's goal is to reduce consumption 10% by 1985. A variety of methods are either already in use or under serious consideration, and they all affect you driving and the cars you will drive. In addition to "down-sizing", the auto industry is using or investigating the use of electronic fuel delivery, electronic engine controls and alternative engines for use in smaller and lighter vehicles, among other alternatives to meet the federally mandated Corporate Average Fuel Economy (CAFE) of 27.5 mpg by 1985. The government, for its part, is considering rationing, mandatory driving curtailments and tax increases on motor vehicle fuel in an effort to reduce consumption. The government's goal of a 10% reduction could be realized — and further government regulation avoided — if every private vehicle could use just 1 less gallon of fuel per week.

How Much Can You Save?

Tests have proven that almost anyone can make at least a 10% reduction in fuel consumption through regular maintenance and tune-ups. When a major manufacturer of spark plugs sur-

TUNE-UP

1. Check the cylinder compression to be sure the engine will really benefit from a tune-up and that it is capable of producing good fuel economy. A tune-up will be wasted on an engine in poor mechanical condition.
2. Replace spark plugs regularly. New spark plugs alone can increase fuel economy 3%.
3. Be sure the spark plugs are the correct type (heat range) for your vehicle. See the Tune-Up Specifications.

Heat range refers to the spark plug's ability to conduct heat away from the firing end. It must conduct the heat away in an even pattern to avoid becoming a source of pre-ignition, yet it must also operate hot enough to burn off conductive deposits that could cause misfiring.

The heat range is usually indicated by a number on the spark plug, part of the manufacturer's designation for each individual spark plug. The numbers in bold-face indicate the heat range in each manufacturer's identification system.

Manufacturer	Typical Designation
AC	R **45** TS
Bosch (old)	WA **145** T30
Bosch (new)	HR **8** Y
Champion	RBL **15** Y
Fram/Autolite	4**15**
Mopar	P-**62** PR
Motorcraft	BRF-**42**
NGK	BP **5** ES-15
Nippondenso	W **16** EP
Prestolite	14GR **5** 2A

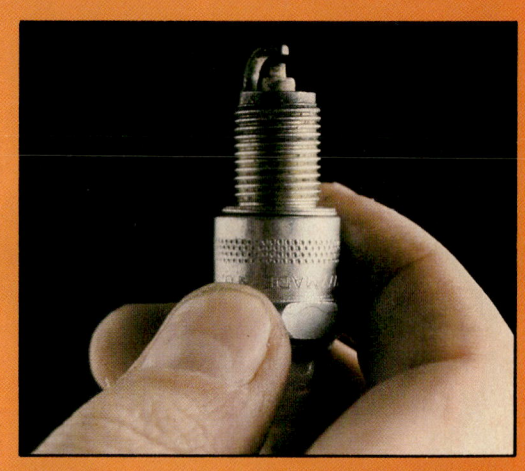

Periodically, check the spark plugs to be sure they are firing efficiently. They are excellent indicators of the internal condition of your engine.

On AC, Bosch (new), Champion, Fram/Autolite, Mopar, Motorcraft and Prestolite, a higher number indicates a hotter plug. On Bosch (old), NGK and Nippondenso, a higher number indicates a colder plug.

4. Make sure the spark plugs are properly gapped. See the Tune-Up Specifications in this book.
5. Be sure the spark plugs are firing efficiently. The illustrations on the next 2 pages show you how to "read" the firing end of the spark plug.
6. Check the ignition timing and set it to specifications. Tests show that almost all cars have incorrect ignition timing by more than 2°.

veyed over 6,000 cars nationwide, they found that a tune-up, on cars that needed one, increased fuel economy over 11%. Replacing worn plugs alone, accounted for a 3% increase. The same test also revealed that 8 out of every 10 vehicles will have some maintenance deficiency that will directly affect fuel economy, emissions or performance. Most of this mileage-robbing neglect could be prevented with regular maintenance.

Modern engines require that all of the functioning systems operate properly for maximum efficiency. A malfunction anywhere wastes fuel. You can keep your vehicle running as efficiently and economically as possible, by being aware of your vehicle's operating and performance characteristics. If your vehicle suddenly develops performance or fuel economy problems it could be due to one or more of the following:

PROBLEM	POSSIBLE CAUSE
Engine Idles Rough	Ignition timing, idle mixture, vacuum leak or something amiss in the emission control system.
Hesitates on Acceleration	Dirty carburetor or fuel filter, improper accelerator pump setting, ignition timing or fouled spark plugs.
Starts Hard or Fails to Start	Worn spark plugs, improperly set automatic choke, ice (or water) in fuel system.
Stalls Frequently	Automatic choke improperly adjusted and possible dirty air filter or fuel filter.
Performs Sluggishly	Worn spark plugs, dirty fuel or air filter, ignition timing or automatic choke out of adjustment.

Check spark plug wires on conventional point type ignition for cracks by bending them in a loop around your finger.

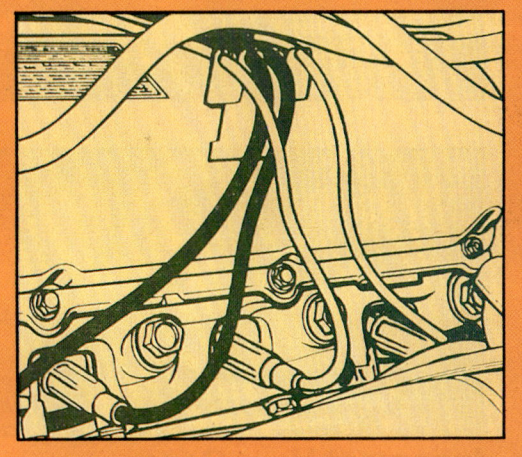

Be sure that spark plug wires leading to adjacent cylinders do not run too close together. (Photo courtesy Champion Spark Plug Co.)

7. If your vehicle does not have electronic ignition, check the points, rotor and cap as specified.

8. Check the spark plug wires (used with conventional point-type ignitions) for cracks and burned or broken insulation by bending them in a loop around your finger. Cracked wires decrease fuel efficiency by failing to deliver full voltage to the spark plugs. One misfiring spark plug can cost you as much as 2 mpg.

9. Check the routing of the plug wires. Misfiring can be the result of spark plug leads to adjacent cylinders running parallel to each other and too close together. One wire tends to pick up voltage from the other causing it to fire "out of time".

10. Check all electrical and ignition circuits for voltage drop and resistance.

11. Check the distributor mechanical and/or vacuum advance mechanisms for proper functioning. The vacuum advance can be checked by twisting the distributor plate in the opposite direction of rotation. It should spring back when released.

12. Check and adjust the valve clearance on engines with mechanical lifters. The clearance should be slightly loose rather than too tight.

SPARK PLUG DIAGNOSIS

Normal

APPEARANCE: This plug is typical of one operating normally. The insulator nose varies from a light tan to grayish color with slight electrode wear. The presence of slight deposits is normal on used plugs and will have no adverse effect on engine performance. The spark plug heat range is correct for the engine and the engine is running normally.

CAUSE: Properly running engine.

RECOMMENDATION: Before reinstalling this plug, the electrodes should be cleaned and filed square. Set the gap to specifications. If the plug has been in service for more than 10-12,000 miles, the entire set should probably be replaced with a fresh set of the same heat range.

Oil Deposits

APPEARANCE: The firing end of the plug is covered with a wet, oily coating.

CAUSE: The problem is poor oil control. On high mileage engines, oil is leaking past the rings or valve guides into the combustion chamber. A common cause is also a plugged PCV valve, and a ruptured fuel pump diaphragm can also cause this condition. Oil fouled plugs such as these are often found in new or recently overhauled engines, before normal oil control is achieved, and can be cleaned and reinstalled.

RECOMMENDATION: A hotter spark plug may temporarily relieve the problem, but the engine is probably in need of work.

Incorrect Heat Range

APPEARANCE: The effects of high temperature on a spark plug are indicated by clean white, often blistered insulator. This can also be accompanied by excessive wear of the electrode, and the absence of deposits.

CAUSE: Check for the correct spark plug heat range. A plug which is too hot for the engine can result in overheating. A car operated mostly at high speeds can require a colder plug. Also check ignition timing, cooling system level, fuel mixture and leaking intake manifold.

RECOMMENDATION: If all ignition and engine adjustments are known to be correct, and no other malfunction exists, install spark plugs one heat range colder.

Carbon Deposits

APPEARANCE: Carbon fouling is easily identified by the presence of dry, soft, black, sooty deposits.

CAUSE: Changing the heat range can often lead to carbon fouling, as can prolonged slow, stop-and-start driving. If the heat range is correct, carbon fouling can be attributed to a rich fuel mixture, sticking choke, clogged air cleaner, worn breaker points, retarded timing or low compression. If only one or two plugs are carbon fouled, check for corroded or cracked wires on the affected plugs. Also look for cracks in the distributor cap between the towers of affected cylinders.

RECOMMENDATION: After the problem is corrected, these plugs can be cleaned and reinstalled if not worn severely.

Photos Courtesy Fram Corporation

MMT Fouled

APPEARANCE: Spark plugs fouled by MMT (Methycyclopentadienyl Maganese Tricarbonyl) have reddish, rusty appearance on the insulator and side electrode.

CAUSE: MMT is an anti-knock additive in gasoline used to replace lead. During the combustion process, the MMT leaves a reddish deposit on the insulator and side electrode.

RECOMMENDATION: No engine malfunction is indicated and the deposits will not affect plug performance any more than lead deposits (see Ash Deposits). MMT fouled plugs can be cleaned, regapped and reinstalled.

High Speed Glazing

APPEARANCE: Glazing appears as shiny coating on the plug, either yellow or tan in color.

CAUSE: During hard, fast acceleration, plug temperatures rise suddenly. Deposits from normal combustion have no chance to fluff-off; instead, they melt on the insulator forming an electrically conductive coating which causes misfiring.

RECOMMENDATION: Glazed plugs are not easily cleaned. They should be replaced with a fresh set of plugs of the correct heat range. If the condition recurs, using plugs with a heat range one step colder may cure the problem.

Ash (Lead) Deposits

APPEARANCE: Ash deposits are characterized by light brown or white colored deposits crusted on the side or center electrodes. In some cases it may give the plug a rusty appearance.

CAUSE: Ash deposits are normally derived from oil or fuel additives burned during normal combustion. Normally they are harmless, though excessive amounts can cause misfiring. If deposits are excessive in short mileage, the valve guides may be worn.

RECOMMENDATION: Ash-fouled plugs can be cleaned, gapped and reinstalled.

Detonation

APPEARANCE: Detonation is usually characterized by a broken plug insulator.

CAUSE: A portion of the fuel charge will begin to burn spontaneously, from the increased heat following ignition. The explosion that results applies extreme pressure to engine components, frequently damaging spark plugs and pistons.

Detonation can result by over-advanced ignition timing, inferior gasoline (low octane) lean air/fuel mixture, poor carburetion, engine lugging or an increase in compression ratio due to combustion chamber deposits or engine modification.

RECOMMENDATION: Replace the plugs after correcting the problem.

Photos Courtesy Champion Spark Plug Co.

EMISSION CONTROLS

13. Be aware of the general condition of the emission control system. It contributes to reduced pollution and should be serviced regularly to maintain efficient engine operation.

14. Check all vacuum lines for dried, cracked or brittle conditions. Something as simple as a leaking vacuum hose can cause poor performance and loss of economy.

15. Avoid tampering with the emission control system. Attempting to improve fuel econ-

FUEL SYSTEM

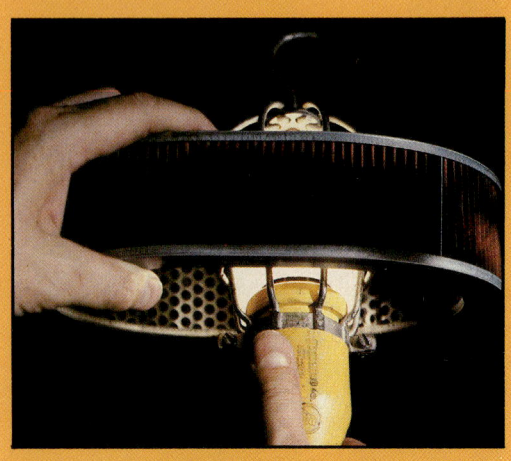

Check the air filter with a light behind it. If you can see light through the filter it can be reused.

Extremely clogged filters should be discarded and replaced with a new one.

18. Replace the air filter regularly. A dirty air filter richens the air/fuel mixture and can increase fuel consumption as much as 10%. Tests show that ⅓ of all vehicles have air filters in need of replacement.

19. Replace the fuel filter at least as often as recommended.

20. Set the idle speed and carburetor mixture to specifications.

21. Check the automatic choke. A sticking or malfunctioning choke wastes gas.

22. During the summer months, adjust the automatic choke for a leaner mixture which will produce faster engine warm-ups.

COOLING SYSTEM

29. Be sure all accessory drive belts are in good condition. Check for cracks or wear.

30. Adjust all accessory drive belts to proper tension.

31. Check all hoses for swollen areas, worn spots, or loose clamps.

32. Check coolant level in the radiator or expansion tank.

33. Be sure the thermostat is operating properly. A stuck thermostat delays engine warm-up and a cold engine uses nearly twice as much fuel as a warm engine.

34. Drain and replace the engine coolant at least as often as recommended. Rust and scale

TIRES & WHEELS

38. Check the tire pressure often with a pencil type gauge. Tests by a major tire manufacturer show that 90% of all vehicles have at least 1 tire improperly inflated. Better mileage can be achieved by over-inflating tires, but never exceed the maximum inflation pressure on the side of the tire.

39. If possible, install radial tires. Radial tires deliver as much as ½ mpg more than bias belted tires.

40. Avoid installing super-wide tires. They only create extra rolling resistance and decrease fuel mileage. Stick to the manufacturer's recommendations.

41. Have the wheels properly balanced.

omy by tampering with emission controls is more likely to worsen fuel economy than improve it. Emission control changes on modern engines are not readily reversible.

16. Clean (or replace) the EGR valve and lines as recommended.

17. Be sure that all vacuum lines and hoses are reconnected properly after working under the hood. An unconnected or misrouted vacuum line can wreak havoc with engine performance.

23. Check for fuel leaks at the carburetor, fuel pump, fuel lines and fuel tank. Be sure all lines and connections are tight.

24. Periodically check the tightness of the carburetor and intake manifold attaching nuts and bolts. These are a common place for vacuum leaks to occur.

25. Clean the carburetor periodically and lubricate the linkage.

26. The condition of the tailpipe can be an excellent indicator of proper engine combustion. After a long drive at highway speeds, the inside of the tailpipe should be a light grey in color. Black or soot on the insides indicates an overly rich mixture.

27. Check the fuel pump pressure. The fuel pump may be supplying more fuel than the engine needs.

28. Use the proper grade of gasoline for your engine. Don't try to compensate for knocking or "pinging" by advancing the ignition timing. This practice will only increase plug temperature and the chances of detonation or pre-ignition with relatively little performance gain.

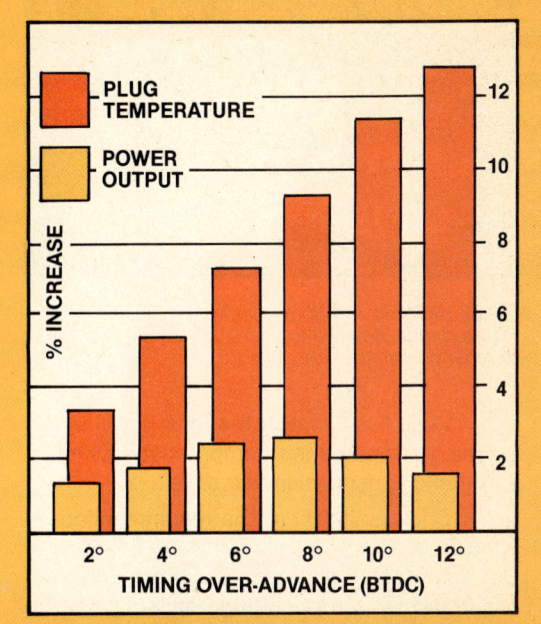

Increasing ignition timing past the specified setting results in a drastic increase in spark plug temperature with increased chance of detonation or preignition. Performance increase is considerably less. (Photo courtesy Champion Spark Plug Co.)

that form in the engine should be flushed out to allow the engine to operate at peak efficiency.

35. Clean the radiator of debris that can decrease cooling efficiency.

36. Install a flex-type or electric cooling fan, if you don't have a clutch type fan. Flex fans use curved plastic blades to push more air at low speeds when more cooling is needed; at high speeds the blades flatten out for less resistance. Electric fans only run when the engine temperature reaches a predetermined level.

37. Check the radiator cap for a worn or cracked gasket. If the cap does not seal properly, the cooling system will not function properly.

42. Be sure the front end is correctly aligned. A misaligned front end actually has wheels going in differed directions. The increased drag can reduce fuel economy by .3 mpg.

43. Correctly adjust the wheel bearings. Wheel bearings that are adjusted too tight increase rolling resistance.

Check tire pressures regularly with a reliable pocket type gauge. Be sure to check the pressure on a cold tire.

GENERAL MAINTENANCE

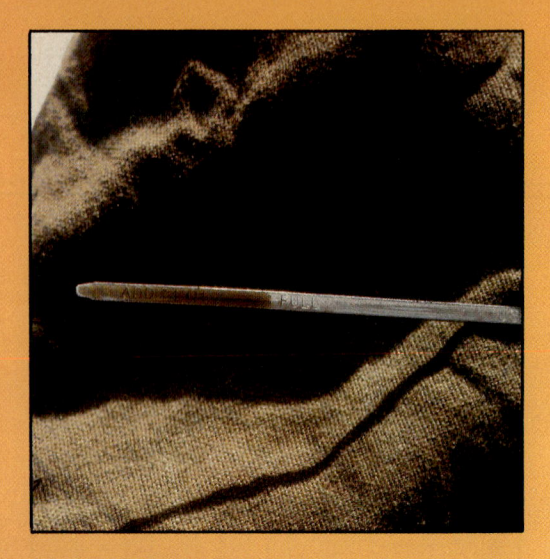

Check the fluid levels (particularly engine oil) on a regular basis. Be sure to check the oil for grit, water or other contamination.

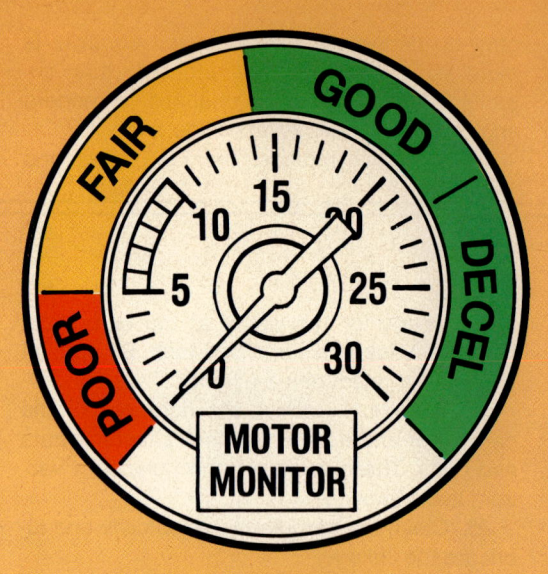

A vacuum gauge is another excellent indicator of internal engine condition and can also be installed in the dash as a mileage indicator.

44. Periodically check the fluid levels in the engine, power steering pump, master cylinder, automatic transmission and drive axle.

45. Change the oil at the recommended interval and change the filter at every oil change. Dirty oil is thick and causes extra friction between moving parts, cutting efficiency and increasing wear. A worn engine requires more frequent tune-ups and gets progressively worse fuel economy. In general, use the lightest viscosity oil for the driving conditions you will encounter.

46. Use the recommended viscosity fluids in the transmission and axle.

47. Be sure the battery is fully charged for fast starts. A slow starting engine wastes fuel.

48. Be sure battery terminals are clean and tight.

49. Check the battery electrolyte level and add distilled water if necessary.

50. Check the exhaust system for crushed pipes, blockages and leaks.

51. Adjust the brakes. Dragging brakes or brakes that are not releasing create increased drag on the engine.

52. Install a vacuum gauge or miles-per-gallon gauge. These gauges visually indicate engine vacuum in the intake manifold. High vacuum = good mileage and low vacuum = poorer mileage. The gauge can also be an excellent indicator of internal engine conditions.

53. Be sure the clutch is properly adjusted. A slipping clutch wastes fuel.

54. Check and periodically lubricate the heat control valve in the exhaust manifold. A sticking or inoperative valve prevents engine warm-up and wastes gas.

55. Keep accurate records to check fuel economy over a period of time. A sudden drop in fuel economy may signal a need for tune-up or other maintenance.

© 1980 Chilton Book Company, Radnor, PA 19089

ENGINE AND ENGINE REBUILDING 59

Engine cooling system

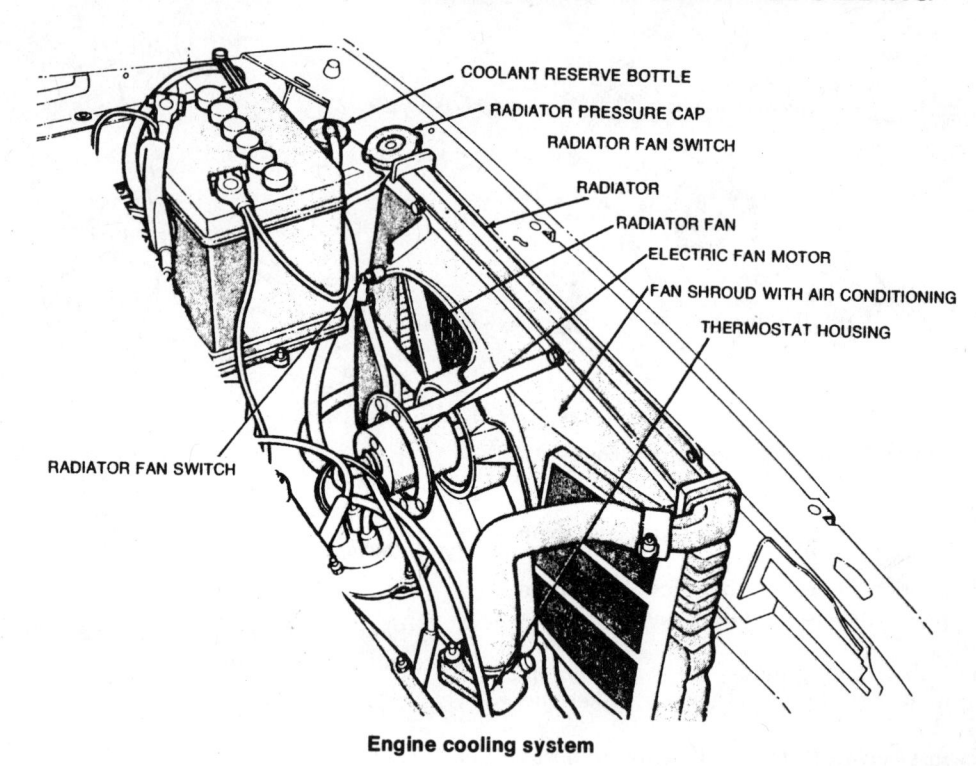

case. Install the separator with the oil holes facing down.

COOLING SYSTEM

The cooling system consists of a radiator, fan shroud, if equipped with air conditioning, overflow tank, water pump, thermostat, coolant temperature switch, electric fan and radiator fan switch. The use of an electric fan is necessitated by the transversely mounted engine. A radiator bypass system is used for faster warmup.

Radiator

REMOVAL AND INSTALLATION

1. Move the temperature selector to full on.
2. Open the radiator drain cock.
3. When the coolant reserve tank is empty, remove the radiator cap.
4. Remove the hoses.
5. If equipped with automatic transmission, disconnect and plug the fluid cooler lines.
6. Remove the upper and lower mounting brackets.
7. Remove the shroud.
8. Remove the fan motor attaching bolts.
9. Remove the top radiator attaching bolts.
10. Remove the bottom radiator attaching bolts.
11. Lift the radiator from the engine compartment.
12. Installation is the reverse of removal.

Water Pump

REMOVAL AND INSTALLATION

1. Drain the cooling system.
2. Remove the drive belts.
3. Remove the water pump pulley.
4. Unbolt the compressor and/or air pump

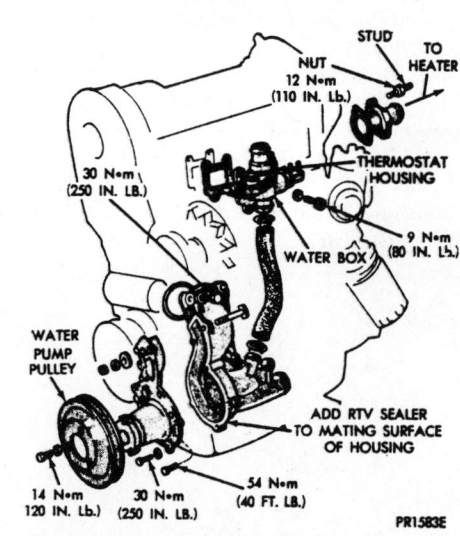

Thermostat Housing and Water Pump—1.7L Engine

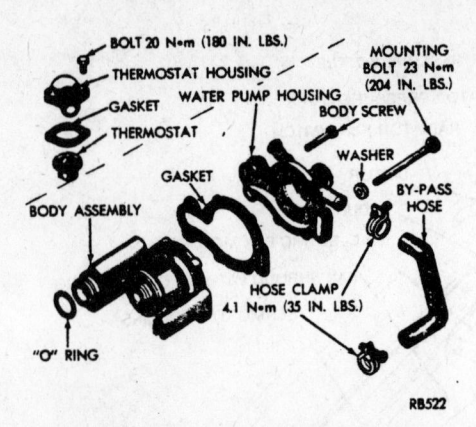

60 ENGINE AND ENGINE REBUILDING

Thermostat Housing and Water Pump—2.6L Engine

brackets from the water pump and secure them out of the way.

5. Position the bypass hose lower clamp in the center of the hose and disconnect the heater hose.

6. Unbolt and remove the water pump. Discard the gasket and clean the gasket surfaces.

7. Installation is the reverse of removal. Torque the water pump bolts to 25–40 ft. lbs., the alternator adjusting bolt to 30–50 ft. lbs.; the pulley bolts to 85–125 in. lbs.

Thermostat

REMOVAL AND INSTALLATION

The thermostat on the 2.2 Liter engine is located in the thermostat housing on the cylinder head. 2.6 Liter engines have the thermostat housing near the intake manifold.

1. Drain the cooling system to a level below the thermostat.
2. Remove the hose from the thermostat housing.
3. Remove the thermostat housing.
4. Remove the thermostat and discard the gasket. Clean both gasket surfaces thoroughly.
5. Position the thermostat in the housing. Install a new gasket and the upper half of the housing. Make sure that the thermostat is properly seated.

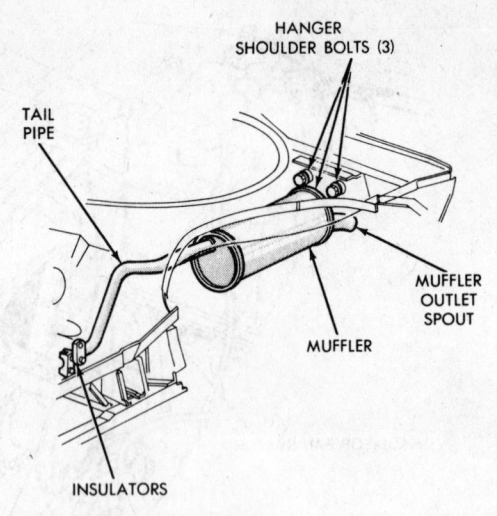

Typical tailpipe and muffler

6. Refill the cooling system, start the engine, and check for leaks.

Exhaust Pipes, Mufflers, and Tailpipes

REMOVAL AND INSTALLATION

1. Support the vehicle securely. Apply penetrating oil to all clamp bolts and nuts you will be working on. Support the vehicle by the body, if possible, to increase working clearances.

2. If the tailpipe is integral with the muffler, and the muffler must be replaced, cut the tail pipe with a hacksaw right near the front of the muffler. The replacement muffler is then installed using a clamp to attach to the tailpipe.

3. Loosen clamps and supports to permit alignment of all parts, and then retighten. Make sure there is adequate clearance so exhaust parts stay clear of underbody parts.

4. Clean the mating surfaces of pipes or the muffler to ensure a tight seal. Use new insulators, clamps, and supports unless the condition of old parts is very good.

Emission Controls and Fuel Systems

4

EMISSION CONTROL SYSTEMS

Several different systems are used on each car. Most require no service and those which may require service also require sophisticated equipment for testing purposes.

Catalytic Converter

Two catalysts are used on each car: A small one located just after the exhaust manifold and a larger one located under the car body. Catalysts promote complete oxidation of exhaust gases through the effect of a platinum coated mass in the catalyst shell. Two things act to destroy the catalyst, functionally: excessive heat and leaded gas. Excessive heat during misfiring and prolonged testing with the ignition system in any way altered is the most common occurence. Test procedures should be accomplished as quickly as possible, and the car, should not be driven when misfiring is noted.

Heated Air Inlet System

All engines are equipped with a vacuum device located in the carburetor air cleaner air intake. A small door is operated by a vacuum diaphragm and a thermostatic spring. When the air temperature outside is 40°F or lower, the door will block off air entering from outside and allow air channelled from the exhaust manifold area to enter the intake. This air is heated by the hot manifold. At 65°F or above, the door fully blocks off the heated air. At temperatures in between, the door is operated in intermediate positions. During acceleration the door is controlled by engine vacuum to allow the maximum amount of air to enter the carburetor.

Exhaust Gas Recirculation System

This system reduces the amount of oxides of nitrogen in the exhaust by allowing a predetermined amount of hot exhaust gases to recirculate and dilute the incoming fuel/air mixture. The principal components of the system are the

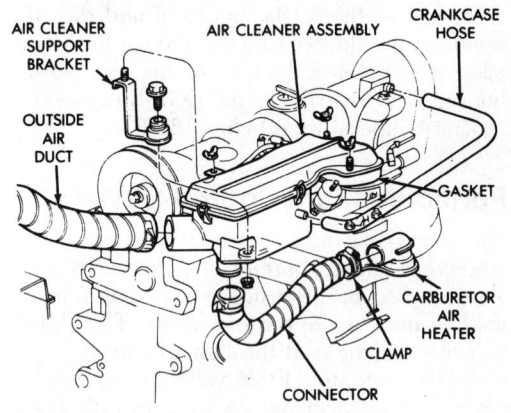

Heated inlet air system—2.2L engine

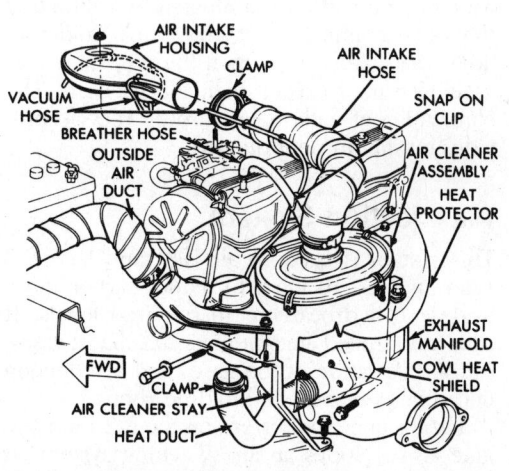

Heated inlet air system—2.6L engine

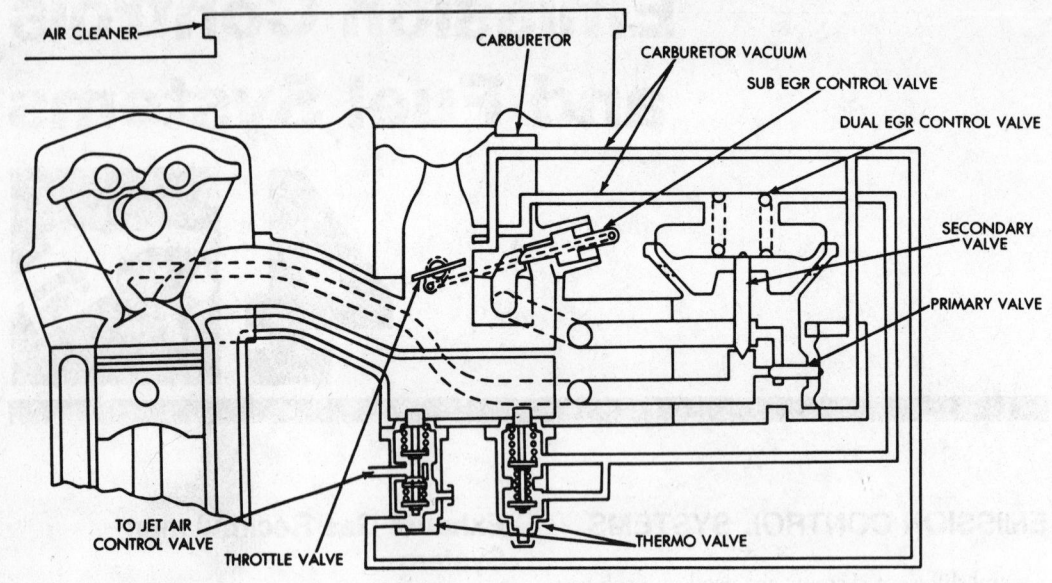

62 EMISSION CONTROLS AND FUEL SYSTEM

EGR system—2.6L engine

EGR valve and the Coolant Control Exhaust Gas Recirculation Valve (CCEGR). The former is located in the intake manifold and directly regulates the flow of exhaust gases into the intake. The latter is located in the thermostat housing and overrides the EGR valve when coolant temperature is below 125°F.

Ported Vacuum Control System

The ported vacuum control system utilizes a type port in the carburetor throttle body which is exposed to an increasing percentage of manifold vacuum as the throttle opens. This throttle bore is connected through an external nipple directly to the EGR valve. Flow rate is dependent on manifold vacuum, throttle position, and exhaust gas back pressure. Recycle at wide open throttle is eliminated by calibrating the valve opening point above manifold vacuums available at wide open throttle, since port vacuum cannot exceed manifold vacuum. The elimination of wide open throttle recycle provides maximum performance.

Air Injection System

This system is used on all 1981 and later 2.2 Liter engines. Its job is to reduce carbon monoxide and hydrocarbons to required levels. It adds a controlled amount of air to exhaust gases, causing oxidation of the gases and a reduction of carbon monoxide and hydrocarbons.

The air injection system on the 2.2 Liter engine also includes an air switching system. It has been designed so that air injection will not interfere with the EGR system to control NOx emissions, and on vehicles equipped with an oxygen sensor, to insure proper air-fuel distribution for maximum fuel economy.

The vehicles produced for sale in the 50 states pump air into the base of the exhaust manifold. The Canadian system pumps air through the head at the exhaust port.

The air injection system consists of a belt-driven air pump, a diverter valve (Canadian engines only) a switch-relief valve, rubber hoses, and check valve tube assemblies to protect the hoses and other components from high temperature exhaust gases.

Pulse Air Feeder System

2.6 Liter Engines

Pulse Air Feeder (PAF) is used for supplying secondary air into the exhaust system between the front and rear catalytic converters, for the purpose of promoting oxidation of exhaust emissions in the rear converter.

The PAF consists of a main red valve and a sub reed valve.

The main reed valve is actuated in response to movement of a diaphragm, which is activated by pressure generated when the piston is in the compression stroke. The sub reed valve is opened on the exhaust stroke.

To inspect the system, remove the hose connected to the air cleaner and check for vacuum, with the engine running. If vacuum is not present, check the lines for leaks and evidence of oil leaks. Periodic maintenance of this system is not required.

EMISSION CONTROLS AND FUEL SYSTEM 63

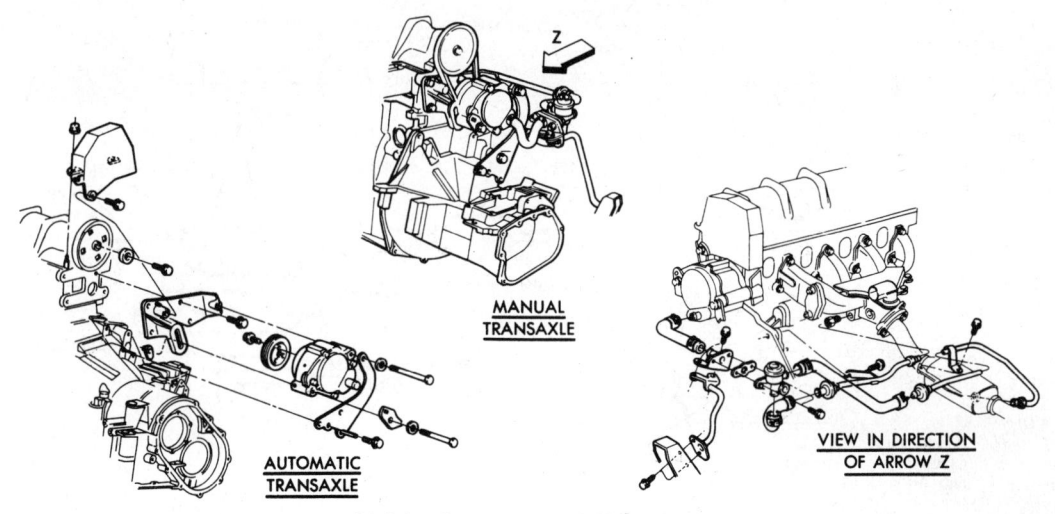

Air injection system—2.2L engine

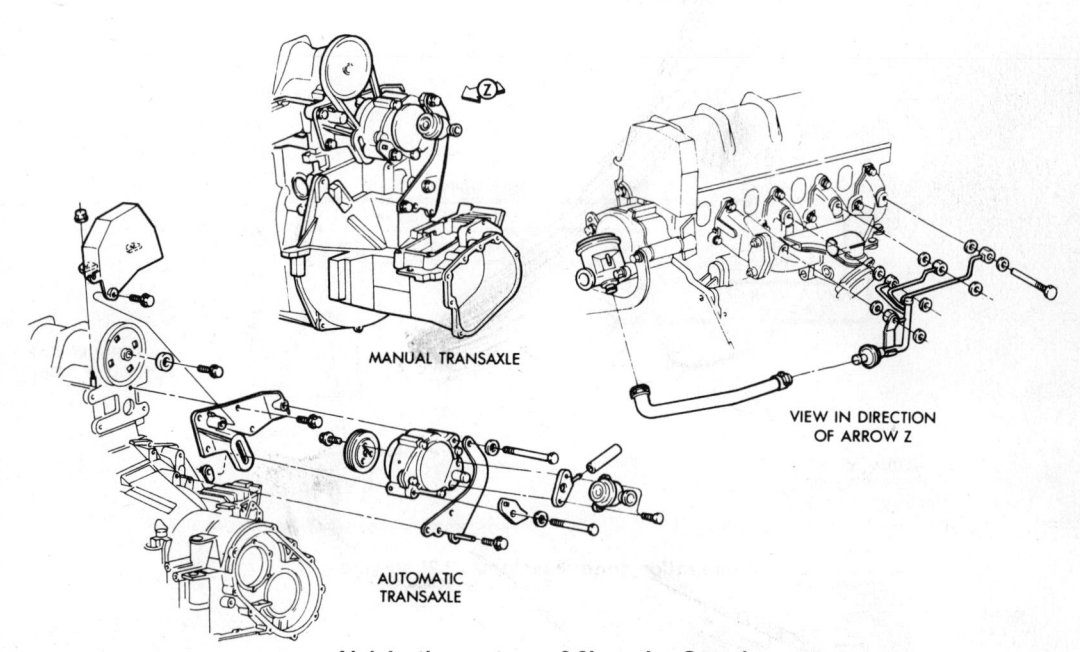

Air injection system—2.2L engine Canada

Evaporation Control System

This system prevents the release of gasoline vapors from the fuel tank and the carburetor into the atmosphere. The system is vacuum operated and draws the fumes into a charcoal canister where they are temporarily held until they are drawn into the intake manifold for burning. For proper operation of the system and to prevent gas tank failure, the lines should never be plugged, and no cap other than the one specified should be used on the fuel tank filler neck.

Diverter Valve

The purpose of the diverter valve is to prevent backfire in the exhaust system during sudden deceleration.

Sudden throttle closure at the beginning of deceleration temporarily creates an air-fuel mixture too rich to burn. This mixture becomes burnable when it reaches the exhaust area and combines with injector air. The next firing of the cylinder will ignite this air-fuel mixture. The valve senses the sudden increase

64 EMISSION CONTROLS AND FUEL SYSTEM

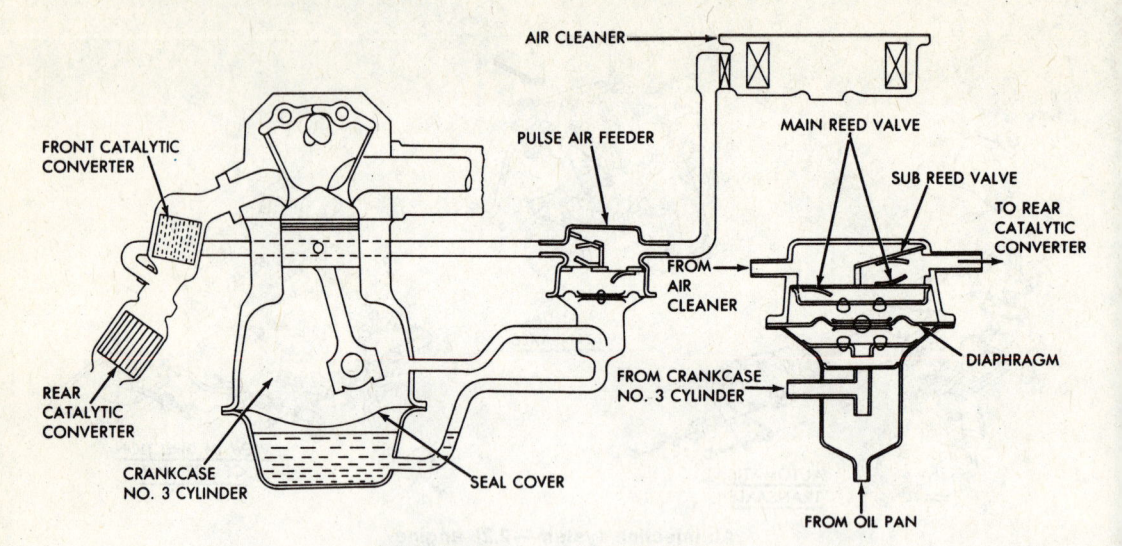

Pulse air feeder system 2.6L engine

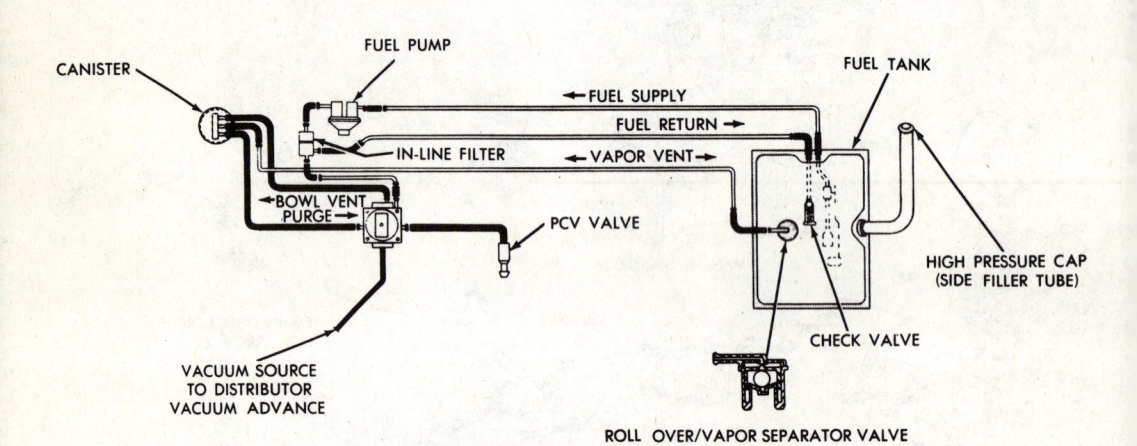

Evaporation control system—2.2L engine

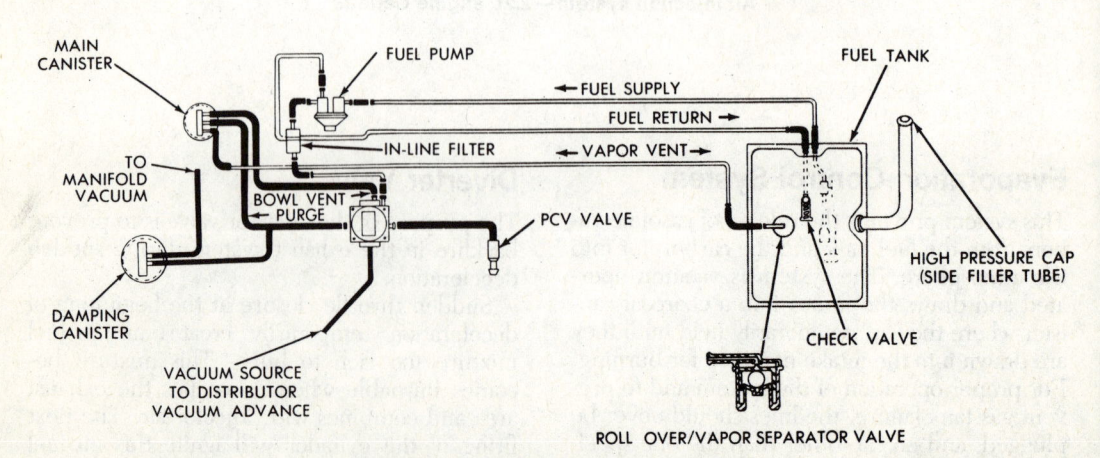

Evaporation control system—2.6L engine

EMISSION CONTROLS AND FUEL SYSTEM

in manifold vacuum causing the valve to open, allowing air from the pump to pass through the valve into the atmosphere.

A pressure relief valve incorporated in the same housing as the diverter valve, controls pressure within the system by diverting excessive pump output at high engine speed to the atmosphere.

Switch-Relief Valve

The purpose of this valve is two-fold. First of all, the valve directs the air injection flow to either the exhaust port location or to the downstream injection point. Second, the valve regulates system pressure by controlling the output of the air pump at high speeds. When the pressure reaches a certain level, some of the output is vented to the atmosphere through the silencer.

Check Valve

A check valve is located in the injection tube assemblies that lead to the exhaust manifold and the catalyst injection points on the 50 state engines and to the exhaust port area, through four hollow bolts on the Canadian engines.

This valve has a one-way diaphragm which prevents hot exhaust gases from backing up into the hose and pump. It also protects the system in the event of pump belt failure, excessively high exhaust system pressure, or air hose ruptures.

Deceleration Spark Advance System

The deceleration spark advance system consists of a solenoid valve and an engine speed sensor.

During vehicle deceleration, ignition timing is advanced by intake manifold vacuum acting on the distributor advance through the solenoid valve. However, when the engine speed sensor detects engine speed at or below 1300 rpm the vacuum acting on the vacuum advance, is changed from the intake manifold to the carburetor ported vacuum by the solenoid valve movement, in order to maintain smooth vehicle operation.

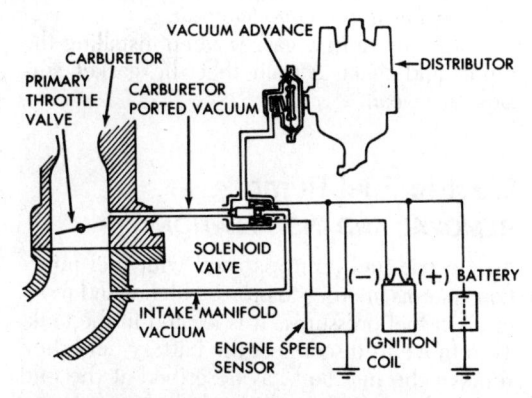

High Altitude Compensation System

A high altitude compensation system is installed on California vehicles. This modification affects the primary metering system as follows:

A small cylindrical bellows chamber mounted on the body panel in the engine compartment and connected to the carburetor with hoses, is vented to the atmosphere at the top of the carburetor. Atmospheric pressure expands and contracts the bellows.

A small brass tapered-seat valve regulates air flow when it is raised off its seat by expanding the bellows.

Some time during engine operation, rarefied atmosphere is encountered, producing a rich airfuel mixture. At a predetermined atmospheric pressure, the bellows open, allowing additional air to enter the main air bleeds. The auxiliary air, along with the present air source, provides the system with the proper amount of air necessary to maintain the correct air-fuel mixture.

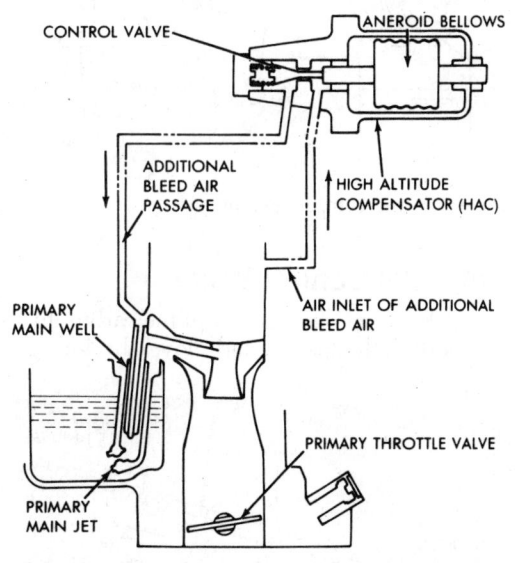

High altitude compensation system

Deceleration spark advance system

Throttle Opener (Idle-UP System)

This system consists of a throttle opener assembly, a solenoid valve, an engine speed sensor,

66 EMISSION CONTROLS AND FUEL SYSTEM

and a compressor switch for the air conditioner unit.

When the compressor switch is turned on and the speed sensor detects engine speed at or below its present level, the solenoid valve is opened slightly by the throttle opener. Consequently, the engine idle speed increases to compensate for the compressor load. When the compressor switch is turned off the throttle stops working and returns to normal idle.

Jet Air Control Valve (JACV)

The jet air control valve system consists of a jet air control valve, which is an integral part of the carburetor, and a thermo-valve which is controlled by coolant temperature.

Its purpose is to help decrease hydrocarbons and carbon monoxide during engine warm-up while the choke is operating.

Carburetor vacuum opens the valve thereby allowing air to flow into the jet air passage preventing an overly rich air-fuel mixture.

The function of the thermo-valve is to stop the jet valve operation when the coolant temperature is above or below a pre-set value.

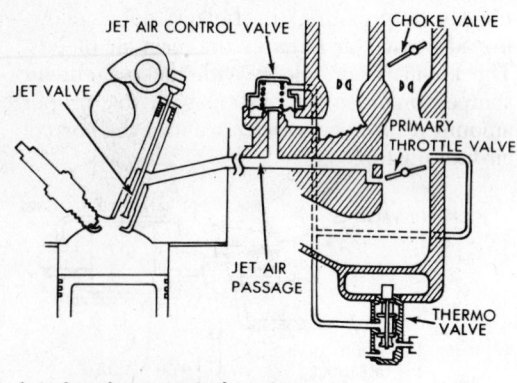

Jet air volume control system

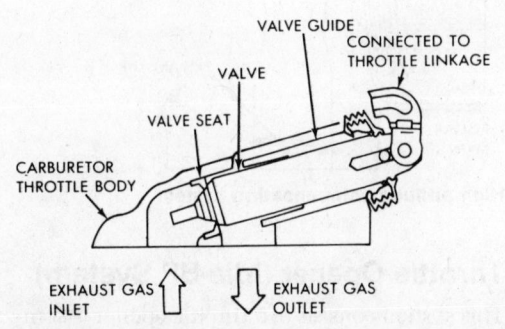

Sub EGR Control Valve

This valve is an integral part of the carburetor, and is directly opened and closed by linkage connected to the throttle valve. In conjunction with the standard EGR system the sub EGR more closely modulates EGR flow in response to the throttle valve opening.

FUEL SYSTEM

Mechanical Fuel Pump

The fuel pump located on the left side of the engine is a mechanical type with an integral vapor separator for satisfactory hot weather performance. The fuel pump is driven by an eccentric cam that is cast on the accessory driveshaft.

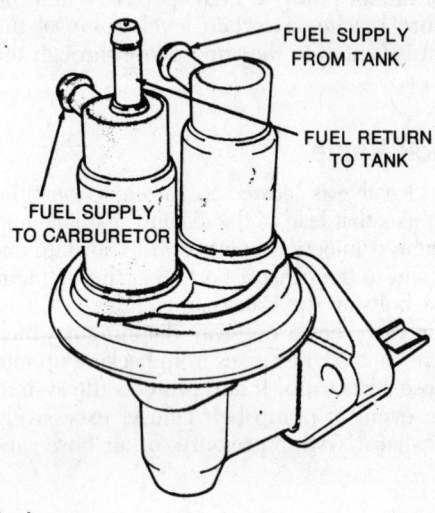

Fuel pump

REMOVAL AND INSTALLATION

1. Disconnect the fuel and vapor lines.
2. Plug the lines to prevent fuel leaks.
3. Remove the attaching bolts and remove the fuel pump.
4. Installation is the reverse of removal.

NOTE: *The pump is not repairable. It must be replaced as a complete unit.*

Always use a new gasket when installing the pump and make certain that the gasket surfaces are clean.

Electric Fuel Pump

REMOVAL AND INSTALLATION

An electric fuel pump is used with fuel injection systems in order to provide higher and more uniform fuel pressures. It is located in the tank. To remove it, disconnect the battery, and then remove the fuel tank, as described at the end of this chapter. Then, with a hammer and *non-*

Sub EGR control valve

EMISSION CONTROLS AND FUEL SYSTEM 67

metallic punch, tap the fuel pump lock ring counterclockwise to release the pump.

To install the pump, first wipe the seal area of the tank clean and install a new O-ring seal. Replace the filter on the end of the pump if it appears to be damaged. Then position the pump in the tank and install the locking ring. Tighten the ring in the same general way in which you loosened it. *Do not* overtighten it, as this can cause leakage. Install the tank as described at the end of this chapter.

Carburetors

REMOVAL AND INSTALLATION

NOTE: *When removing the carburetor on the 2.2 Liter engine, it should not be necessary to disturb the isolator, unless it has been determined that there is a leak in it.*

1. Disconnect the negative battery terminal.
2. Remove the air cleaner.
3. Remove the gas cap.

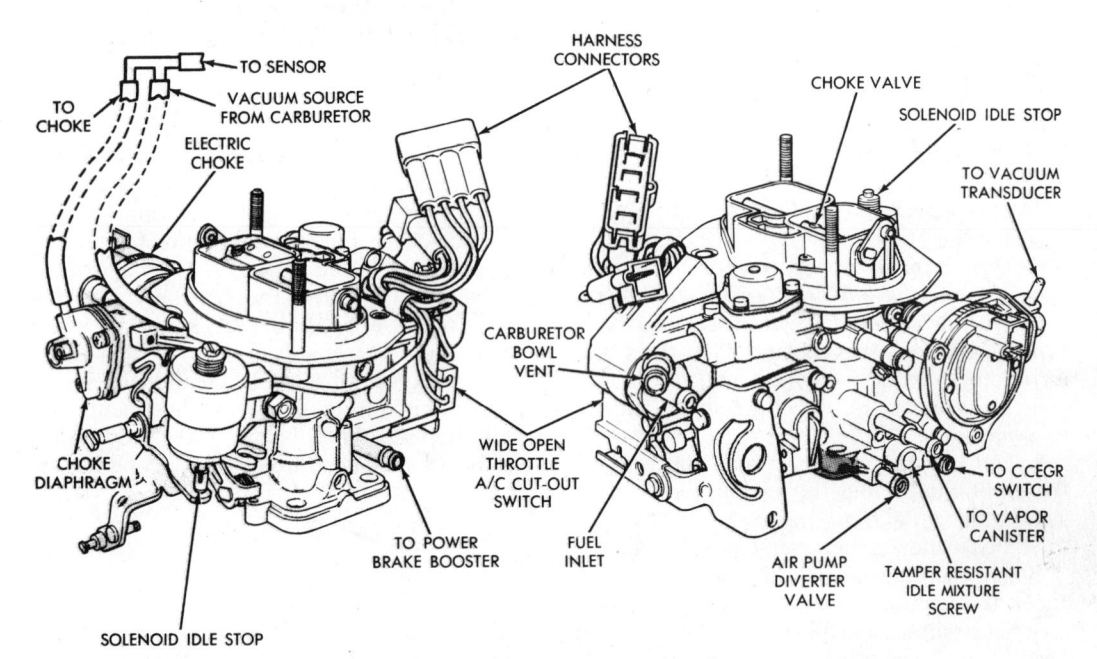

Details of the 2.2L carburetor

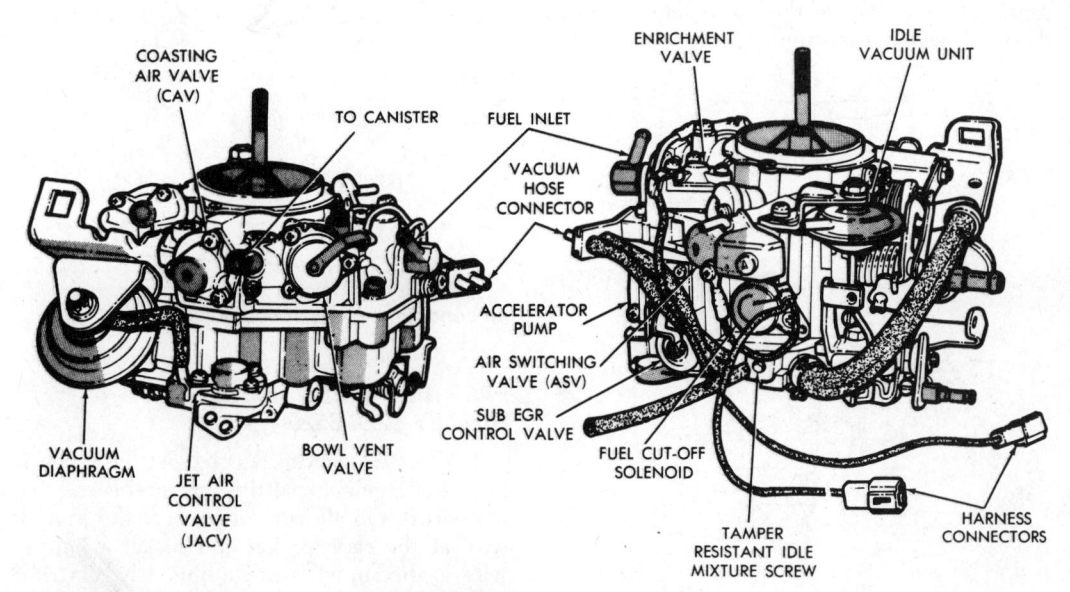

Details of the 2.6L carburetor

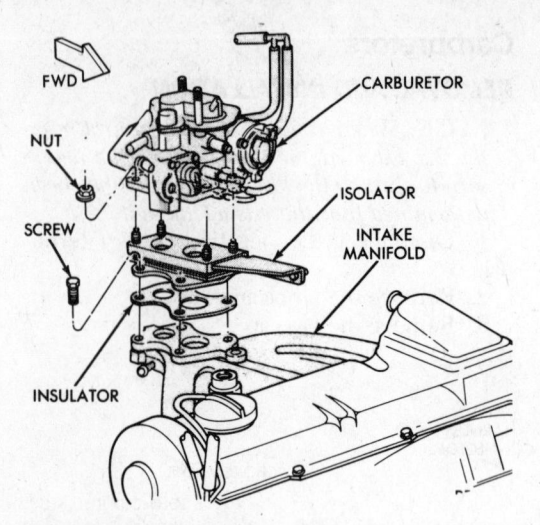

68 EMISSION CONTROLS AND FUEL SYSTEM

Carburetor—2.2L engine

4. Disconnect the fuel intact line and all necessary wiring.

NOTE: *It may be necessary to drain the coolant on the 2.6 Liter engine before removing the coolant lines at the carburetor.*

5. Disconnect the coolant lines from the carburetor, (2.6 Liter engines only).
6. Disconnect the throttle linkage and all vacuum hoses.
7. Remove the mounting nuts and remove the carburetor. Hold the carburetor level to avoid spilling fuel from the bowl.
8. Installation is the reverse of removal.

Before checking and adjusting any idle speed, check the ignition timing and adjust if necessary. Disconnect and plug the EGR vacuum hose. Unplug the connector at the radiator fan and install a jumper wire so the fan will run continuously. Remove the PCV valve. Allow the PCV valve to draw under hood air and plug the ³⁄₁₆ in. diameter hose at the canister. Connect a tachometer and start the engine.

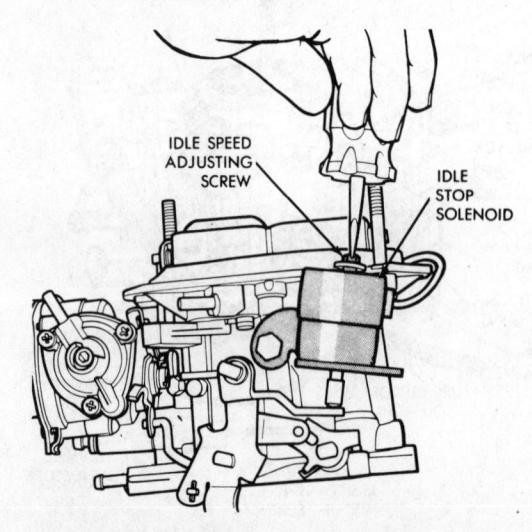

NOTE: *Do not remove the air cleaner.*

IDLE ADJUSTMENT—HOLLEY 5220/6520

1. On air conditioned vehicles, allow the engine to stabilize after performing the idle speed adjustments.
2. If your tachometer indicates the rpm is not set to specifications, turn the idle speed screw until the correct rpm is achieved. See the under hood sticker for correct idle speed.

AIR CONDITIONING IDLE SPEED ADJUSTMENT—HOLLEY 5220/6520

1. Turn the air conditioner on and set the blower on low. Disconnect and plug the EGR valve vacuum hose.
2. Remove the adjusting screw and spring from the top of the air conditioning solenoid.
3. Insert a ⅛ in. Allen wrench into the solenoid and adjust to obtain the correct idle speed as per the under hood sticker. This adjustment is required on 1981–82 models only. On later models, just verify that the A/C idle speed kicker works.
4. Make sure that the air conditioning clutch is operating during the speed adjustments.
5. Replace the adjusting screw and spring on the solenoid and turn off the air conditioner.

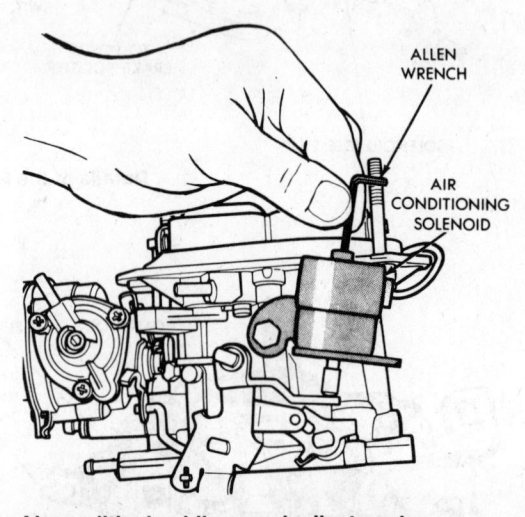

Air conditioning idle speed adjustment

FAST IDLE SPEED ADJUSTMENT—HOLLEY 5220/6520

1. On 1981–82 cars, disconnect the two-way electrical connector at the carburetor (red and tan wires). On all cars, disconnect the jumper wire at the radiator fan and install a jumper wire so the fan will run continuously. On 1983 and later cars: Pull the PCV valve out of the

Idle set rpm adjustment

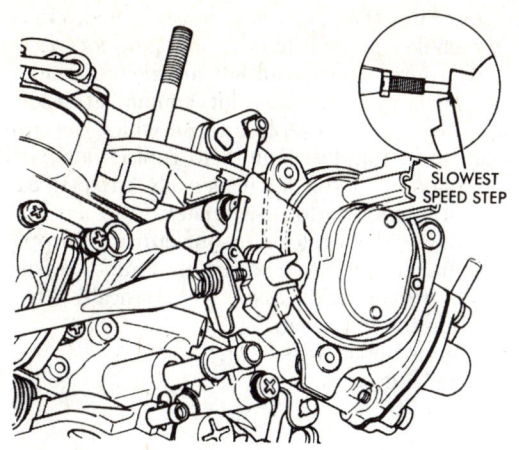

EMISSION CONTROLS AND FUEL SYSTEM 69

Fast idle speed adjustment

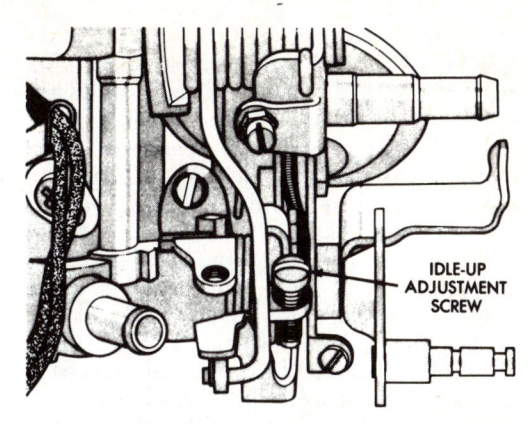

Adjusting the idle-up (air conditioner-on) on the Mikuni carburetor

valve cover and allow it to draw underhood air; disconnect the O₂ system connector located on the left fender shield near the shock tower; and ground the carburetor switch with a jumper wire.

2. Open the throttle slightly and place the adjustment screw on the slowest speed step of the fast idle cam. With the choke fully open adjust the fast idle speed to comply with the under-hood sticker. Return the vehicle to idle, then replace the adjusting screw on the slowest speed step of the fast idle cam to verify fast idle speed. Re-adjust as necessary.

4. Turn the engine off, remove the jumper wire and reconnect the fan. Reinstall the PCV valve and remove the tachometer.

On 1983 and later models, reconnect the O₂ system connector, and remove the jumper wire at the carburetor.

IDLE ADJUSTMENT—MIKUNI CARBURETOR (2.6L ENGINE)

1. Place the transaxle in neutral, set the parking brake, and turn off all accessories. Disconnect the radiator fan. Run the engine until it reaches operating temperature. On 1983 and earlier models, allow the engine to idle for one minute to stabilize RPM.

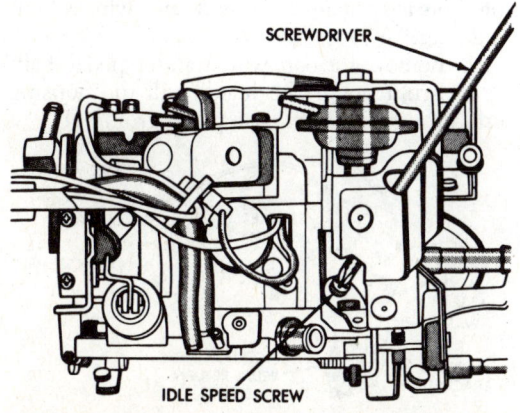

2. On 1984 models, turn the engine off, and then disconnect the negative battery cable for three seconds and then reconnect it. Disconnect the engine harness lead from the O₂ sensor at the bullet connector. Don't pull on the sensor wire in doing this. Restart the engine. On 1984 and 1985 vehicles, run the engine at 2,500 rpm for 10 seconds. Then, wait two minutes before checking idle speed.

3. Check the idle speed with a tachometer. If not to specifications, on 1983–84 models, disconnect idle switch connector if the idle speed must be adjusted. Now, adjust the idle speed with the idle screw.

4. On A/C models, turn on the air conditioning with the temperature control lever set to the coldest setting. If the RPM is not 900, turn the idle-up screw to obtain this reading.

5. Turn off the engine and reconnect all connectors.

MIXTURE ADJUSTMENT

Chrysler recommends the use of a propane enrichment procedure to adjust the mixture. The equipment needed for this procedure is not readily available to the general public.

> NOTE: *Mixture screws are sealed under tamperproof plugs. The only time mixture adjustments are necessary is during a major carburetor overhaul. Refer to the instructions supplied with the overhaul kit.*

OVERHAUL

Efficient carburetion depends greatly on careful cleaning and inspection during overhaul, since dirt, gum, water, or varnish in or on carburetor parts are often responsible for poor performance.

Adjusting idle speed on the Mikuni carburetor (2.6 L engine)

EMISSION CONTROLS AND FUEL SYSTEM

Overhaul your carburetor in a clean, dust-free area. Carefully disassemble the carburetor, referring often to the exploded views and directions packaged with the rebuilding kit. Keep all similar and look-alike parts segregated during disassembly and cleaning to avoid accidental interchange during assembly. Make a note of all jet sizes.

When the carburetor is disassembled, wash all parts (except diaphragms, electric choke units, pump plunger, and any other plastic, leather, fiber, or rubber parts) in clean carburetor solvent. Do not leave parts in the solvent any longer than is necessary to sufficiently loosen the deposits. Excessive cleaning may remove the special finish from the float bowl and choke valve bodies, leaving these parts unfit for service. Rinse all parts in clean solvent and blow them dry with compressed air or allow them to air dry. Wipe clean all cork, plastic, leather, and fiber parts with a clean, lint-free cloth.

Blow out all passages and jets with compressed air and be sure that there are no restrictions or blockages. Never use wire or similar tools to clean jets, fuel passages, or air bleeds. Clean all jets and valves separately to avoid accidental interchange.

Check all parts for wear or damage. If wear or damage is found, replace the defective parts. Especially check the following.

1. Check the float needle and seat for wear. If wear is found, replace the complete assembly.
2. Check the float hinge pin for wear and the float(s) for dents or distortion. Replace the float if fuel has leaked into it.
3. Check the throttle and choke shaft bores for wear or an out-of-round condition. Damage or wear to the throttle arm, shaft, or shaft bore will often require replacement of the throttle body. These parts require a close tolerance of fit; wear may allow air leakage, which could affect starting and idling.

NOTE: *Throttle shafts and bushings are not included in overhaul kits. They can be purchased separately.*

4. Inspect the idle mixture adjusting needles for burrs or grooves. Any such condition requires replacement of the needle, since you will not be able to obtain a satisfactory idle.
5. Test the accelerator pump check valves. They should pass air one way but not the other. Test for proper seating by blowing and sucking on the valve. Replace the valve as necessary. If the valve is satisfactory, wash the valve again to remove breath moisture.
6. Check the bowl cover for warped surfaces with a straightedge.
7. Closely inspect the valves and seats for wear and damage, replacing as necessary.
8. After the carburetor is assembled, check the choke valve for freedom of operation.

Carburetor overhaul kits are recommended for each overhaul. These kits contain all gaskets and new parts to replace those which deteriorate most rapidly. Failure to replace all parts supplied with the kit (especially gaskets) can result in poor performance later.

Some carburetor manufacturers supply overhaul kits of three basic types: minor repair; major repair; and gasket kits. Basically, they contain the following:

Minor Repair Kits:
- All gaskets
- Float needle valve
- All diaphragms
- Spring for the pump diaphragm

Major Repair Kits:
- All jets and gaskets
- All diaphragms
- Float needle valve
- Pump ball valve
- Float
- Complete intermediate rod
- Intermediate pump lever
- Some cover hold-down screws and washers

Gasket Kits:
- All gaskets

After cleaning and checking all components, reassemble the carburetor, using new parts and referring to the exploded view. When reassembling, make sure that all screws and jets are tight in their seats, but do not overtighten as the tips will be distorted. Tighten all screws gradually, in rotation. Do not tighten needle valves into their seats; uneven jetting will result. Always use new gaskets. Be sure to adjust the float level when reassembling.

THROTTLE CABLE REMOVAL AND INSTALLATION

1. From inside the vehicle, remove the cable housing retainer clip and core wire retaining plug.
2. Remove the core wire from the pedal shaft.
3. From under the hood, pull the housing end-fitting out of the dash panel grommet.

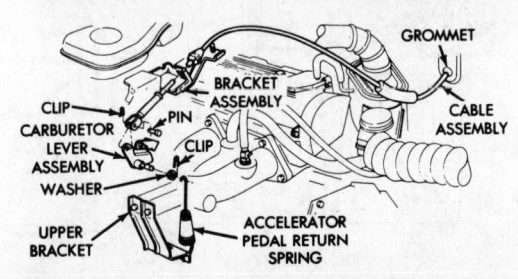

Throttle cable attachment to carburetor 2.6L engine

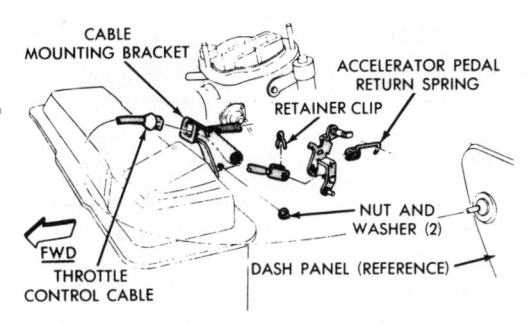

EMISSION CONTROLS AND FUEL SYSTEM

Throttle cable attachment 2.2L engine

4. Remove the cable clevis from the carburetor lever stud. Now the cable mounting bracket will separate by using wide-jaw pliers to compress the end-fitting tabs.

5. Installation is the reverse of removal. Adjust the cable as necessary.

Throttle body injection system
GENERAL INFORMATION

This electronic fuel injection system is a computer regulated single point fuel injection system that provides precise air/fuel ratio for all driving conditions. At the center of this system is a digital preprogrammed computer known as a logic module that regulates ignition timing, air-fuel ratio, emission control devices and idle speed. This component has the ability to update and revise its programming to meet changing operating conditions.

Various sensors provide the input necessary for the logic module to correctly regulate the fuel flow at the fuel injector. These include the manifold absolute pressure, throttle position, oxygen feedback, coolant temperature, charge temperature and vehicle speed sensors. In addition to the sensors, various switches also provide important information. These include the neutral-safety, heated back lite, air conditioning, air conditioning clutch switches, and an electronic idle switch.

All inputs to the logic module are converted into signals sent to the power module. These signals cause the power module to change either the fuel flow at the injector or ignition timing or both.

The logic module tests many of its own input and output circuits. If a fault is found in a major system this information is stored in the logic module. Information on this fault can be displayed to a technician by means of a flashing light emitting diode (LED) or by connecting a diagnostic read out and reading a numbered display code which directly relates to a specific fault.

NOTE: *Experience has shown that most complaints that may occur with EFI can be traced to poor wiring or hose connections. A visual check will help spot these most com-*

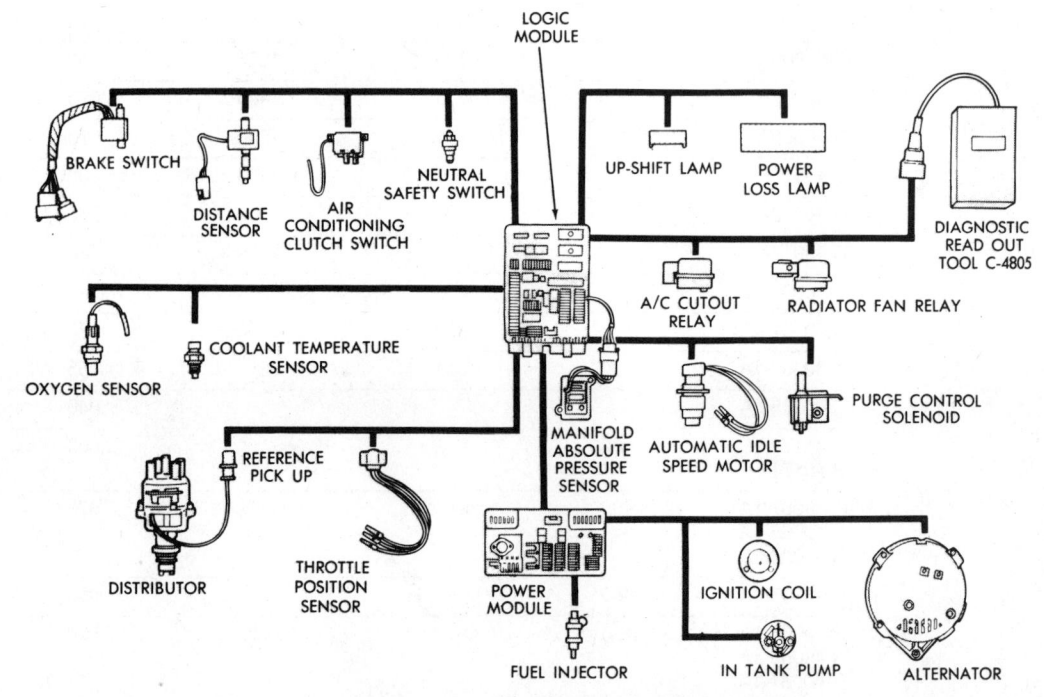

Diagram of the Single-Point EFI system

EMISSION CONTROLS AND FUEL SYSTEM

Carburetor Specifications
Holley 6520

Year	Carb. Part No.	Dry Float Setting (in.)	Solenoid Idle Stop (rpm)	Fast Idle Speed (rpm)	Vacuum Kick (in.)
1981	R9060A R9061A	.480	850	1100	.030
	R9125A R9126A	.480	850	1200	.030
	R9052A R9053A	.480	850	1400	.070
	R9054A R9055A	.480	850	1400	.040
	R9602A R9603A	.480	850	1500	.065
	R9604A R9605A	.480	850	1600	.065
1982	R9824A	.480	900	1400	.065
	R9503A R9504A R9750A R9751A	.480	850	1300	.085
	R9822A R9823A	.480	850	1400	.080
	R9505A R9506A R9752A R9753A	.480	900	1600	.100
1983	R-40003A	.480	775	1400	.070
	R-40004A		900	1500	.080
	R-40005A		900	1350	.080
	R-40006A		850	1275	.080
	R-40007A		775	1400	.070
	R-40008A		900	1600	.070
	R-40010A		900	1500	.080
	R-40012A		900	1600	.070
	R-40014A		850	1275	.080
	R-40080A		850	1400	.045
	R-40081A		850	1400	.045
1984	R-40060-1A	.480	see	see	.055
	R-40085-1A				.040
	R-40170A R-40171A	.480			.060
	R-40067-1A R-40068-1A R-40058-1A	.480	underhood	underhood	.070
	R-40107-1A	.480			.055
	R-40064-1A R-40065-1A R-40081-1A R-40082-1A	.480	sticker	sticker	.080

EMISSION CONTROLS AND FUEL SYSTEM 73

Carburetor Specifications (cont.)
Holley 6520

Year	Carb. Part No.	Dry Float Setting (in.)	Solenoid Idle Stop (rpm)	Fast Idle Speed (rpm)	Vacuum Kick (in.)
1984	R-40071A R-40122A				
1985	R40058A	.480	see	see	.070
	R40060A	.480			.055
	R40116A R40117A	.480	underhood	underhood	.095
	R40134A R40135A R40138A R40139A	.480	sticker	sticker	.075

mon faults and save unnecessary test and diagnosis time.

ADJUSTMENTS

Ignition Timing

1. Connect a power timing light to the number one cylinder, or a magnetic timing unit to the engine. (Use a 10° degree offset when required).
2. Connect a tachometer to the engine and turn selector to the proper cylinder position.
3. Start engine and run until operating temperature is reached.
4. Disconnect and reconnect the water temperature sensor connector on the thermostat housing. The loss of power lamp on the dash must come on and stay on. Engine rpm should be within emission label specifications.
5. Aim power timing light at timing hole in bell housing or read the magnetic timing unit.
6. Loosen distributor and adjust timing to emission label specifications if necessary.
7. Shut engine off, disconnect and reconnect positive battery quick disconnect. Start vehicle, the loss of power lamp should be off.
8. Shut engine off, then turn ignition on, off, on, off, on. Fault codes should be clear with 88–51–55 shown.
9. Increase engine to 2000 rpm.
10. Read timing it should be approximately 40 degrees.
11. If timing advance does not reach specifications, have the logic module replaced.

Idle Speed

1. Before adjusting the idle on an electronic fuel injected vehicle the following items must be checked.
   a. AIS motor has been checked for operation.
   b. Engine has been checked for vacuum or EGR leaks.
   c. Engine timing has been checked and set to specifications.
   d. Coolant temperature sensor has been checked for operation.
2. Connect a tachometer and timing light to engine.
3. Disconnect throttle body 6-way connector. Remove brown with white tracer AIS wire from connector and rejoin connector.
4. Connect one end of a jumper wire to AIS wire and other end to battery positive post for 5 seconds.
5. Connect a jumper to radiator fan so that it will run continuously.
6. Start and run engine for 3 minutes to allow speed to stabilize.
7. Using tool C-4804 or equivalent, turn idle speed adjusting screw to obtain 800 ± 10 rpm (Manual) 725 ± 10 rpm (Automatic) with transaxle in neutral.
NOTE: *If idle will not adjust down, check for binding linkage, speed control servo cable adjustments, or throttle shaft binding.*
8. Check that timing is 18 ± 2° BTDC (Manual) 12 ± 2° BTDC (Automatic).
9. If timing is not to above specifications turn idle speed adjusting screw until correct idle speed and ignition timing are obtained.
10. Turn off engine, disconnect tachometer and timing light, reinstall AIS wire and remove jumper wire.

Multi-port Electronic Fuel Injection

GENERAL INFORMATION

The turbocharged multi-point Electronic Fuel Injection system combines an electronic fuel and spark advance control system with a turbocharged intake system. At the center of this

74 EMISSION CONTROLS AND FUEL SYSTEM

system is a digital pre-programmed computer known as a Logic Module that regulates ignition timing, air-fuel ratio, emission control devices and idle speed. This component has the ability to update and revise its programming to meet changing operating conditions.

Various sensors provide the input necessary for the Logic Module to correctly regulate fuel flow at the fuel injectors. These include the Manifold Absolute Pressure, Throttle Position, Oxygen Feedback, Coolant Temperature, Charge Temperature, and Vehicle Speed Sensors. In addition to the sensors, various switches also provide important information. These include the Transmission Neutral-Safety, Heated Backlite, Air Conditioning, and the Air Conditioning Clutch Switches.

Inputs to the Logic Module are converted into signals sent to the Power Module. These signals cause the Power Module to change either the fuel flow at the injector or ignition timing or both. The Logic Module tests many of its own input and output circuits. If a fault is found in a major circuit, this information is stored in the Logic Module. Information on this fault can be displayed to a technician by means of the instrument panel power loss lamp or by connecting a diagnostic readout and observing a numbered display code which directly relates to a general fault.

NOTE: *Most complaints that may occur with turbocharged multi-point Electronic Fuel Injection can be traced to poor wiring or hose connections. A visual check will help spot these faults and save unnecessary test and diagnosis time.*

ADJUSTMENTS
Ignition Timing

1. Connect a power timing light to the number one cylinder, or a magnetic timing unit to the engine. (Use a 10° degree offset when required).
2. Connect a tachometer to the engine and turn selector to the proper cylinder position.
3. Start engine and run until operating temperature is reached.
4. Disconnect and reconnect the water temperature sensor connector on the thermostat housing. The loss of power lamp on the dash must come on and stay on. Engine rpm should be within emission label specifications.
5. Aim power timing light at timing hole in bell housing or read the magnetic timing unit.
6. Loosen distributor and adjust timing to emission label specifications if necessary.
7. Shut engine off, disconnect and reconnect positive battery quick disconnect. Start vehicle, the loss of power lamp should be off.
8. Shut engine off, then turn ignition on, off, on, off, on. Fault codes should be clear with 88–51–55 shown.

Idle Speed

Before adjusting the idle on an electronic fuel injected vehicle the following items must be checked:
   a. AIS motor has been checked for operation
   b. Engine has been checked for vacuum or EGR leaks.
   c. Engine timing has been checked and set to specifications.
   d. Coolant temperature sensor has been checked for operation.
1. Install a tachometer.
2. Warm up engine to normal operating temperature (accessories off).
3. Shut engine off and disconnect radiator fan.
4. Disconnect Throttle Body 6-way connector. Remove the brown with white tracer AIS wire from the connector and reconnect connector.
5. Start engine with transaxle selector in park or neutral.
6. Apply 12 volts to AIS brown with white tracer wire. This will drive the AIS fully closed and the idle should drop.
7. Disconnect then reconnect coolant temperature sensor.
8. With transaxle in neutral, idle speed should be 775 ± 25 (700 ± 25 green engine).
9. If idle is not to specifications adjust idle air bypass screw.
10. If idle will not adjust down, check for

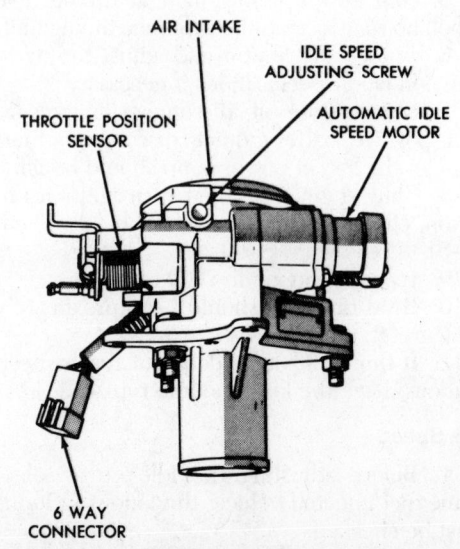

Location of idle speed adjusting screw on the throttle body of the multi-port injection system

EMISSION CONTROLS AND FUEL SYSTEM 75

vacuum leaks, AIS motor damage, throttle body damage, or speed control cable adjustment.

Fuel Tank

REMOVAL AND INSTALLATION

1. Jack up your vehicle and support it with jack stands.
2. Disconnect the negative battery terminal.
3. Remove the gas cap to relieve any pressure in the tank.
4. Disconnect the fuel supply line at the right front shockabsorber tower, and drain the fuel tank.
5. Remove the screws that hold the filler tube to the quarter panel.
6. Remove the right rear wheel and disconnect the wiring from the tank.
7. Remove the screws from the exhaust pipe to fuel tank shield, and allow this shield to rest on the exhaust pipe.
8. Support the tank with a jack and remove the tank strap bolts.
9. Lower the tank slightly, and carefully remove the filler tube from the tank.
10. Lower the fuel tank, disconnect the vapor separator rollover valve hose, and remove the fuel tank and insulator pad.
11. Installation is the reverse of removal.

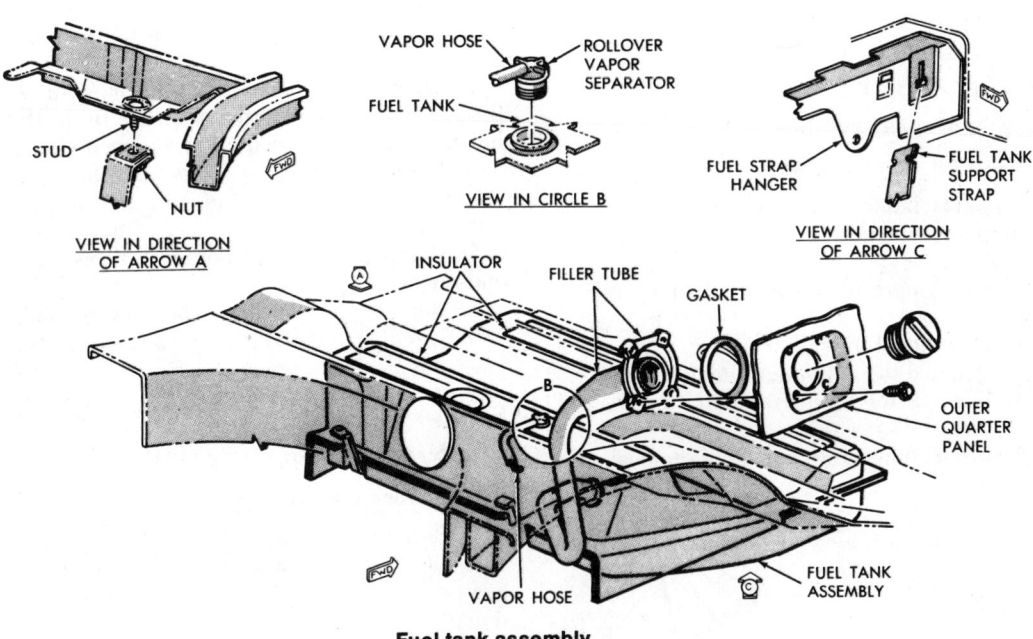

Fuel tank assembly

Chassis Electrical

5

HEATER

Blower Motor

REMOVAL AND INSTALLATION

Without Air Conditioning

The blower motor is located under the instrument panel on the left side of the heater assembly.

1. Disconnect the negative battery terminal.
2. Disconnect the motor wiring.
3. Remove the left outlet duct if necessary.
4. Remove the motor retaining screws and the motor.
5. Installation is the reverse of removal.

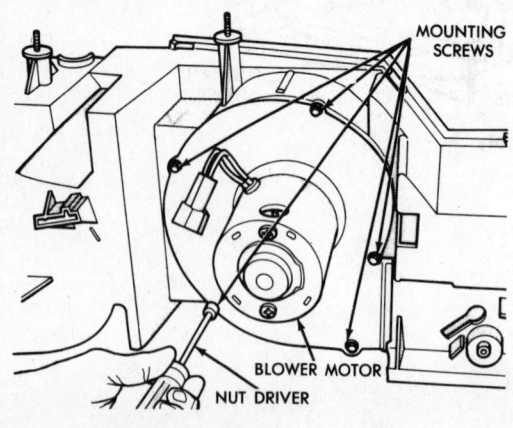

Removing blower motor

Air Conditioned Cars

1. Disconnect the negative battery terminal.
2. Remove the three screws securing the glovebox to the instrument panel.
3. Disconnect the wiring from the blower and case.
4. Remove the blower vent tube from the case.
5. Loosen the recirculating door from its bracket and remove the actuator from the housing. Leave the vacuum lines attached.
6. Remove the seven screws attaching the recirculating housing to the A/C unit and remove the housing.
7. Remove the three mounting flange nuts and washers.
8. Remove the blower motor from the unit.
9. Installation is the reverse of removal. Replace any damaged sealer.

Heater Core

REMOVAL AND INSTALLATION

Without Air Conditioning

1. Remove the heater assembly.
2. Remove the padding from around the heater core outlets and remove the upper core mounting screws.
3. Pry loose the retaining snaps from around the outer edge of the housing cover.

NOTE: *If a retaining snap should break, the housing cover has provisions for mounting screws.*

4. Remove the housing top cover.
5. Remove the bottom heater core mounting screw.
6. Slide the heater core out of the housing.
7. Installation is the reverse of removal.

Air Conditioned Cars

Removal of the Heater-Evaporator Unit is required for core removal. Two people will be required to perform the operation. Discharge, evacuation and recharge and leak testing of the refrigerant sytem is necessary. This work should only be performed by a trained technician. Have the system discharged before attempting removal. During installation, a small can of refrigerant oil will be necessary.

1. Disconnect the battery ground.
2. Drain the coolant.
3. Disconnect the temperature door cable from the heater-evaporator unit.
4. Disconnect the temperature door cable from the retaining clips.
5. Remove the glovebox.
6. Disconnect the vacuum harness from the control head.
7. Disconnect the blower motor lead and anti-diesel relay wire.
8. Remove the seven screws fastening the right trim bezel to the instrument panel. Starting at the right side, swing the bezel clear and remove it.
9. Remove the three screws on the bottom of the center distribution duct cover and slide the cover rearward and remove it.
10. Remove the center distribution duct.
11. Remove the defroster duct adaptor.
12. Remove the H-type expansion valve, located on the right side of the firewall:
   a. remove the 5/18 in. bolt in the center of the plumbing sealing plate.
   b. carefully pull the refrigerant lines toward the front of the car, taking care to avoid scratching the valve sealing surfaces.
   c. remove the two Allenhead capscrews and remove the valve.
13. Cap the pipe openings at once. Wrap the valve in a plastic bag.
14. Disconnect the hoses from the core tubes.
15. Disconnect the vacuum lines at the intake manifold and water valve.
16. Remove the unit-to-firewall retaining nuts.
17. Remove the panel support bracket.
18. Remove the right cowl lower panel.
19. Remove the instrument panel pivot bracket screw from the right side.
20. Remove the screws securing the lower instrument panel at the steering column.
21. Pull back the carpet from under the unit as far as possible.
22. Remove the nut from the evaporator-heater unit-to-plenum mounting brace and blower motor ground cable. While supporting the unit, remove the brace from its stud.
23. Lift the unit, pulling it rearward to allow clearance. These operations may require two people.
24. Slowly lower the unit taking care to keep the studs from hanging-up on the insulation.
25. When the unit reaches the floor, slide it rearward until it is out from under the instrument panel.
26. Remove the unit from the car.
27. Place the unit on a workbench. On the inside-the-car-side, remove the nut from the mode door actuator on the top cover and the two retaining clips from the front edge of the cover. To remove the mode door actuator, remove the two screws securing it to the cover.
28. Remove the screws attaching the cover to the assembly and lift off the cover. Lift the mode door out of the unit.
29. Remove the screw from the core retaining bracket and lift out the core.

To install:

30. Place the core in the unit and install the bracket.
31. Install the actuator arm.

CAUTION: *When installing the unit in the car, care must be taken that the vacuum lines to the engine compartment do not hang-up on the accelerator or become trapped between the unit and the firewall. If this happens, kinked lines will result and the unit will have to be removed to free them. Proper routing of these lines will require two people. The portion of the vacuum harness which is routed through the steering column support MUST be positioned BEFORE the distribtuion housing is installed. The harness MUST be routed ABOVE the temperature control cable.*

32. Place the unit on the floor as far under the panel as possible.
33. Raise the unit carefully, at the same time pull the lower instrument panel rearward as far as possible.
34. Position the unit in place and attach the brace to the stud.
35. Install the lower ground cable and attach the nut.
36. Install and tighten the unit-to-firewall nuts.
37. Reposition the carpet and install, but do not tighten the right instrument panel pivot bracket screw.
38. Place a piece of sheet metal or thin cardboard against the evaporator-heater assembly to center the assembly duct seal.
39. Position the center distributor duct in place making sure that the upper left tab comes in through the left center A/C outlet opening and that each air take-off is properly inserted in its respective outlet.

NOTE: *Make sure that the radio wiring connector does not interfere with the duct.*

40. Install and tighten the screw securing the upper left tab of the center air distribution duct to the instrument panel.
41. Remove the sheet metal or cardboard from between the unit and the duct.

NOTE: *Make sure that the unit seal is properly aligned with the duct opening.*

42. Install and tighten the two lower screws fastening the center distribution duct to the instrument panel.

78 CHASSIS ELECTRICAL

43. Install and tighten the screws securing the lower instrument panel at the steering column.
44. Install and tighten the nut securing the instrument panel to the support bracket.
45. Make sure that the seal on the unit is properly aligned and seated against the distribution duct assembly.
46. Tighten the instrument panel pivot bracket screw and install the right cowl lower trim.
47. Slide the distributor duct cover assembly onto the center distribution duct so that the notches lock into the tabs and the tabs slide over the rear and side ledges of the center duct assembly.
48. Install the three screws securing the ducting.
49. Install the right trim bezel.
50. Connect the vacuum harness to the control head.
51. Connect the blower lead and the anti-diesel wire.
52. Install the glovebox.
53. Connect the temperature door cable.
54. Install new O-rings on the evaporator plate and the plumbing plate. Coat the new O-rings with clean refrigerant oil.
55. Place the H-valve against the evaporator sealing plate surface and install the two through-bolts. Torque to 6–10 ft. lb.
56. Carefully hold the refrigerant line connector against the valve and install the bolt. Torque to 14–20 ft. lb.
57. Install the heater hoses at the core tubes.
58. Connect the vacuum lines at the manifold and water valve.
59. Install the condensate drain tube.
60. Have the system evacuated, charged and leak tested by a trained technician.

Heater Assembly

All Chrysler K- and E-cars use a "Blend-Air" type heater. Outside air enters the heater through the cowl opening and passes through a plenum chamber to the heater unit.

NOTE: *The air intake, located on the hood, must be kept free of ice, snow, and other obstructions for the heater to draw in sufficient outside air.*

A blend air door in the heater housing directs incoming air through the heater core and/or the heater core by-pass. The amount of blended air is determined by the setting of the temperature lever on the heater control panel.

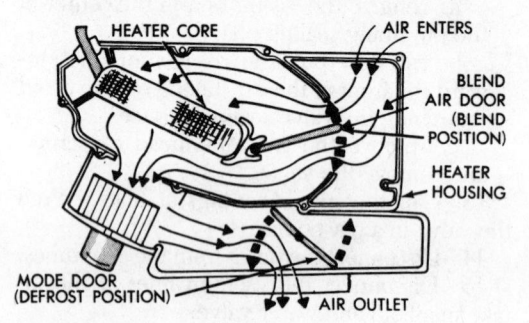

Blend air heater system—typical

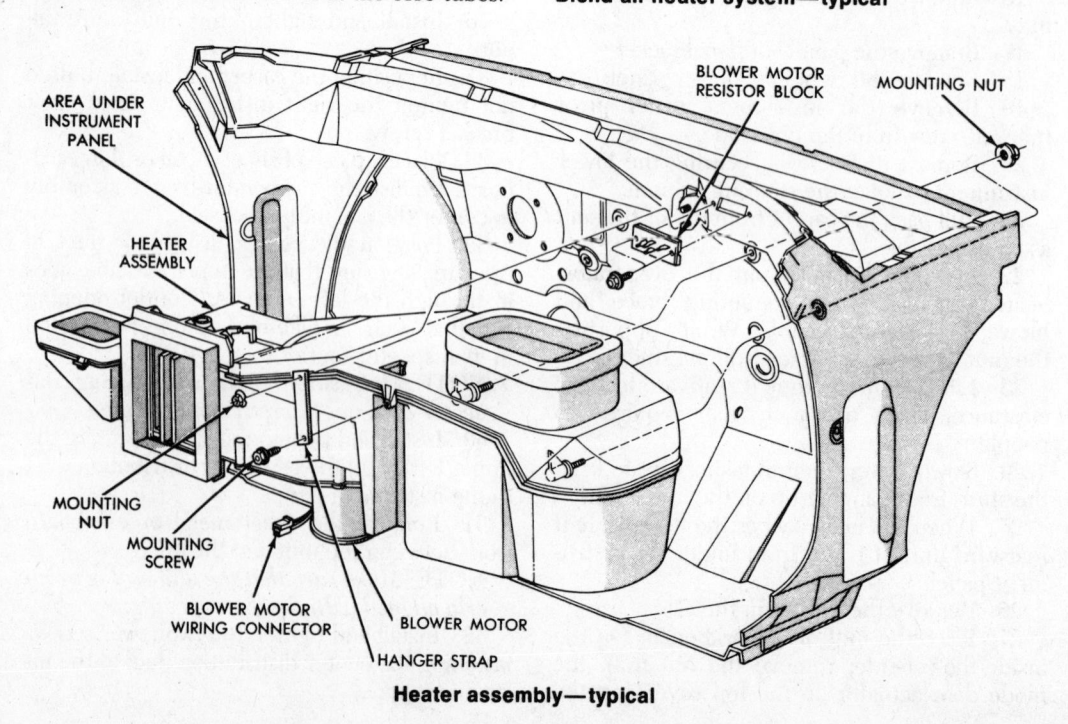

Heater assembly—typical

CHASSIS ELECTRICAL

REMOVAL AND INSTALLATION
Without Air Conditioning

1. Disconnect the negative battery cable and drain the radiator.
2. Disconnect the blower motor wiring connector.
3. Reach under the unit, depress the tab on the mode door and temperature control cables, pull the flags from the receivers, and remove the self-adjust clip from the crank arm.
4. Remove the glove box assembly.
5. Disconnect the heater hoses to the unit on the engine side and seal the heater core tube openings and hoses.
6. Through the glove box opening, remove the screw attaching the hanger strap to the heater assembly.
7. Remove the nut attaching the hanger strap to the dash panel and remove the hanger strap.
8. Remove the two nuts attaching the heater assembly to the dash panel. The nuts are on the engine side.
9. Pull out the bottom of the instrument panel and slide out the heater assembly.
10. Installation is the reverse of removal.

RADIO

AM, AM/FM monaural, or AM/FM stereo multiplex units are available. All radios are trimmed at the factory and should require no further adjustment. However, after repair or if the antenna trim is to be verified, proceed as follows:

1. Turn radio on.
2. Manually tune the radio to a weak station between 1400 and 1600 KHz on AM.
3. Increase the volume and set the tone control to full treble (clockwise).
4. Viewing the radio from the front, the trimmer control is a slot-head located at the rear of the right side. Adjust it carefully by turning it back and forth with a screwdriver until maximum loudness is achieved.

REMOVAL AND INSTALLATION

1. Remove the bezel.
2. If equipped with a mono-speaker, remove the instrument panel top cover, speaker, and disconnect the wires from the radio.
3. Remove the two screws attaching the radio to the base panel.
4. Pull the radio thru the front of the base, then disconnect the wiring harness, antenna lead and ground strap.
5. Installation is the reverse of removal.

WINDSHIELD WIPERS

The windshield wipers can be operated with the wiper switch only when the ignition switch is in the Accessory or Ignition position. A circuit breaker, integral with the wiper switch protects the circuitry of the wiper system and the vehicle.

Motor

REMOVAL AND INSTALLATION
Front

1. Disconnect the negative battery terminal.
2. Disconnect the linkage from the motor crank arm.
3. Remove the wiper motor plastic cover.
4. Disconnect the wiring harness from the motor.
5. Remove the three mounting bolts from the motor mounting bracket and remove the motor.
6. Installation is the reverse of removal.

Rear

1. Disconnect the negative battery terminal.
2. Remove the blade and arm assembly.
3. Open the liftgate.
4. Remove the motor cover and disconnect the wiring connector.
5. Remove the four bracket retaining screws and remove the motor.
6. Installation is the reverse of removal.

WIPER BLADE REPLACEMENT

1. Lift the wiper arm away from the glass.
2. Depress the release lever on the bridge and remove the blade assembly from the arm.
3. Lift the tab and pinch the end bridge to release it from the center bridge.
4. Slide the end bridge from the blade ele-

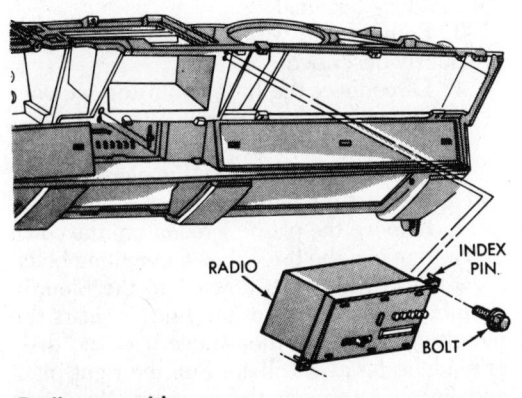

Radio assembly

80 CHASSIS ELECTRICAL

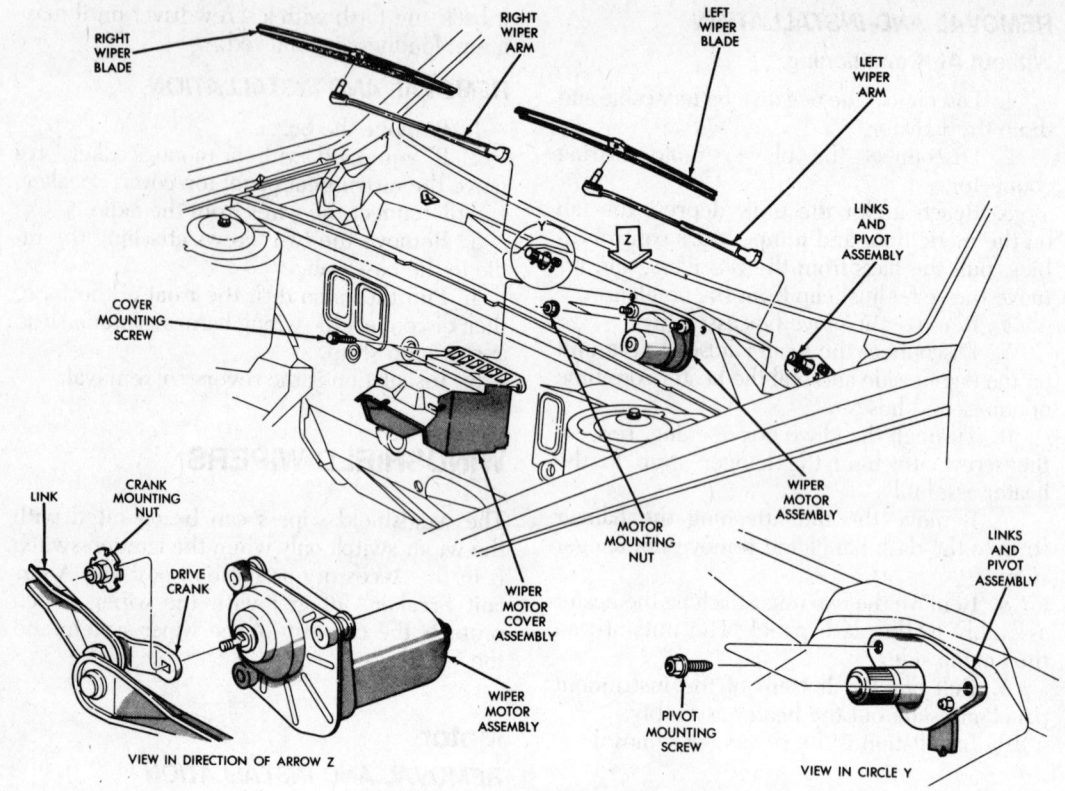

Windshield wiper motor and linkage

ment and the element from the opposite end bridge.

5. Assembly is the reverse of removal. Make sure that the element locking tabs are securely locked in position.

Wiper Arm

REMOVAL AND INSTALLATION

Front

1. Lift the arm so that the latch can be pulled out to the holding position and then release the arm. The arm will remain off the windshield in this position.
2. Remove the arm off the pivot using a rocking motion.
3. When installing, the motor should be in the park position and the tips of the blades 1½" above the bottom of the windshield moulding.

Rear

1. To remove the rear wiper arm assembly the use of special tool C-3982 is necessary.
   NOTE: *The use of a screwdriver is not recommended as it will distort and damage the arm.*
2. With the tool installed on the arm, lift the arm then remove it from the output shaft.

3. To install, the wiper motor should be in the park position.
4. Install the arm so that the tip of the blade is about 1.3 inches above the lower liftgate gasket.

Linkage

REMOVAL AND INSTALLATION

1. Put the windshield wipers in the park position.
2. Raise the hood and disconnect the negative battery terminal.
3. Remove the wiper arms and blades as previously described.
4. Disconnect the hoses from the tee connector.
5. Remove the pivot screws.
6. Remove the wiper motor plastic cover, and disconnect the wiring harness.
7. Remove the plastic screen from the cowl.
8. Remove the three motor mounting bolts.
9. Push the pivots down into the plenum chamber. Pull the motor out until it clears the mounting studs and then move it to the driver's side as far as it will go. Pull the right pivot and link out through the opening, then shift

CHASSIS ELECTRICAL 81

the motor to the right and remove the motor, the left link and pivot.

NOTE: *Do not rotate the motor output shaft from the park position.*

10. Installation is the reverse of removal.

INSTRUMENT CLUSTER

REMOVAL AND INSTALLATION

Conventional Cluster

1. Disconnect the negative battery terminal.
2. Place the gearshift lever in position "1".
3. Remove the instrument panel trim strip.
4. Remove the left upper and lower cluster bezel screws.
5. Remove the right lower cluster bezel screw and retaining clip.
6. Remove the instrument cluster bezel by snapping the bezel off of the five retaining clips.
7. Remove the seven retaining screws and remove the upper right bezel.
8. Remove the four rear instrument panel top cover mounting screws.
9. Lift the rear edge of the panel top cover and remove the two screws attaching the upper trim strip retainer and cluster housing to the base panel.

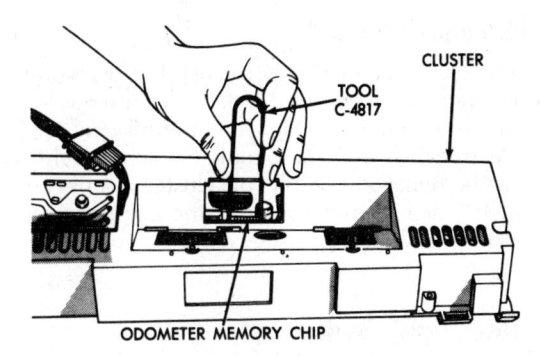

Removing/installing the odometer memory chip in the electronic instrument cluster

10. Remove the trim strip retainer.
11. Remove the two screws attaching the cluster housing to the base panel of the lower cluster.
12. Lift the rearward edge of the panel top cover and slide the cluster housing rearward.
13. Disconnect the right printed circuit board connector from behind the cluster housing.
14. Disconnect the speedometer cable connector.
15. Disconnect the left printed circuit connector.
16. Remove the cluster assembly.
17. Installation is the reverse of removal.

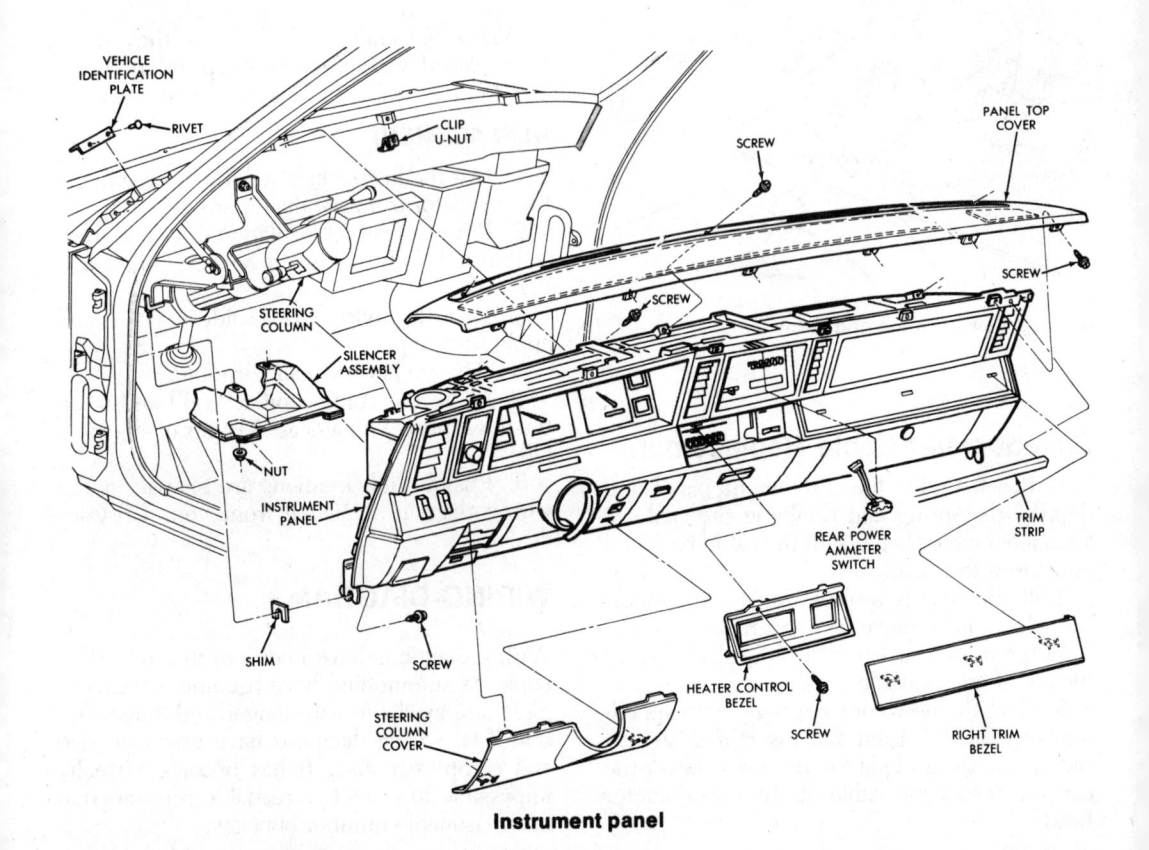

Instrument panel

82 CHASSIS ELECTRICAL

Electronic Cluster

The electronic cluster is removed in the same manner as the conventional cluster, except for the speedometer cable. When replacing the electronic cluster, the odometer memory chip can be removed from the old cluster and placed in the new one. To remove the chip, special tool C-4817 must be used.

Headlight Switch

REMOVAL AND INSTALLATION

1. Remove the three screws securing the headlamp switch mounting plate to the base panel.
2. Pull the switch and plate rearward and disconnect the wiring connector.
3. Depress the button on the switch and remove the knob and stem.
4. Snap out the escutcheon, then remove the nut that attaches the switch to the mounting plate.
5. Installation is the reverse of removal.

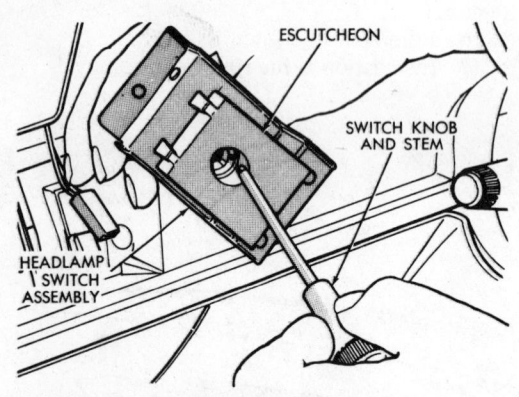

Headlight switch knob and stem

Speedometer Cable Replacement

1. Reach under the instrument panel and depress the spring clip retaining the cable to the speedometer head. Pull the cable back and away from the head.
2. If the core is broken, raise and support the vehicle and remove the cable retaining screw from the cable bracket. Carefully slide the cable out of the transaxle.
3. Coat the new core sparingly with speedometer cable lubricant and insert it in the cable. Install the cable at the transaxle, lower the car and install the cable at the speedometer head.

HEADLIGHTS

REMOVAL AND INSTALLATION

1. Remove the headlight bezel.
2. Unhook the spring from the headlight retaining ring if so equipped.
3. Unscrew the retaining ring and remove it.
   NOTE: *Do not disturb the two long aiming screws.*
4. Unplug the old sealed beam.
5. Connect the replacement bulb and install into the receptacle.
6. Install the retaining ring and connect the spring.
7. Install the headlight bezel.

FUSIBLE LINKS

CAUTION: *Do not replace blown fusible links with standard wire. Only fusible type wire with hypalon insulation can be used, or damage to the electrical system will occur.*

When a fusible link blows it is very important to find out why. They are placed in the electrical system for protection against dead shorts to ground, which can be caused by electrical component failure or various wiring failures.

CAUTION: *Do not just replace the fusible link to correct a problem.*

When replacing all fusible links, they are to be replaced with the same type of prefabricated link available from your Chrysler dealer.

REPLACEMENT

1. Cut the fusible link including the connection insulator from the main harness wire.
2. Remove 1 in. of insulation from both new fusible link, and the main harness, and wrap together.
3. Heat the splice with a soldering gun, and apply rosin type solder.
   NOTE: *Do not use acid core solder.*
4. Allow the connection to cool, and wrap the new splice with at least 3 layers of electrical tape.
5. Fusible link locations are shown on the wiring diagram available from your Chrysler dealer.

WIRING DIAGRAMS

Wiring diagrams have been omitted from this book. As automobiles have become more complex, and available with longer and longer option lists, wiring diagrams have grown in size and complexity also. It has become virtually impossible to provide a readable reproduction in a reasonable number of pages.

Clutch and Transaxle 6

MANUAL TRANSAXLE

REMOVAL AND INSTALLATION

A-412

NOTE: *Anytime the differential cover is removed, a new gasket should be formed from RTV sealant. See Chapter 1.*

1. Remove the engine timing mark access plug.
2. Rotate the engine to align the drilled mark on the flywheel with the pointer on the engine.
3. Disconnect the battery ground.
4. Disconnect the shift linkage rods.
5. Disconnect the starter and ground wires.
6. Disconnect the backup light switch wire.
7. Remove the starter.
8. Disconnect the clutch cable.
9. Disconnect the speedometer cable.
10. Support the weight of the engine from above, preferably with a shop hoist or the fabricated holding fixture.
11. Raise and support the vehicle.
12. Disconnect the drive shafts and support them out of the way.
13. Remove the left splash shield.
14. Drain the transaxle.
15. Unbolt the left engine mount.
16. Remove the transaxle-to-engine bolts.
17. Slide the transaxle to the left until the mainshaft clears, then, carefully lower it from the car.
18. Installation is the reverse of removal.
19. Adjust the clutch cable.
20. Adjust the shift linkage.
21. Fill the transaxle.

465, 525

1. Disconnect the battery.
2. Install a shop crane and lifting eye under the #4 cyl. exhaust manifold bolt.
3. Disconnect the shift linkage.
4. Remove both front wheels.
5. Remove the left front splash shield, and left engine mount.
6. Follow the procedures under Halfshaft Removal and Installation in the next paragraph.
7. The removal of the unit is the same as that for the automatic transaxle, except that no torque converter is used.
8. Installation is the reverse of removal. Always use new self-locking nuts on the shift linkage. Observe the following torques:
   - Shift housing-to-case: 21 ft. lb.
   - Strut-to-block: 70 ft. lb.
   - Strut-to-case: 70 ft. lb.
   - Flywheel-to-crankshaft: 65 ft. lb.
   - Transaxle-to-block: 70 ft. lb.

Halfshaft

REMOVAL AND INSTALLATION

The driveshaft assemblies are three piece units. Each driveshaft has an inner sliding constant velocity (Tripod) joint bolted to the transaxle, and an outer constant velocity (Rzeppa) joint with a stub shaft splined into the hub. The connecting shafts for the C/V joints are unequal in length and construction. The left side is a short solid shaft and the right is longer and tubular.

NOTE: *Driveshafts on Aries/Reliant models are interchangeable from manual to automatic transmission models.*

A-412 Manual Transmission

1. With the vehicle on the floor and the brakes applied, loosen the hub nut.

NOTE: *The hub and driveshaft are splined together and retained by the hub nut which is torqued to at least 180 ft. lbs.*

2. Raise and support the vehicle and remove the hub nut and washer.

CLUTCH AND TRANSAXLE

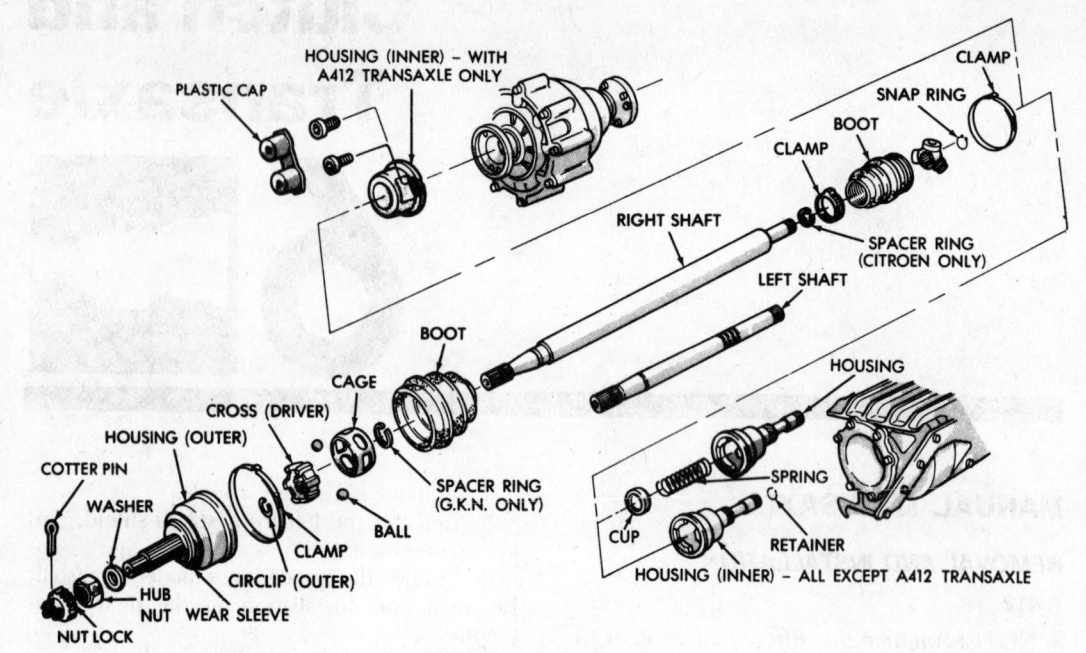

Driveshaft components

NOTE: *Always support both ends of the driveshaft during removal.*

3. Disconnect the lower control arm ball joint stud nut from the steering knuckle.

4. Remove the six 1/18 inch Allenhead screws which secure the CV joint to the transmission flange.

5. Holding the CV housing, push the outer joint and knuckle assembly outward while disengaging the inner housing from the flange face. Quickly turn the open end of the joint upward to retain as much lubricant as possible, then carefully pull the outer joint spline out of the hub. Cover the joint with a clean towel to prevent dirt contamination.

NOTE: *The outer joint and shaft must be supported during disengagement of the inner joint.*

6. Before installation, make sure that any lost lubricant is replaced. The only lubricant specified is Chrysler part number 4131389. No other lubricant of any type is to be used, as premature failure of the joint will result.

7. Clean the joint body and mating flange face.

8. Install the outer joint splined shaft into the hub. Do not secure with the nut and washer.

9. Early production vehicles were built with a cover plate between the hub and flange face. This cover is not necessary and should be discarded.

10. Position the inner joint in the transmission drive flange and secure it with *six* new screws. Torque the screws to 37–40 ft. lb.

11. Connect the lower control arm to the knuckle.

12. Install the outer joint and secure it with a *new* nut and washer. Torque the nut with the car on the ground and the brake set. Torque is 180 ft. lbs. Reinstall the cotter pin and locknut.

13. After attaching the driveshaft, if the inboard boot appears to be collapsed or deformed, vent the inner boot by inserting a round-tipped, small diameter rod between the boot and the shaft. As venting occurs, boot will return to its original shape.

A-460 465, 525 Manual Transmission and Automatic Transmission

The inboard CV joints are retained by circlips in the differential side gears. The circlip tangs are located on a machined surface on the inner end of the stub shaft.

1. With the car on the ground, loosen the hub nut.

2. Drain the transaxle differential and remove the cover.

NOTE: *Anytime the transaxle differential cover is removed, a new gasket should be formed from RTV sealant.*

3. To remove the right-hand driveshaft, disconnect the speedometer cable and remove the cable and gear before removing the driveshaft.

4. Rotate the driveshaft to expose the circlip tangs.

5. Compress the circlip with needle nose

CLUTCH AND TRANSAXLE

pliers and push the shaft into the side gear cavity.

6. Remove the clamp bolt from the ball stud and steering knuckle.

7. Separate the ball joint stud from the steering knuckle, by prying against the knuckle leg and control arm.

8. Separate the outer CV joint splined shaft from the hub by holding the CV housing and moving the hub away. Do not pry on the slinger or outer CV joint.

9. Support the shaft at the CV joints and remove the shaft. Do not pull on the shaft.

NOTE: *Removal of the left shaft may be made easier by inserting the blade of a thin prybar between the differential pinion shaft and prying against the end face of the shaft.*

10. Installation is the reverse of removal. Be sure the circlip tangs are positioned against the flattened end of the shaft before installing the shaft. A quick thrust will lock the circlip in the groove. Tighten the hub nut with the wheels on the ground to 180 ft. lbs.

HALFSHAFT OVERHAUL

1. With the driveshaft assembly removed from the vehicle, remove the clamps and boot.

2. Depending on the unit (GKN or Citroën) separate the tripod assembly from the housing, as follows:

Citroën

Since the trunion ball rollers are not retained on bearing studs a retaining ring is used to prevent accidental tripod/housing separation, which would allow roller and needle bearings to fall away.

In the case of the spring loaded inner C/V joints, if it weren't for the retaining ring, the spring would automatically force the tripod out of the housing whenever the shaft was not installed in the vehicle.

Separate the tripod from the housing by slightly deforming the retaining ring in 3 places, with a suitable tool.

CAUTION: *Secure the rollers to the studs, during separation. With the tripod out of the housing secure the assembly with tape.*

GKN

The non-spring loaded GKN inboard joint tripods will slide right out of the housing. There is no retaining ring to prevent their removal. Spring loaded GKN inboard C/V joints have tabs on the can cover that prevent the spring from forcing the tripod out of the housing. These tabs must be bent back with a pair of pliers before the tripod can be removed. Under normal conditions it is not necessary to secure the GKN rollers to their studs during separation due to the presence of a retainer ring on the end of each stud. This retention force can easily be overcome if the rollers are pulled or impacted. It is also possible to pull the rollers off by removing or installing the tripod with the connecting shaft at too high an angle, relative to the housing.

Remove the snapring from the shaft end groove then remove the tripod with a brass punch.

DISASSEMBLY

1. Remove the boot clamps and discard them.

2. Wipe away the grease to expose the joint.

3. Support the shaft in a vice. Hold the outer joint, and using a plastic hammer, give a sharp tap to the top of the joint body to dislodge it from the internal circlip.

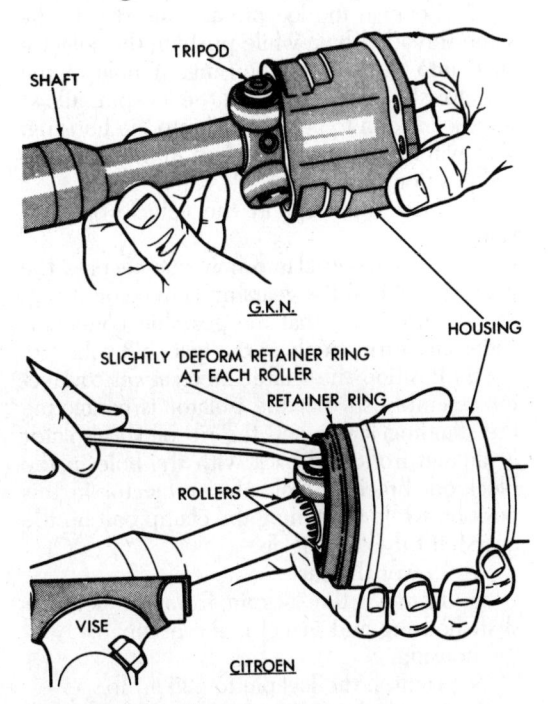

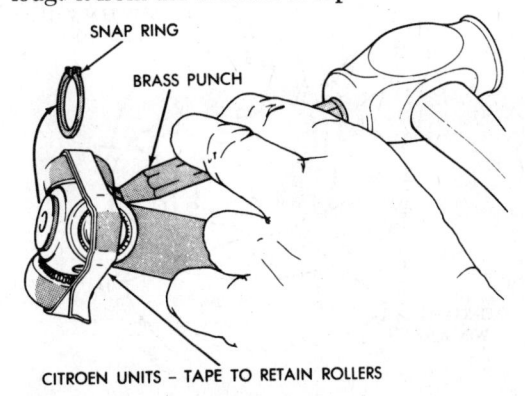

Separate tripod from housing

Remove snapring—then tripod

86 CLUTCH AND TRANSAXLE

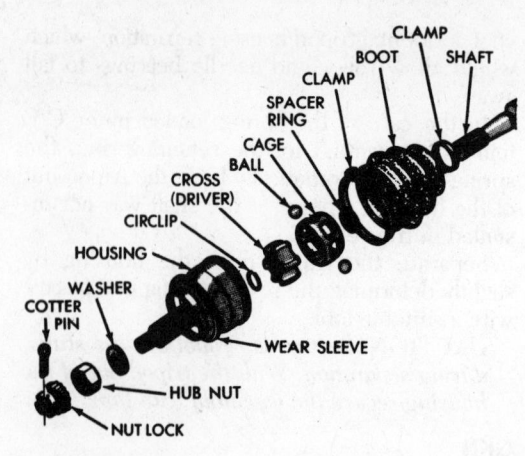

Outer CV joint

4. If the shaft is bent carefully pry the wear sleeve from the C/V joint machined ledge.
5. Remove the circlip from the shaft and discard it.
NOTE: *Replacement boot kits will contain this circlip.*
6. Unless the shaft is damaged do not remove the heavy spacer ring from the shaft.
NOTE: *If the shaft must be replaced, care must be taken that the new shaft is of the proper construction, depending on whether the inner joint is spring loaded or not.*
If the C/V joint was operating satisfactorily, and the grease does not appear contaminated, just replace the boot. If the outer joint is noisy or badly worn, replace the entire unit. The repair kit will include boot, clamps, retaining ring (circlip) and lubricant.
7. Wipe off the grease and mark the position of the inner cross, cage and housing with a dab of paint.
8. Hold the joint vertically in a vise. Do not crush the splines on the shaft.

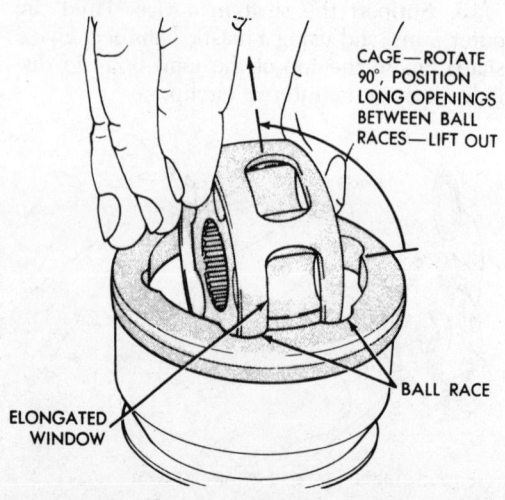

Removing cage and cross assembly from housing

9. Press down on one side of the inner race to tilt the cage and remove the balls from the opposite side.
10. If the joint is tight, use a hammer and brass drift pin to tap the inner race. Repeat this step until all balls have been removed.
CAUTION: *Do not hit the cage.*
11. Tilt the cage and inner race assembly vertically and position the two opposing, elongated cage windows in the area between the ball grooves. Pull the cage out of the housing.
12. Turn the inner cross 90° and align the race lands with an elongated hole in the cage. Remove the inner race.
13. Installation is the reverse of removal.
NOTE: *Spring loaded parts and non-spring loaded parts are not interchangeable.*

SHIFTER ADJUSTMENT
Model A-412

1. Place the transmission in neutral at the 3-4 position.
2. Loosen the shift tube clamp.
3. Place a ⅝ inch spacer between the slider and blocker bracket.
4. Tighten the shift tube clamp remove the spacer.

A-460, 465, 525

1. From the left side of the car, remove the lockpin from the transaxle selector shaft housing.
2. Reverse the lockpin and insert it in the same threaded hole while pushing the selector shaft into the selector housing. A hole in the selector shaft will align with the lockpin, allowing the lockpin to be screwed into the housing. This will lock the selector shaft in the 1-2 neutral position.
3. Raise and support the vehicle on jackstands.
4. Loosen the clamp bolt that secures the gearshift tube to the gearshift connector.
5. Make sure that the gearshift connector slides and turns freely in the gearshift tube.
6. Position the shifter mechanism connector assembly so that the isolator is contacting the standing flange and the rib on the isolator is aligned front and back with the hole in the block-out bracket. Hold the connector in this position while tightening the clamp bolt on the gearshift tube to 14 ft. lb.
7. Lower the car.
8. Remove the lockpin from the selector shaft housing and install it the original way in the housing.
9. Tighten the lockpin to 105 in. lb.
10. Check shifter action.

CLUTCH AND TRANSAXLE

CLUTCH

The clutch is a dry disc unit, with no adjustment for wear provided in the clutch itself. Adjustment is made through an adjustable sleeve in the pedal linkage.

REMOVAL AND INSTALLATION

A-412 Transaxle

NOTE: *Chrysler recommends the use of special tool L-4533 for disc alignment.*

1. Remove the transaxle.
2. Loosen the flywheel-to-pressure plate bolts diagonally, one or two turns at a time to avoid warpage.
3. Remove the flywheel and clutch disc from the pressure plate.
4. Remove the retaining ring and release plate.
5. Diagonally loosen the pressure plate-to-crankshaft bolts. Mark all parts for reassembly.
6. Remove the bolts, spacer and pressure plate.
7. The flywheel and pressure plate surfaces should be cleaned thoroughly with fine sandpaper.
8. Align marks and install the pressure plate, spacer and bolts. Coat the bolts with thread compound and torque them to 55 ft. lbs.
9. Install the release plate and retaining ring.
10. Using special tool L-4533 or its equivalent, install the clutch disc and flywheel on the pressure plate.

CAUTION: *Make certain that the drilled mark on the flywheel is at the top, so that the two dowels on the flywheel align with the proper holes in the pressure plate.*

11. Install the six flywheel bolts and tighten them to 15 ft. lbs.
12. Remove the aligning tool.

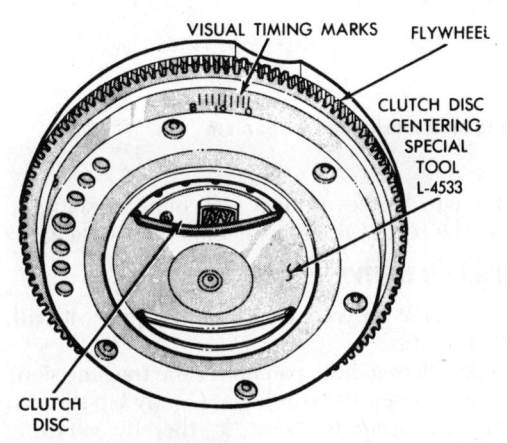

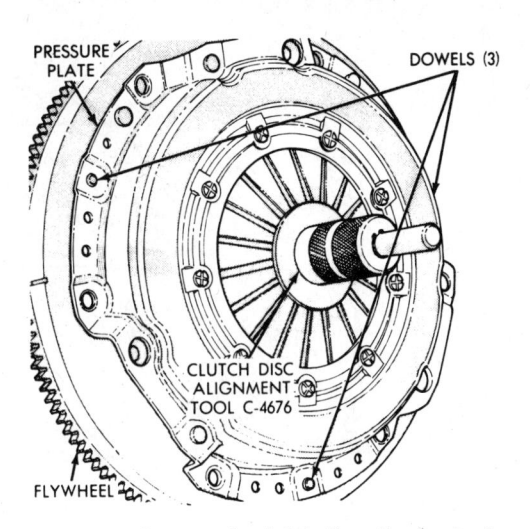

A-460 manual transaxle clutch disc aligning tool

13. Install the transmission.
14. Adjust the freeplay.

A-460 465, 525 Transaxle

NOTE: *Chrysler recommends the use of special tool #C4676 for disc alignment.*

1. Remove the transaxle.
2. Matchmark the clutch cover and flywheel for easy reinstallation.
3. Insert special tool C4676 or its equivalent to hold the clutch disc in place.
4. Loosen the cover attaching bolts. Do this procedure in a diagonal manner, a few turns at a time to prevent warping the cover.
5. Remove the cover assembly and disc from the flywheel.
6. Remove the clutch release shaft and slide the release bearing off the input shaft seal retainer.
7. Remove the fork from the release bearing thrust plate.
8. Installation is the reverse of removal. Upon reinstallation tighten the clutch cover bolts to 21 ft. lbs.

FREEPLAY ADJUSTMENT

A-412 Transaxle

NOTE: *The A-460 465 and 525 Transaxles are equipped with a self-adjusting clutch release mechanism.*

1. Pull up on the clutch cable.
2. While holding the cable up, rotate the adjusting sleeve downward until a snug contact is made against the grommet.
3. Rotate the sleeve slightly to allow the end of the sleeve to seat in the rectangular hole in the grommet.

Centering clutch disc

88 CLUTCH AND TRANSAXLE

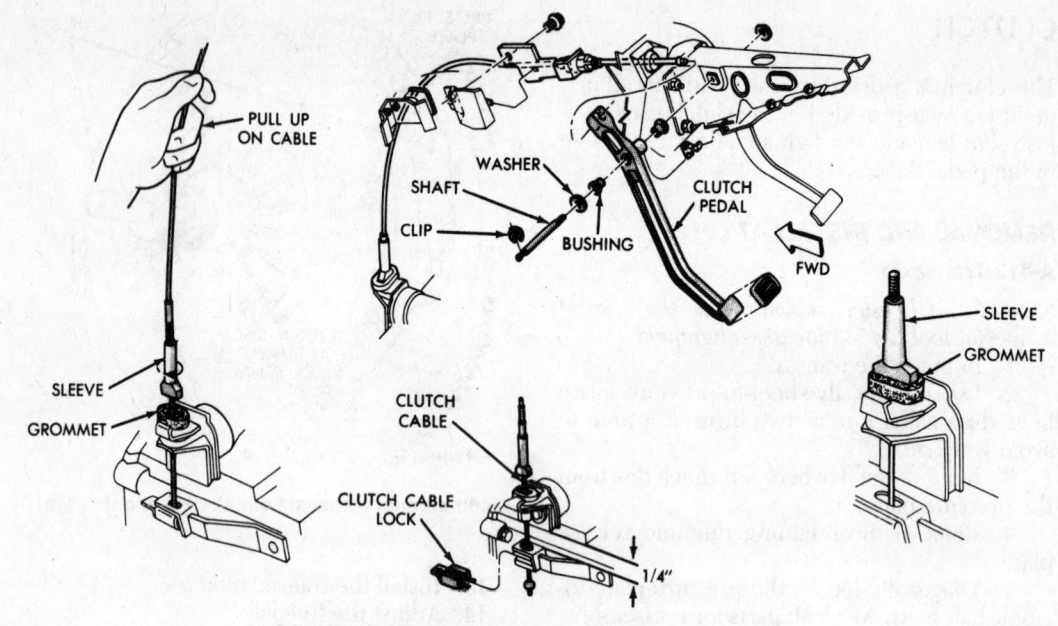

Adjusting clutch free play—A-412 manual transaxle

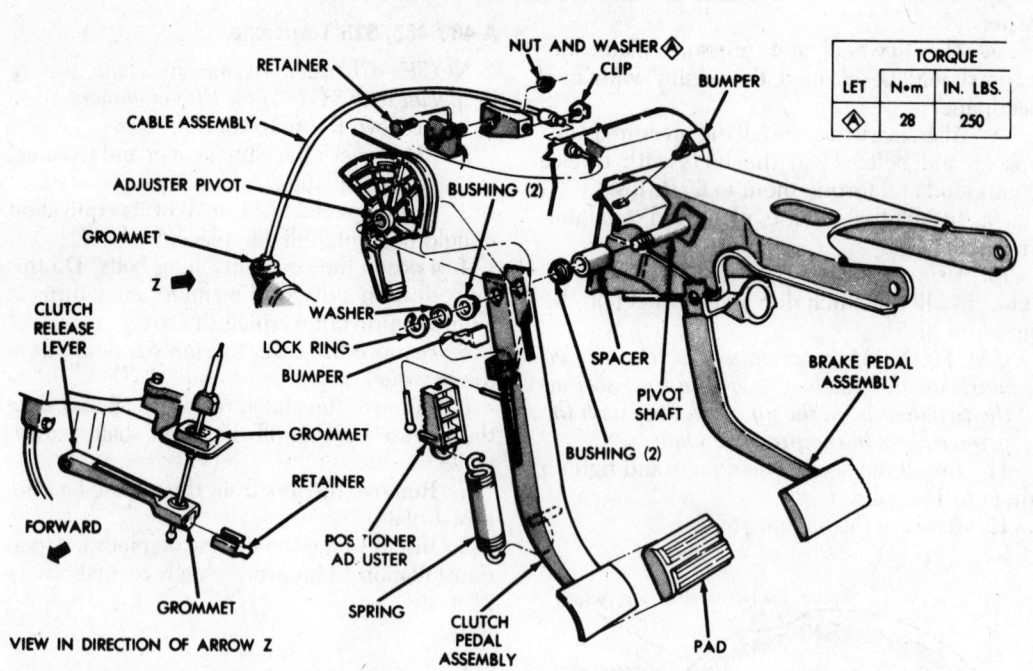

A-460 manual transaxle self-adjusting clutch release mechanism

TORQUE		
LET	N•m	IN. LBS.
◊	28	250

AUTOMATIC TRANSAXLE

The transaxle combines a torque converter, a fully automatic 3 speed transmission, final drive gearing and a differential, into a compact front wheel drive system.

Transaxle operation requirements are different for each vehicle and engine combination. Some internal parts will be different to provide for this. When you order replacement parts, refer to the seven digit part number stamped on the rear of the transmission oil pan flange.

FILTER SERVICE

1. Jack up your vehicle and support it with jack stands.
2. Place a drain pan under the transmission.
3. Loosen the pan bolts. Gently tap the pan at one corner to loosen it, thereby, allowing the fluid to drain.

CLUTCH AND TRANSAXLE 89

Automatic transaxle

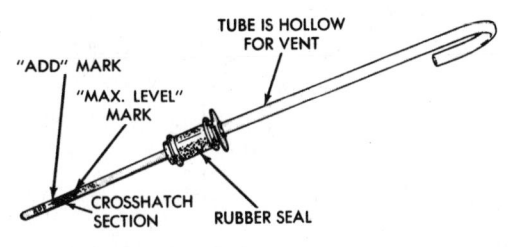

Dipstick and transmission vent

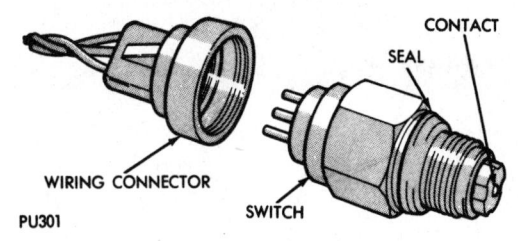

Neutral start and back-up light switch

4. Remove the pan and the oil filter.
5. Install a new filter and tighten the filter bolts to 40 in. lbs.
6. Reinstall the pan and tighten the bolts to 14 ft. lbs.
7. Put 4 quarts of Dexron II® transmission fluid in the transaxle.
8. Start the engine and allow it to run for at least 2 minutes. While the engine is running, hold your foot on the service brake, apply the emergency brake and shift the transmission through all gears.
9. Check the fluid in the neutral or park position, and add more if necessary. Recheck the fluid after it has reached normal operating temperature. The fluid level should be between the "Max" and "Add" lines on the dipstick.

NEUTRAL SAFETY/BACK-UP LIGHT SWITCH ADJUSTMENT

The neutral safety switch is the center terminal of the three terminal switch, located on the transaxle. The back-up light switch uses the two outside terminals. The center terminal provides a ground for the starter solenoid circuit through the selector level in the Park and Neutral positions only.

1. Disconnect the negative battery terminal.
2. Unscrew the switch from the transaxle, and allow the fluid to drain into a pan.
3. Move the selector lever to see that the switch operating the lever fingers are centered in the switch opening.
4. Install the new switch and seal. Tighten the switch to 24 ft. lbs.

SHIFT LINKAGE ADJUSTMENT

NOTE: *When it is necessary to disassemble the linkage cable from the lever, which uses plastic grommets as retainers, the grommets should be replaced with new ones.*

1. Make sure that the adjustable swivel block is free to slide on the shift cable.
2. Place the shift lever in Park.
3. With the linkage assembled, and the swivel lock bolt loose, move the shift arm on the transaxle all the way to the front detent.
4. Hold the shift arm in this position with a force of about 10 lbs. and tighten the adjust swivel lock bolt to 8 ft. lb.
5. Check the linkage action.

NOTE: *The automatic transmission gear selector release button may pop up in the knob when shifting from PARK to DRIVE. This is caused by inadequate retention of the selector release knob retaining tab. The release button will always work but the loose button can be annoying. A sleeve (Chrysler Part No. 5211984) and washers (Chrysler Part No. 6500380) are available to cure this condition. If these are unavailable, do the following:*

1. Remove the release button.
2. Cut and fold a standard paper match stem as shown.
3. Using tweezers, insert the folded match as far as possible into the clearance slot as shown. The match should be below the knob surface.
4. Insert the button, taking care not to break the button stem.

THROTTLE CABLE ADJUSTMENT

NOTE: *This adjustment should be performed while the engine is at normal operating temperature. Make sure that the carburetor is not on fast idle by disconnecting the choke.*

90 CLUTCH AND TRANSAXLE

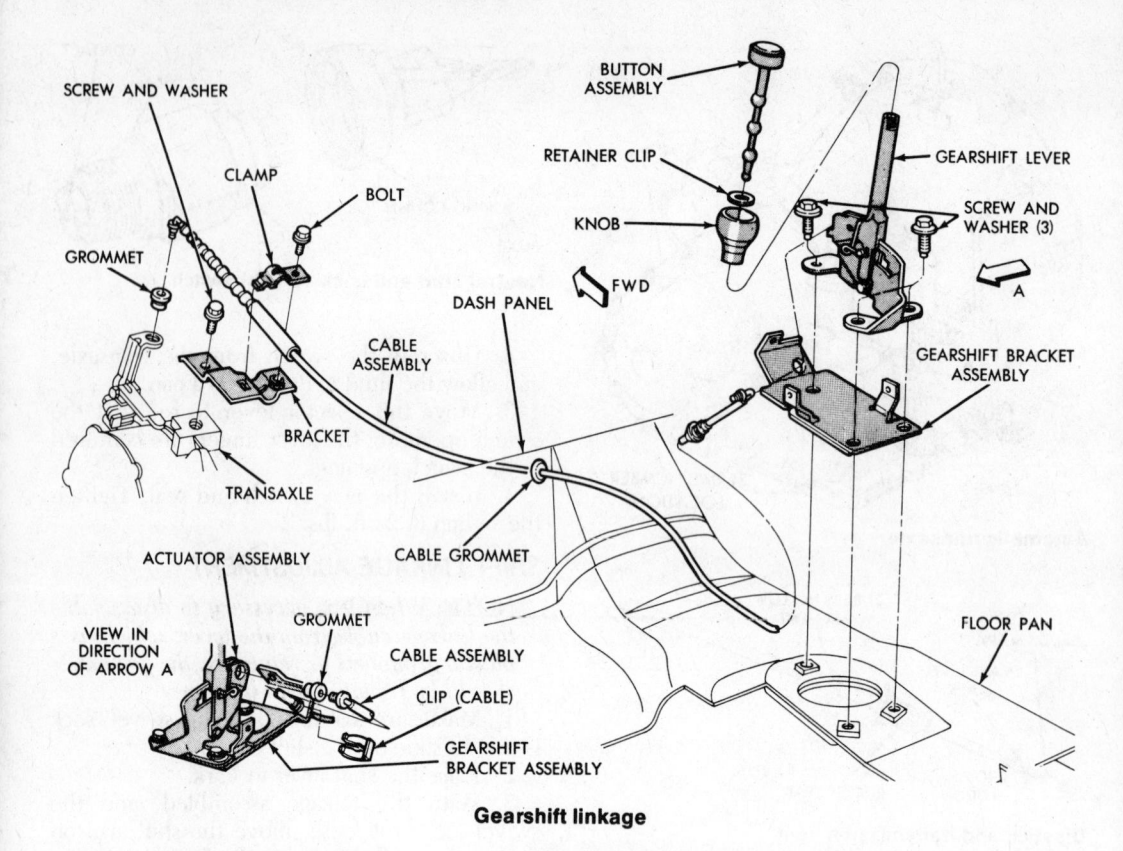

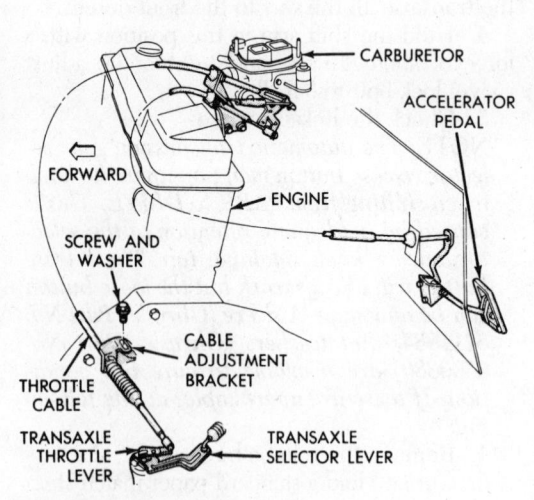

Gearshift linkage

Throttle control (typical)

1. Loosen the adjustment bracket lock screw.
2. To insure proper adjustment, the bracket must be free to slide on its slot.
3. Hold the throttle lever firmly to the left (toward the engine) against its internal stop and tighten the adjusting bracket lock to 105 in. lbs. (8¾ ft. lb.)
4. Reconnect the choke. Test the cable operation by moving the throttle lever forward and slowly releasing it to confirm it will return fully rearward.

FRONT BAND ADJUSTMENT

The kickdown band adjusting screw is located on the left side (top front) of the transaxle case.

1. Loosen the locknut and back off the nut approximately 5 turns. Test the adjusting screw for free turning in the transaxle case.
2. Using special tool #C-3380-A or its equivalent, tighten the adjusting screw to 72 in. lbs. If adapter C-3705 is used with the tool, tighten the adjusting screw to 50 in. lb.
3. Back off the adjusting screw 3 turns (A-404); 2½ turns (A-413 and A-470). Hold the adjusting screw in this position and tighten the locknut to 35 ft. lbs.

REAR BAND ADJUSTMENT
A-404

1. Remove the oil pan and pressurize the low-reverse servo with 30 psi of air pressure.
2. Measure the gap between the band ends. If the gap is less than .080 in., the band has worn excessively and should be replaced. Band replacement is best left to a qualified repair facility.
3. Loosen and back off the locknut approximately 5 turns.
4. Tighten the adjusting screw to 41 in. lbs.

CLUTCH AND TRANSAXLE

5. Back off the adjusting screw 3½ turns.
6. Tighten the locknut to 20 ft. lbs.

A-413 & A-470

NOTE: *Prior to adjustment, check the end-gap as in the A-404 procedure.*

1. Loosen the locknut 5 turns.
2. Tighten the adjusting screw to 41 in. lb.
3. Back off the screw 3½ turns.
4. Tighten the locknut to 10 ft. lb.

REMOVAL AND INSTALLATION

The automatic transaxle can be removed with the engine installed in the car, but, the transaxle and torque converter must be removed as an assembly. Otherwise the drive plate, pump bushing or oil seal could be damaged. The drive plate will not support a load—no weight should be allowed to bear on the drive plate.

1. Disconnect the positive battery cable.
2. Disconnect the throttle and shift linkage from the transaxle.
3. Raise and support the car. Remove the front wheels. Refer to the following chapter to remove or install the driveshafts.
4. Remove the upper oil cooler tube.
5. Remove the left splash shield. Drain the differential and remove the cover.
6. Remove the speedometer adaptor, cable and gear.
7. Remove the sway bar.
8. Remove both lower ball joint-to-steering knuckle bolts.
9. Pry the lower ball joint from the steering knuckle.
10. Remove the driveshaft from the hub.
11. Rotate both driveshafts to expose the circlip ends. Note the flat surface on the inner ends of both axle tripod shafts. Pry the circlip out.
12. Remove both driveshafts.
13. Matchmark the torque converter and drive plate. Remove the torque converter mounting bolts. Remove the access plug in the right splash shield to rotate the engine.
14. Remove the lower cooler tube and the wire to the neutral safety switch.
15. Install some means of supporting the engine.
16. Remove the upper bell-housing bolts.
17. Remove the engine mount bracket from the front crossmember.
18. Support the transmission.
19. Remove the front mount insulator through-bolts and the bell housing mount
20. Remove the long through-bolt from the left-hand engine mount.
21. Raise the transaxle and pry it away from the engine.
22. Installation is the reverse of removal. Fill the differential with DEXRON® automatic transmission fluid before lowering the car. Form a new gasket from RTV sealant when installing the differential cover. See Chapter 1.

Suspension and Steering

FRONT SUSPENSION

A MacPherson Type front suspension, with vertical shock absorbers attached to the upper fender reinforcement and the steering knuckle, is used. Lower control arms, attached inboard to a cross-member and outboard to the steering knuckle through a ball joint, provide lower steering knuckle position. During steering manuevers, the upper strut and steering knuckle turns as an assembly.

Strut Damper
REMOVAL AND INSTALLATION

1. Jack up your vehicle and support it with jack stands.
2. Remove the tire and wheel assembly.
3. Remove the cam adjusting bolt, through bolt, and brake hose bracket screw.
4. Remove the strut mounting nuts and the strut.
5. Installation is the reverse of removal.
NOTE: *If the original strut is to be reinstalled mark the adjusting bolt prior to removal.*

The following torques are necessary for reinstallation: Strut mounting nuts 20 ft. lbs.; Brake hose bracket screw 10 ft. lbs.; Cam bolts 45 ft. lbs. plus ¼ turn; and the wheel nuts to 80 ft. lbs.

Ball Joints

The lower front suspension ball joints operate with no free play. The ball joint housing is pressed into the lower control arm with the joint stud retained in the steering knuckle with a (clamp) bolt.

INSPECTION

With the weight of the vehicle resting on the ground, grasp the ball joint grease fitting, and attempt to move it. If the ball joint is worn the grease fitting will move easily. If movement is noted, replacement of the ball joint is recommended.

REMOVAL AND INSTALLATION

1. Pry off the seal.
2. Position a receiving cup, special tool #C-4699-2 or its equivalent to support the lower control arm.
3. Install a 1 1/16 inch deep socket over the stud and against the joint upper housing.
4. Press the joint assembly from the arm.
5. To install, position the ball joint housing into the control arm cavity.
6. Position the assembly in a press with special tool #C-4699-1 or its equivalent, supporting the control arm.
7. Align the ball joint assembly, then press it until the housing ledge stops against the control arm cavity down flange.
8. To install a new seal, support the ball joint housing with tool #C-4699-2 and place a new seal over the stud, against the housing.
9. With a 1½ inch socket, press the seal onto the joint housing with the seat against the control arm.

Spring
REMOVAL AND INSTALLATION

1. Remove the struts as previously outlined.
2. Compress the spring, using a reliable coil spring compressor.
3. Hold the strut rod and remove the rod nut.
4. Remove the retainers and bushings.
5. Remove the spring.
NOTE: *Springs are not interchangeable from side to side.*
CAUTION: *When removing the spring from the compressor, open the compressor evenly and not more than 9¼ inches.*

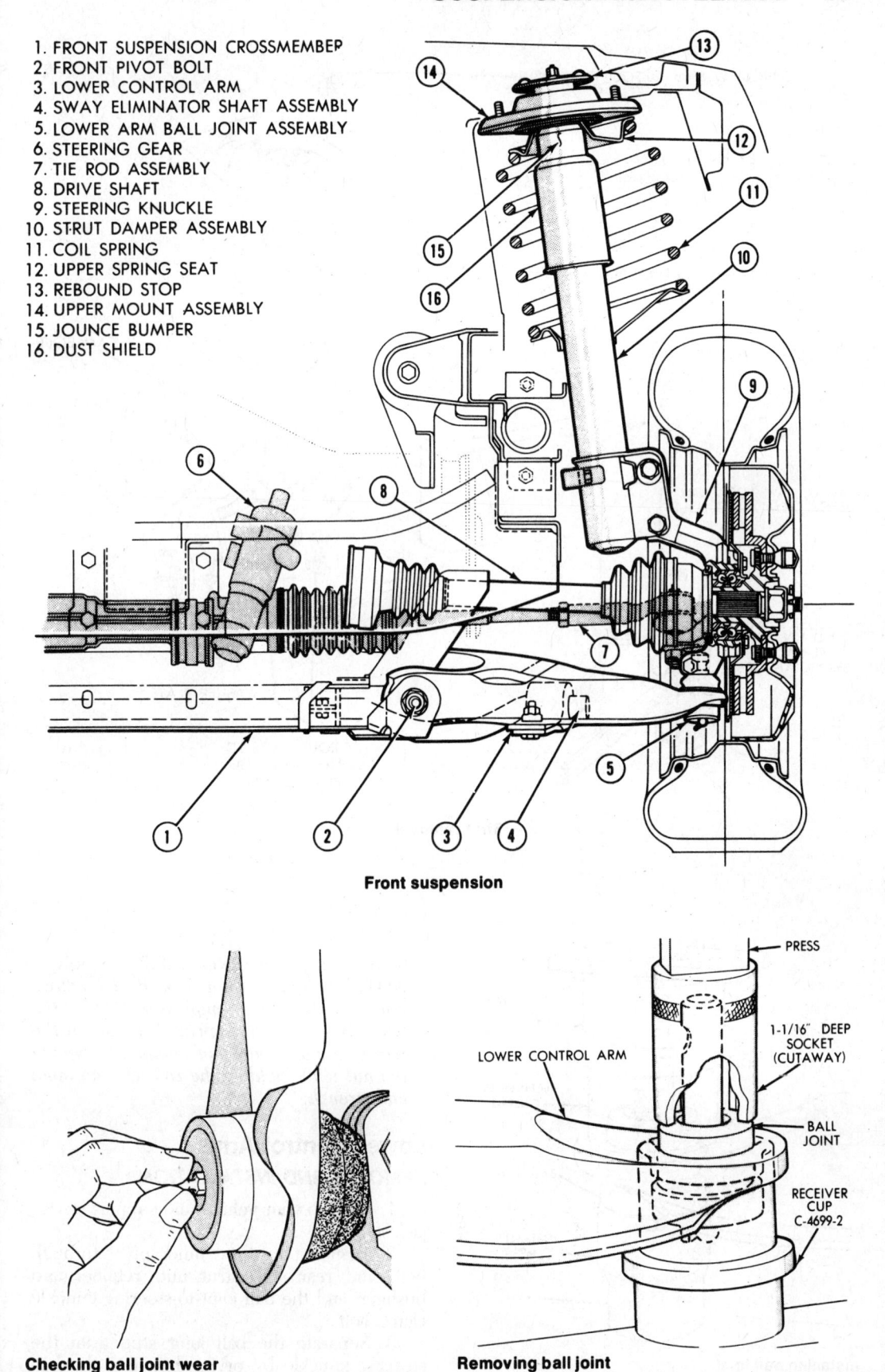

SUSPENSION AND STEERING 93

1. FRONT SUSPENSION CROSSMEMBER
2. FRONT PIVOT BOLT
3. LOWER CONTROL ARM
4. SWAY ELIMINATOR SHAFT ASSEMBLY
5. LOWER ARM BALL JOINT ASSEMBLY
6. STEERING GEAR
7. TIE ROD ASSEMBLY
8. DRIVE SHAFT
9. STEERING KNUCKLE
10. STRUT DAMPER ASSEMBLY
11. COIL SPRING
12. UPPER SPRING SEAT
13. REBOUND STOP
14. UPPER MOUNT ASSEMBLY
15. JOUNCE BUMPER
16. DUST SHIELD

Front suspension

Checking ball joint wear

Removing ball joint

94 SUSPENSION AND STEERING

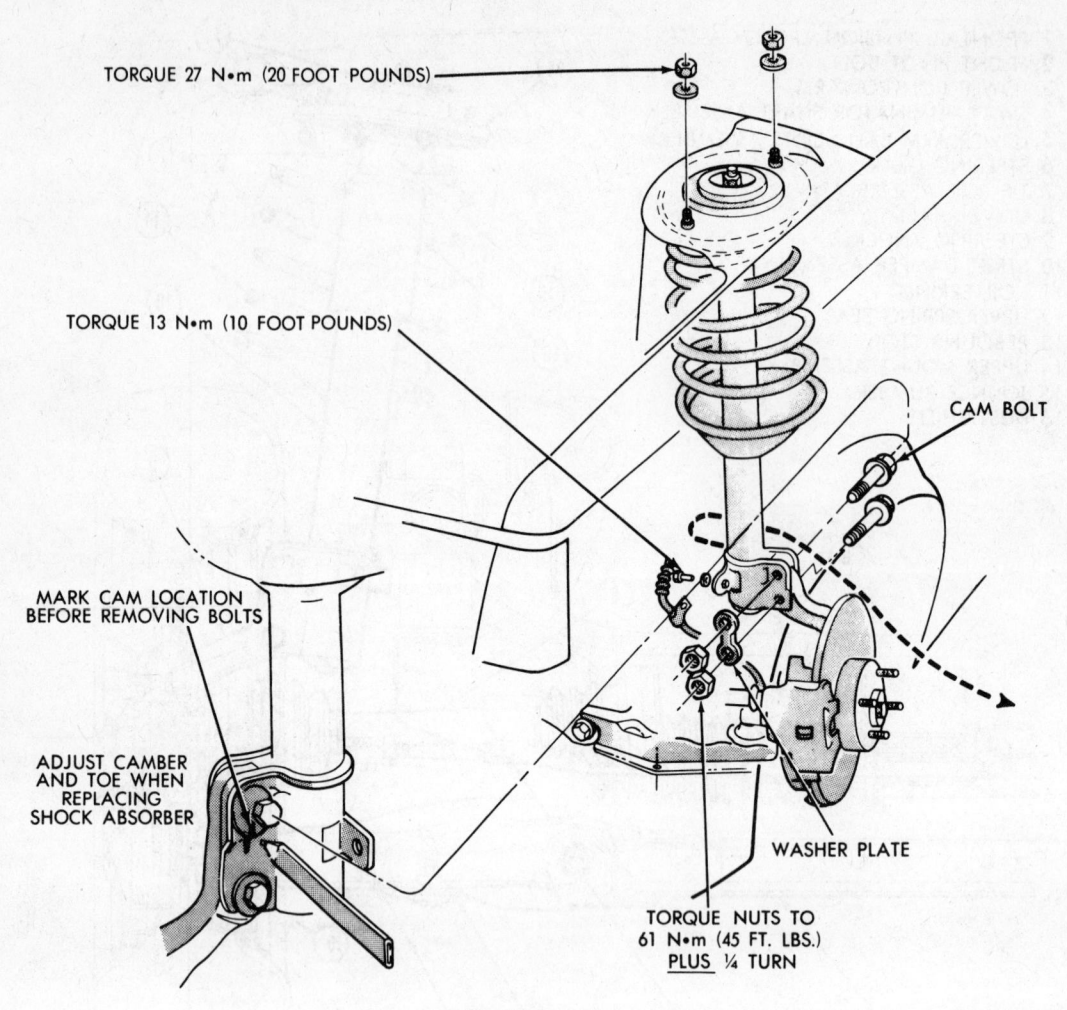

Strut removal

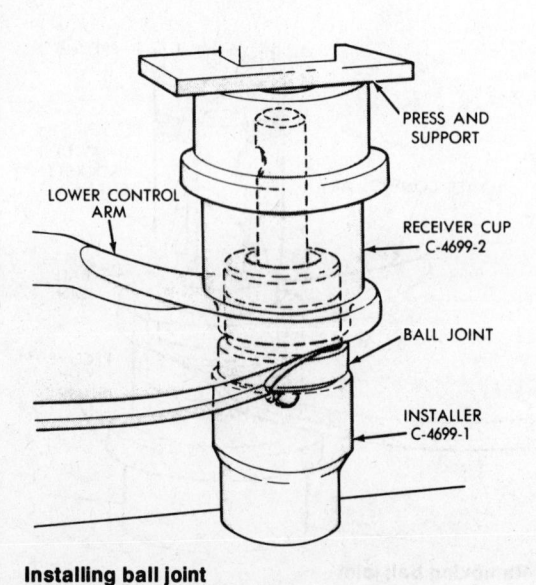

Labels: TORQUE 27 N•m (20 FOOT POUNDS); TORQUE 13 N•m (10 FOOT POUNDS); CAM BOLT; MARK CAM LOCATION BEFORE REMOVING BOLTS; ADJUST CAMBER AND TOE WHEN REPLACING SHOCK ABSORBER; WASHER PLATE; TORQUE NUTS TO 61 N•m (45 FT. LBS.) PLUS ¼ TURN

Installing ball joint

Labels: PRESS AND SUPPORT; LOWER CONTROL ARM; RECEIVER CUP C-4699-2; BALL JOINT; INSTALLER C-4699-1

6. Assembly is the reverse of disassembly.
NOTE: *Torque rod nut to 55 ft. lbs. before removing the spring compressor. Be sure the lower coil end of the spring is seated in the recess. Use a "crow's foot" adaptor to tighten the nut while holding the rod with an open end wrench.*

Lower Control Arm
REMOVAL AND INSTALLATION

1. Jack up your vehicle and support it with jack stands.
2. Remove the front inner pivot through bolt, and rear stub strut nut, retainer and bushing, and the ball joint-to-steering knuckle clamp bolt.
3. Separate the ball joint stud from the steering knuckle by prying between the ball

SUSPENSION AND STEERING

stud retainer on the knuckle and the lower, control arm.

CAUTION: *Pulling the steering knuckle out from the vehicle after releasing it from the ball joint can separate the inner C/V joint.*

4. Remove the sway bar-to-control arm nut and reinforcement and rotate the control arm over the sway bar. Remove the rear stub strut bushing, sleeve and retainer.

NOTE: *The substitution of fasteners other than those of the grade originally used is not recommended.*

5. Install the retainer, bushing and sleeve on the stub strut.
6. Position the control arm over the sway bar and install the rear stub strut and front pivot into the crossmember.
7. Install the front pivot bolt and loosely install the nut.
8. Install the stub strut bushing and retainer and loosely assemble the nut.
9. Install the ball joint stud into the steering knuckle and install the clamp bolt. Torque the clamp bolt to 70 ft. lb.
10. Position the sway bar bracket and stud through the control arm and install the retainer nut. Tighten the nut to 25 ft. lb.
11. Lower the car so that it is resting on the wheels. Tighten the front pivot bolt to 105 ft. lb. and the stub strut nut to 70 ft. lb.

Front End Alignment

Front wheel alignment is the proper adjustment of all the inter-related suspension angles affecting the running and steering of the front wheels.

There are six basic factors which are the foundation of front wheel alignment, height, caster camber, toe-in, steering axis inclination, and toe-out on turns. Of these basic factors, only camber and toe are mechanically adjustable.

CAMBER ADJUSTMENT

1. Check the tire air pressure. Adjust if necessary.
2. Check the front wheels for radial run out.
3. Inspect the lower ball joints and steering linkage for looseness.
4. Check for broken or weak springs, front and rear.

5. Loosen the cam and through bolts.
6. Rotate the upper cam bolt to move the wheel in or out to the specified camber.
7. Tighten the bolts to 45 ft. lbs. plus ¼ turn.

TOE-IN ADJUSTMENT

1. Follow steps 1–4 from the previous procedure.
2. Center the steering wheel and hold it.
3. Loosen the tie rod lock nuts. Rotate the rods to align the toe to specifications.

CAUTION: *Do not twist the tie rod to steering gear rubber boots during alignment.*

4. Tighten the tie rod lock nuts to 55 ft. lbs.

REAR SUSPENSION

All these use a flexible beam axle with trailing links and coil springs. One shock absorber on each side is mounted outside the coil spring and attached to the body and the beam axle. Wheel spindles are bolted to the outer ends of the axle.

Springs

REMOVAL AND INSTALLATION

1. Jack up your vehicle and support it with jack stands.
2. Support the rear axle with a floor jack.
3. Remove the bottom bolt from both rear shock absorbers.
4. Lower the axle assembly until the spring and upper isolator can be removed.

NOTE: *Do not stretch the brake hoses.*

5. Remove the spring and isolator
6. Installation is the reverse of removal. Torque the lower shock bolts to 40 ft. lb.

Shock Absorbers

TESTING

Shock absorbers require replacement if the car fails to recover quickly after hitting a large bump or if it sways excessively following a directional change.

A good way to test the shock absorbers is to intermittently apply downward pressure to the

Wheel Alignment Specifications
(Caster is not adjustable)

Year	Front Camber Range (deg.)	Front Camber Preferred	Rear Camber Range (deg.)	Rear Camber Preferred	Toe-Out (in.) Front	Toe-Out (in.) Rear
'81–'85	¼N to ¾P	5/16P	1N-O	½N	7/32 out to ⅛ in	3/16 out to 3/16 in

96 SUSPENSION AND STEERING

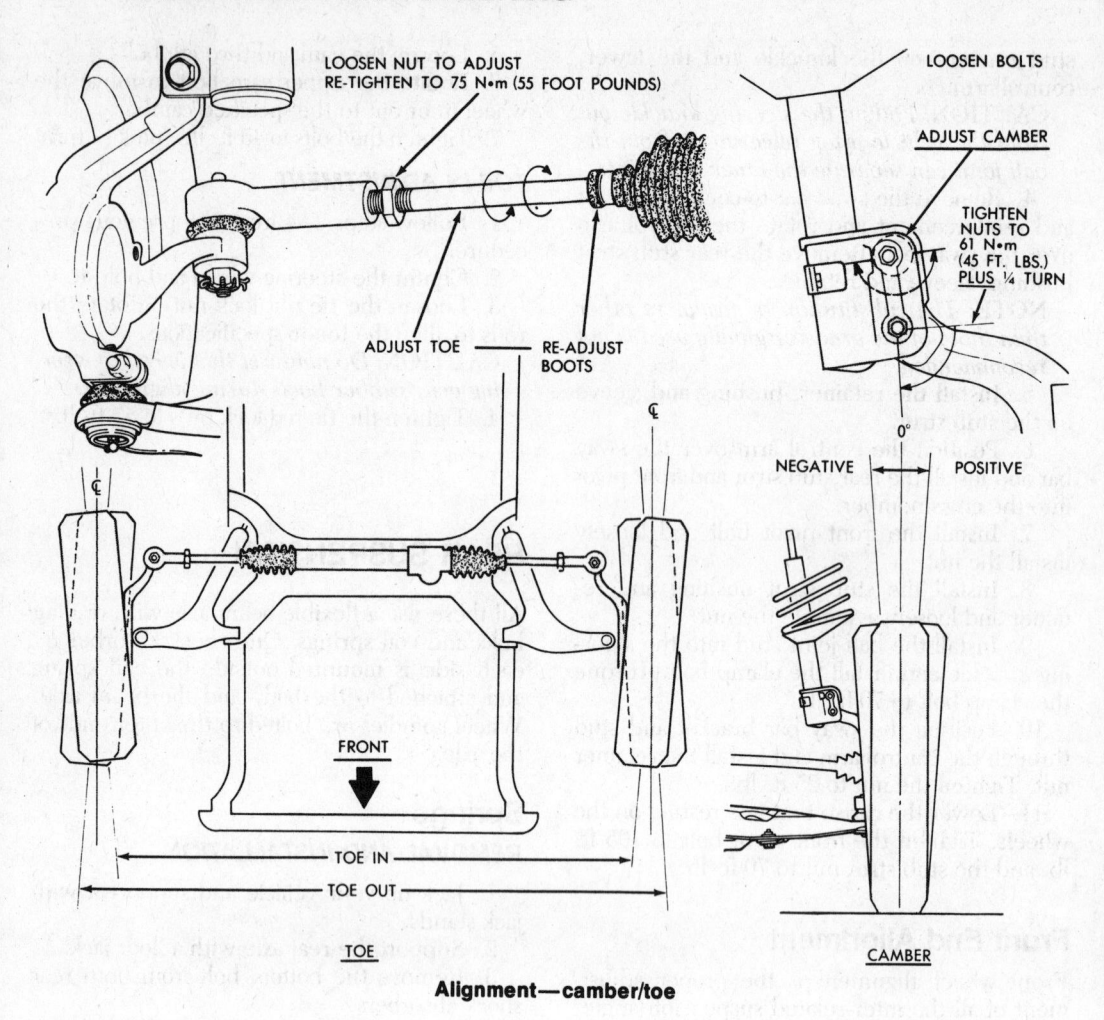

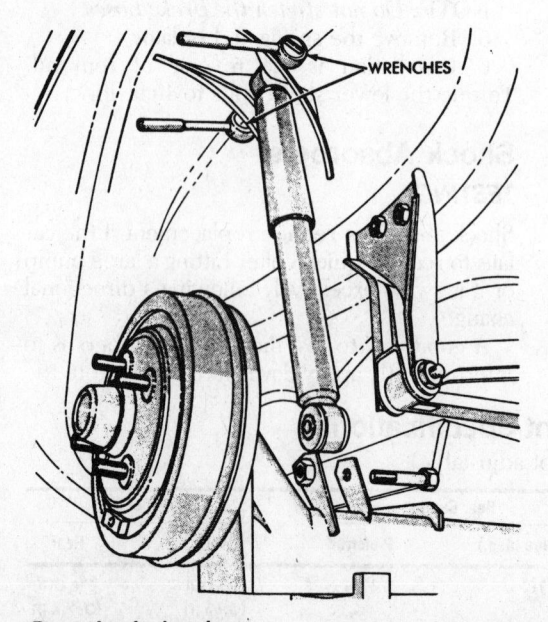

Alignment—camber/toe

Rear shock absorbers

side of the car until it is moving up and down for almost its full suspension travel. Release it and observe its recovery. If the car bounces once or twice after having been released and then comes to a rest, the shocks are alright. If the car continues to bounce, the shocks will probably require replacement.

REMOVAL AND INSTALLATION

1. Jack up your vehicle and support it with jack stands.
2. Support the rear axle with a floor jack.
3. Remove the top and bottom shock absorber bolts.
4. Remove the shock absorbers.
5. Installation is the reverse of removal. Torque the upper and lower bolts to 40 ft. lb.

Rear Axle Alignment

Chrysler K- and E-Cars are equipped with a rear suspension, using wheel spindles, thereby,

SUSPENSION AND STEERING 97

TORQUE		
Ⓐ	54 N•m	40 FT. LBS.
Ⓑ	108 N•m	80 FT. LBS.
Ⓒ	61 N•m	45 FT. LBS.
Ⓓ	8 N•m	70 IN. LBS.

Rear suspension

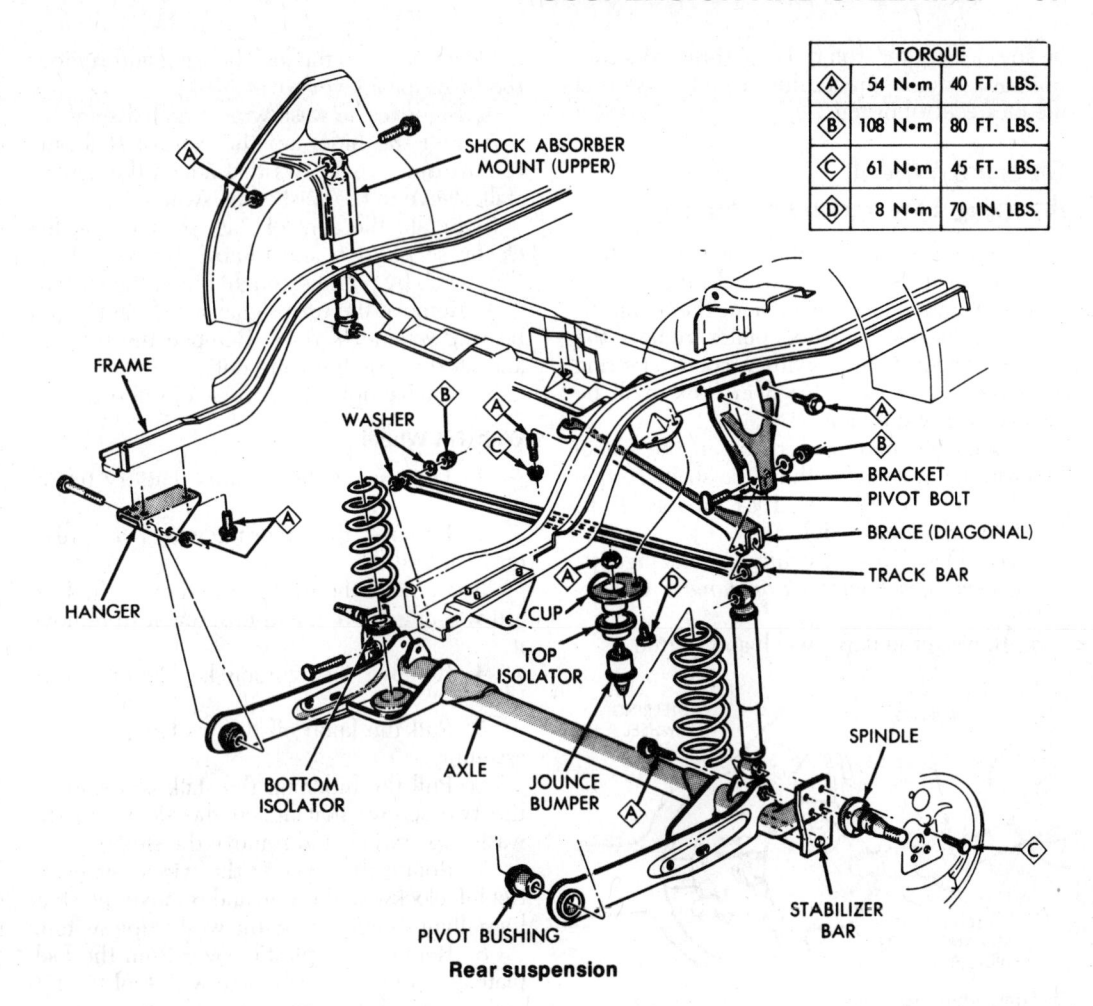

making it possible to align the camber and toe of the rear wheels.

Alignment adjustment, if required, is made by adding shims (Part #5205114 or equivalent) between the spindle mounting surface and axle mounting plate.

Because of the specialized equipment needed to perform this procedure it is best left to your Chrysler dealer or a reliable repair facility.

STEERING

The manual steering system consists of a tube which contains the toothed rack, a pinion, the rack slipper, and the rack slipper spring. Steering effect is transmitted to the steering arms by the tie rods which are coupled to the ends of the rack, and tie rod ends. The connection between the ends of the rack and the tie rod is protected by a bellows type oil seal which retains the gear lubricant.

The power steering system consists of four major parts: the power gear, power steering pump, pressure hose and the return hose. As with the manual system, the turning of the steering wheel is converted into linear travel through the meshing of the helical pinion teeth with the rack teeth. Power assist is provided

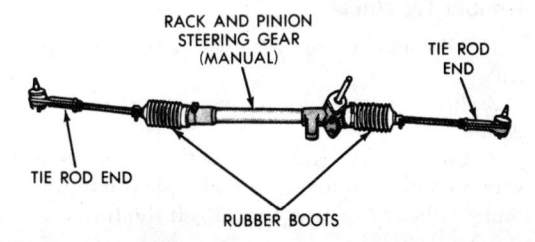

Manual steering gear

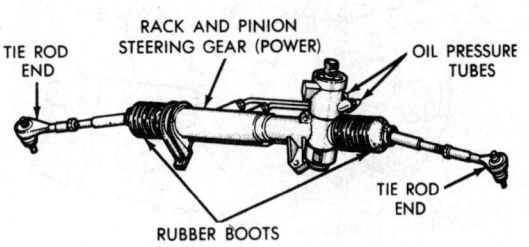

Power steering gear

98 SUSPENSION AND STEERING

by an open center, rotary type, three-way control valve which directs fluid to either side of the rack control piston.

Steering Wheel
REMOVAL AND INSTALLATION

1. Remove the horn button and horn switch.
2. Remove the steering wheel nut, and, on cars with automatic transmission, the damper.
3. Using a steering wheel puller, remove the steering wheel. On cars with a "sport" steering wheel, two 3/8 × 18 SAE × 5 in. bolts will be needed with the puller.
4. Align the master serration in the wheel hub with the missing tooth on the shaft. Torque the shaft nut to 60 ft. lbs. 1981 models, 45 ft. lbs. 1982 and later models.
CAUTION: *Do not torque the nut against the steering column lock or damage will occur.*
5. Replace the horn switch and button.

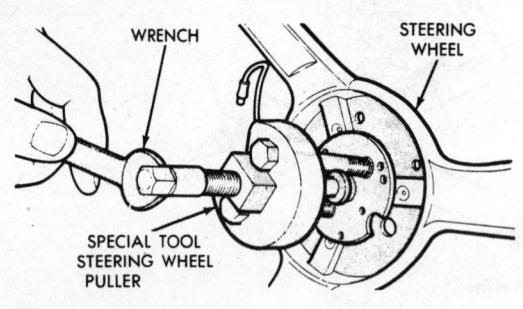

Steering wheel removal

Turn Signal Switch
REMOVAL AND INSTALLATION
Without Tilt Wheel

1. Disconnect the negative battery terminal.
2. Remove the steering wheel as described earlier.
3. On vehicles equipped with intermittent wipe or intermittent wipe with speed control, remove the two screws that attach the turn signal lever cover to the lock housing and remove the turn signal lever cover.
4. Remove the wash/wipe switch assembly.
5. Pull the hider up the control stalk and remove the two screws that attach the control stalk sleeve to the wash/wipe switch.
6. Rotate the control stalk shaft to the full clockwise position and remove the shaft from the switch by pulling straight out of the switch.
7. Remove the turn signal switch and upper bearing retainer screws. Remove the retainer and lift the switch up and out.
8. Installation is the reverse of removal.

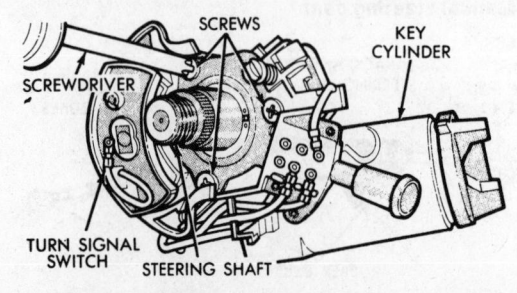

With Tilt Wheel

1. Disconnect the negative battery terminal.
2. Remove the steering wheel as previously described.
3. Remove the tilt lever and push the hazard warning knob in and unscrew it to remove it.
4. Remove the ignition key lamp assembly.
5. Pull the knob off the wash/wipe switch assembly.
6. Pull the hider up the stalk and remove the two screws that attach the sleeve to the wash/wipe switch and remove the sleeve.
7. Rotate the shaft in the wiper switch to the full clockwise position and remove the shaft by pulling straight out of the wash/wipe switch.
8. Remove the plastic cover from the lock plate. Depress the lock plate with tool C-4156 and pry the retaining ring out of the groove. Remove the lock plate, canceling cam and upper bearing spring.
9. Remove the switch actuator screw and arm.
10. Remove the three turn signal switch attaching screws and place the shift bowl in low position. Wrap a piece of tape around the connector and wires to prevent snagging then remove the switch and wires.
11. Installation is the reverse of removal.

Ignition Switch and Keylock
REMOVAL AND INSTALLATION
Without Tilt Wheel

1. Follow the turn signal switch removal procedure previously described.
2. Unclip the horn and key light ground wires.
3. Remove the retaining screw and move the ignition key lamp assembly out of the way.
4. Remove the four screws that hold the bearing housing to the lock housing.
5. Remove the snap ring from the upper end of the steering shaft.

Turn signal switch removal

SUSPENSION AND STEERING

6. Remove the bearing housing from the shaft.
7. Remove the lock plate spring and lock plate from the steering shaft.
8. Remove the ignition key, then remove the screw and lift out the buzzer/chime switch.
9. Remove the two screws attaching the ignition switch to the column jacket.
10. Remove the ignition switch by rotating the switch 90 degrees on the rod then sliding off the rod.
11. Remove the two mounting screws from the dimmer switch and disengage the switch from the actuator rod.
12. Remove the two screws that mount the bellcrank and slide the bellcrank up in the lock housing until it can be disconnected from the ignition switch actuator rod.
13. To remove the lock cylinder and lock levers place the cylinder in the lock position and remove the key.
14. Insert a small diameter screwdriver or similar tool into the lock cylinder release holes and push into the release spring loaded lock retainers. At the same time pull the lock cylinder out of the housing bore.
15. Grasp the lock lever and spring assembly and pull straight out of the housing.
16. If necessary the lock housing may be removed from the column jacket by removing the hex head retaining screws.
17. Installation is the reverse of removal. If the lock housing was removed tighten the lock housing screws to 90 inch pounds.
18. To install the dimmer switch, firmly seat the push rod into the switch. Compress the switch until two .093 inch drill shanks can be inserted into the alignment holes. Reposition the upper end of the push rod in the pocket of the wash/wipe switch. With a light rearward pressure on the switch, install the two screws.
19. Grease and assemble the two lock levers, lock lever spring and pin.
20. Install the lock lever assembly in the lock housing. Seat the pin firmly into the bottom of the slots and make sure the lock lever spring leg is firmly in place in the lock casting notch.
21. Install the ignition switch actuator rod from the bottom through the oblong hole in the lock housing and attach it to the bellcrank. Position the bellcrank assembly into the lock housing while pulling the ignition switch rod down the column, install the bellcrank onto its mounting surface. The gearshift lever should be in the park position.
22. Place the ignition switch on the ignition switch actuator rod and rotate it 90 degrees to lock the rod into position.
23. To install the ignition lock, turn the key to the lock position and remove the key. Insert the cylinder far enough into the housing to contact the switch actuator. Insert the key and press inward and rotate the cylinder. When the parts align the cylinder will move inward and lock into the housing.
24. With the key cylinder in the lock position and the ignition switch in the lock position (second detent from top) tighten the ignition switch mounting screws.
25. Feed the buzzer/chime switch wires behind the wiring post and down through the space between the housing and the jacket. Remove the ignition key and position the switch in the housing and tighten the mounting screws. The ignition key should be removed.
26. Install the lock plate on the steering shaft.
27. Install the upper bearing spring, then the upper bearing housing.
28. Install the upper bearing snap ring on the steering shaft, locking the assembly in place.
29. Install the four screws attaching the bearing housing to the lock housing.
30. Install the key lamp and turn signal switch, following the procedure given previously.

Lock Cylinder

REMOVAL AND INSTALLATION

With Tilt Wheel

1. Remove the turn signal switch as previously described.
2. Place the lock cylinder in the lock position.
3. Insert a thin tool into the slot next to the switch mounting screwing boss (right hand slot) and depress the spring latch at the bottom of the slot and remove the lock.
4. Installation is the reverse of removal. Turn the ignition lock to the "Lock" position and remove the key. Insert the cylinder until the spring loaded retainer snaps into place.

Ignition Switch

REMOVAL AND INSTALLATION

With Tilt Wheel

Due to the complexity of the ignition switch removal procedure and the necessity of special tools it is recommended that the switch be replaced by a qualified repair shop.

Tie Rod Ends

REMOVAL AND INSTALLATION

1. Jack up your car and support it with jack stands.
2. Loosen the jam nut which connects the tie rod end to the rack.

SUSPENSION AND STEERING

3. Mark the tie rod position on the threads.
4. Remove the tie rod cotter pin and nut.
5. Using a puller, remove the tie rod from the steering knuckle.
6. Unscrew the tie rod end from the rack.
7. Install a new tie rod end, and retighten the jam nut.
8. Recheck the wheel alignment.

Brakes

BRAKES

A conventional front disc/rear drum setup is used. The front discs are single piston caliper types; the rear drums are activated by a conventional top mounted wheel cylinder. Disc brakes require no adjustments, the drum brakes are self adjusting by means of the parking brake cable. The system is diagonally balanced, that is, the front left and right rear are on one system and the front right and left rear on the other. No proportioning valve is used. Power brakes are optional.

Master Cylinder

REMOVAL AND INSTALLATION

With Power Brakes

1. Disconnect the primary and secondary brake lines from the master cylinder. Plug the openings.
2. Remove the nuts attaching the cylinder to the power brake booster.
3. Slide the master cylinder straight out, away from the booster.
4. Installation is the reverse of removal. Torque the mounting bolts to 15–25 ft. lb.
5. Remember to bleed the brake system.

With Non-Power Brakes

1. Disconnect the primary and secondary brake lines and install plugs in the master cylinder openings.
2. Disconnect the stoplight switch mounting bracket from under the instrument panel. Pull the stop light switch out of the way to prevent switch damage.
3. Pull the brake pedal backward to disengage the pushrod from the master cylinder piston.
   NOTE: *This will destroy the grommet.*
4. Remove the master cylinder-to-fire-wall nuts.
5. Slide the master cylinder out and away from the firewall. Be sure to remove all pieces of the broken grommet.
6. Install the boot on the pushrod.
7. Install a new grommet on the pushrod.
8. Apply a soap and water solution to the grommet and slide it firmly into position in the primary piston socket. Move the pushrod from side to side to make sure it's seated.
9. From the engine side, press the pushrod through the master cylinder mounting plate and align the mounting studs with the holes in the cylinder.
10. Install the nuts and torque them to 250 in. lbs.
11. From under the instrument panel, place the pushrod on the pin on the pedal and install a new retaining clip.
    CAUTION: *Be sure to lubricate the pin.*
12. Install the brake lines on the master cylinder.
13. Bleed the system.

OVERHAUL

1. Remove the master cylinder as previously outlined.
2. Clean the housing and reservoir.
3. Remove the caps and empty the brake fluid.
4. Remove the reservoir by rocking it from side to side.
5. Remove the housing-to-reservoir grommets.
6. Use needle-nose pliers to remove the secondary piston stop pin from inside the master cylinder housing.
7. Remove the snapring from the outer end of the cylinder bore.
8. Slide the piston out of the cylinder bore.
9. Gently tap the end of the master cylinder on the bench to remove the secondary piston.
   NOTE: *If the piston sticks in the bore use*

BRAKES

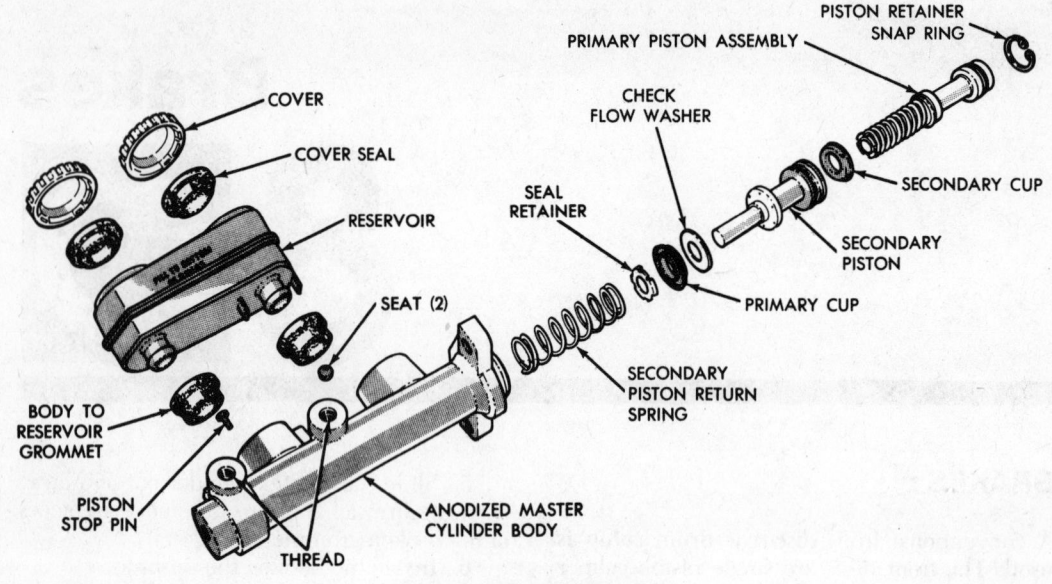

Master cylinder assembly

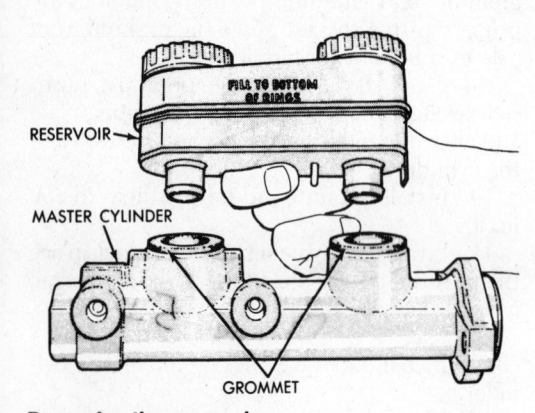

Removing the reservoir

air pressure to force the piston out. New cups must be installed, if air pressure is used to force the piston out.

10. Remove the rubber cups from the pistons, after noting the position of the cup lips.

NOTE: *Do not remove the primary cup of the primary piston. If the cup is damaged the entire piston assembly must be replaced.*

11. If the brass tube seats are not reusable, remove them with an Easy-out®, and insert new ones.

12. Wash the cylinder bore with clean brake fluid. Check for scoring, pitting or scratches. If any of these conditions exist replace the master cylinder. Replace the pistons if they are corroded. Replace the cups and seals. Discard all used rubber parts. Upon installation, coat all components with clean brake fluid.

13. Installation is the reverse of removal.

BLEEDING

1. Place the master cylinder in a vise.
2. Connect two lines to the fluid outlet orifices, and into the reservoir.
3. Fill the reservoir with brake fluid.
4. Using a wooden dowel, depress the pushrod slowly, allowing the pistons to return. Do this several times until the air bubbles are all expelled.
5. Remove the bleeding tubes from the master cylinder, plug the outlets and install the caps.

NOTE: *It is not necessary to bleed the entire system after replacing the master cylinder, provided the master cylinder has been bled and filled upon installation.*

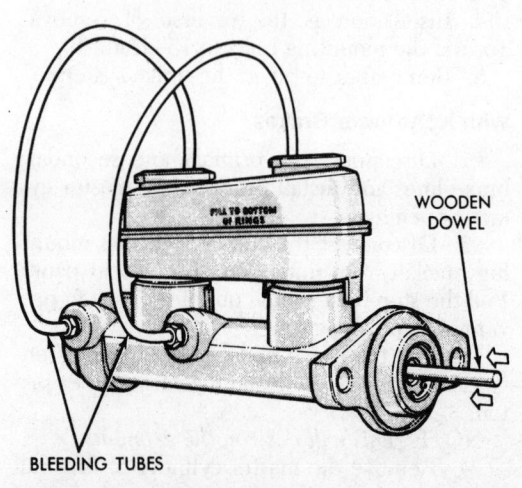

Bleeding the master cylinder

Brake Booster

REMOVAL AND INSTALLATION

1. Remove the brake lines from the master cylinder.
2. Remove the nuts attaching the master cylinder to the brake booster, and remove the master cylinder.
3. Disconnect the vacuum line to the brake booster.
4. Underneath the instrument panel, remove the retainer clip from the brake pedal pin. Discard the retainer clip.
5. Remove the brake light switch and striker plate.
6. Remove the four power booster attaching nuts.
7. Remove the booster from the car.
8. Installation is the reverse of removal.

NOTE: *Remember to bleed the brake system.*

CAUTION: *The power brake booster is not repairable. Do not attempt to disassemble it.*

Tighten the brake booster mounting bolts to 21 ft. lb., the master cylinder bolts 14–20 ft. lbs.

Bleeding

The purpose of bleeding the brakes is to expel air trapped in the hydraulic system. The system must be bled whenever the pedal feels spongy, indicating that compressible air has entered the system. It must also be bled whenever the system has been opened or repaired. You will need a helper for this job.

CAUTION: *Never reuse brake fluid which has been bled from the brake system.*

1. The sequence for bleeding is right rear, left front, left rear and right front. If the car has power brakes, remove the vacuum by applying the brakes several times. Do not run the engine while bleeding the brakes.
2. Clean all the bleeder screws. You may want to give each one a shot of penetrating solvent to loosen it up; seizure is a common problem with bleeder screws, which then break off, sometimes requiring replacement of the part to which they are attached.
3. Fill the master cylinder with DOT 3 brake fluid.

NOTE: *Brake fluid absorbs moisture from the air. Don't leave the master cylinder or the fluid container uncovered any longer than necessary. Be careful handling the fluid—it eats paint.*

Check the level of the fluid often when bleeding, and refill the reservoirs as necessary. Don't let them run dry, or you will have to repeat the process.

4. Attach a length of clear vinyl tubing to the bleeder screw on the wheel cylinder. Insert the other end of the tube into a clear, clean jar half filled with brake fluid.
5. Have your assistant slowly depress the brake pedal. As this is done, open the bleeder screw $\frac{1}{3}$ to $\frac{1}{2}$ of a turn, and allow the fluid to run through the tube. Then close the bleeder screw before the pedal reaches the end of its travel. Have your assistant slowly release the pedal. Repeat this process until no air bubbles appear in the expelled fluid.
6. Repeat the procedure on the other three brakes, checking the level of fluid in the master cylinder reservoir often.

After you're done, there should be no sponginess in the brake pedal feel. If there is, either there is still air in the line, in which case the process should be repeated, or there is a leak somewhere, which of course must be corrected before the car is moved.

HYDRAULIC SYSTEM

A hydraulic system is used to actuate the brakes. The system transports the power required to force the frictional surfaces of the braking system together from the pedal to the individual braking units at each wheel. A hydraulic system is used for three reasons. First, fluid under pressure can be carried to all parts of the automobile by small hoses—some of which are flexible—without taking up a significant amount of room or posing routing problems. Second, liquid is noncompressible; a hydraulic system can transport force without modifying or reducing that force. Third, a great mechanical advantage can be given to the brake pedal end of the system, and the foot pressure required to actuate the brakes can be reduced by making the surface area of the master cylinder pistons smaller than that of any of the pistons in the wheel cylinders or calipers.

The master cylinder consists of a fluid reservoir and a double cylinder and piston assembly. Double type master cylinders are designed to separate the front and rear braking systems hydraulically in case of a leak.

Steel lines carry the brake fluid to a point on the vehicle's frame near each of the vehicle's wheels. The fluid is then carried to the slave cylinders by flexible tubes in order to allow for suspension and steering movements.

In drum brake systems, the slave cylinders are called wheel cylinders. Each wheel cylinder contains two pistons, one at either end, which push outward in opposite directions. In disc brake systems, the slave cylinders are part of the calipers. One or four cylinders are used to force the brake pads against the disc, but all cylinders contain one piston only. All slave cylinder pistons employ some type of seal, usually made of rubber, to minimize the leakage of fluid around the piston. A rubber dust boot seals the outer end of the cylinder against dust and dirt. The boot fits around the outer end of the piston on disc brake calipers, and around the brake actuating rod on wheel cylinders.

The hydraulic system operates as follows: When at rest, the entire system, from the pistons in the master cylinder to those in the wheel cylinders or calipers, is full of brake fluid. Upon application of the brake pedal, fluid trapped in front of the master cylinder pistons is forced through the lines to the slave cylinders. Here, it forces the pistons outward, in the case of drum brakes, and inward toward the disc, in the case of disc brakes. The motion of the pistons is opposed by return springs mounted outside the cylinders in drum brakes, and by internal springs or spring seals in disc brakes.

Upon release of the brake pedal, a spring located inside the master cylinder immediately returns the master cylinder pistons to the normal position. The pistons contain check valves and the master cylinder has compensating ports drilled in it. These are uncovered as the pistons reach their normal position. The piston check valves allow fluid to flow toward the wheel cylinders or calipers as the pistons withdraw. Then, as the return springs force the brake pads or shoes into the released position, the excess fluid returns to the master cylinder fluid reservoir through the compensating ports. It is during the time the pedal is in the released position that any fluid that has leaked out of the system will be replaced through the compensating ports.

Dual circuit master cylinders employ two pistons, located one behind the other, in the same cylinder. The primary piston is actuated directly by mechanical linkage from the brake pedal. The secondary piston is actuated by fluid trapped between the two pistons. If a leak develops in front of the secondary piston, it moves forward until it bottoms against the front of the master cylinder, and the fluid trapped between the pistons will operate the rear brakes. If the rear brakes develop a leak, the primary piston will move forward until direct contact with the secondary piston takes place, and it will force the secondary piston to actuate the front brakes. In either case, the brake pedal moves farther when the brakes are applied, and less braking power is available.

All dual-circuit systems use a distributor switch to warn the driver when only half of the brake system is operational. This switch is located in a valve body which is mounted on the master cylinder. A hydraulic piston receives pressure from both circuits, each circuit's pressure being applied to one end of the piston. When the pressures are in balance, the piston remains stationary. When one circuit has a leak, however, the greater pressure in that circuit during application of the brakes will push the piston to one side, closing the distributor switch and activating the brake warning light.

In disc brake systems, this valve body also contains a metering valve and, in some cases, a proportioning valve. The metering valve keeps pressure from traveling to the disc brakes on the front wheels until the brake shoes on the rear wheels have contacted the drums, ensuring that the front brakes will never be used alone. The proportioning valve throttles the pressure to the rear brakes so as to avoid rear wheel lock-up during very hard braking.

These valves may be tested by removing the lines to the front and rear brake systems and installing special brake pressure testing gauges. Front and rear system pressures are then compared as the pedal is gradually depressed. Specifications vary with the manufacturer and design of the brake system.

Brake system warning lights may be tested by depressing the brake pedal and holding it while opening one of the wheel cylinder bleeder screws. If this does not cause the light to go on, substitute a new lamp, make continuity checks, and, finally, replace the switch as necessary.

The hydraulic system may be checked for leaks by applying pressure to the pedal gradually and steadily. If the pedal sinks very slowly to the floor, the system has a leak. This is not to be confused with a springy or spongy feel due to the compression of air within the lines. If the system leaks, there will be a gradual change in the position of the pedal with a constant pressure.

Check for leaks along all lines and at wheel cylinders. If no external leaks are apparent, the problem is inside the master cylinder.

FRONT DISC BRAKES

Disc Brake Pads and Calipers
REMOVAL AND INSTALLATION
ATE System

1. Raise and support the front end on jackstands.
2. Remove the front wheels.
3. Remove the caliper holddown spring by pushing in on the center of the spring and pushing outward.
4. Loosen, but do not remove the guide

BRAKES 105

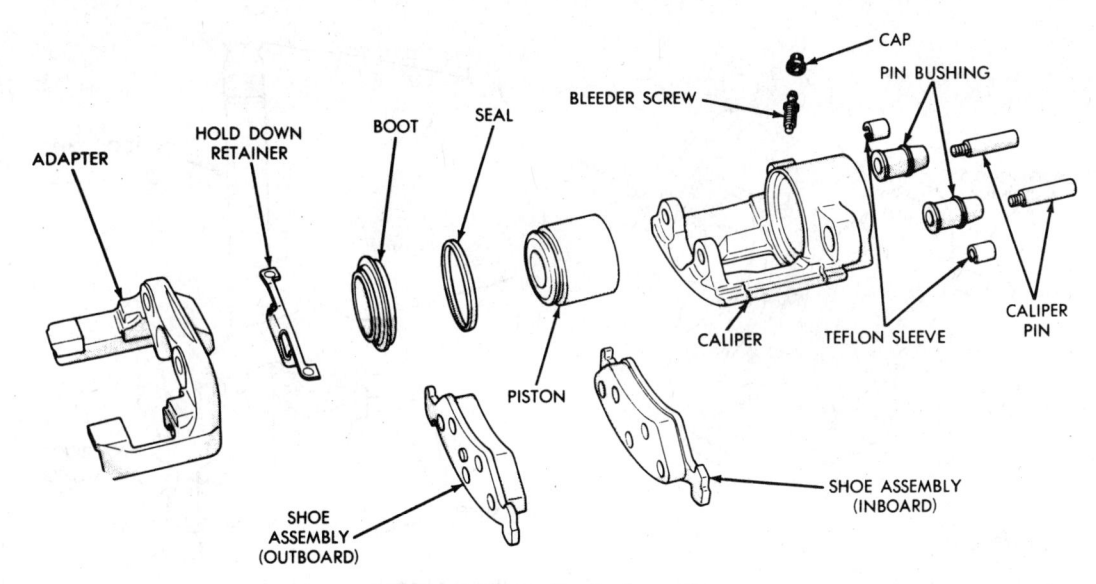

Exploded view—disc brake caliper

pins, until the caliper is free. Remove the guide pins only if the bushings are being replaced.

5. Lift the caliper away from the rotor. The inboard shoe will remain with the caliper. Remove the shoe.

6. If the caliper is being removed, disconnect and cap the brake line. If only the pads are being removed, support the caliper with wire.

7. Lubricate both busing channels with silicone lubricant.

8. Remove the protective backing from the noise suppression gasket on the inner shoe assembly.

9. Install the new inboard shoe in the caliper, entering the retainer in the piston bore.

10. Remove the protective backing from the noise suppression gasket on the outboard shoe and position the shoe on the adapter.

11. Carefully lower the caliper over the rotor and inboard shoe.

12. Install the guide pins and torque to 18–22 ft. lb.

CAUTION: *The guide pins are easy to crossthread.*

13. Install the holddown spring.

14. Install the wheels and torque the lugs to ½ torque in a crossing pattern, then torque them to the full torque of 95 ft. lb.

Kelsey-Hayes System

1. Raise and support the front end on jackstands.

2. Remove the front wheels.

3. Remove the caliper guide pin.

4. Using a small prybar, wedge the caliper away from the rotor, breaking the adhesive seals.

5. Slowly slide the caliper off of the rotor.

6. Remove the outboard, then the inboard shoe.

7. If the caliper is to be removed, disconnect and cap the brake line.

8. Lubricate both bushing channels with silicone grease.

9. Remove the protective paper backing from the anti-squeal surfaces and install the inboard shoe on the adapter. Install the outboard shoe in the caliper and carefully slide it into place over the rotor.

10. Install the guide pin and torque it to 35 ft. lb.

11. Install the wheels and torque the lugs to half torque in a crossing pattern. Torque the lugs to full torque (95 ft. lb.).

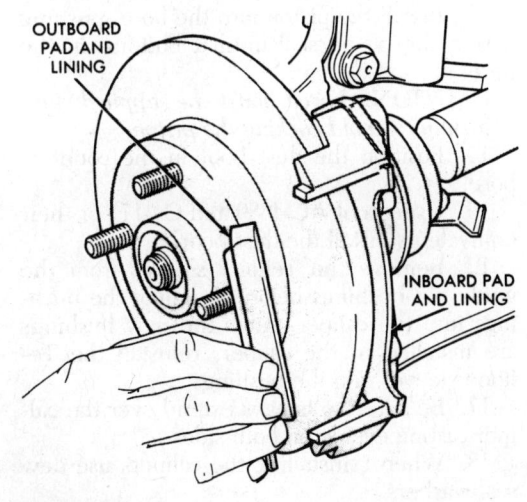

Outer disc pad

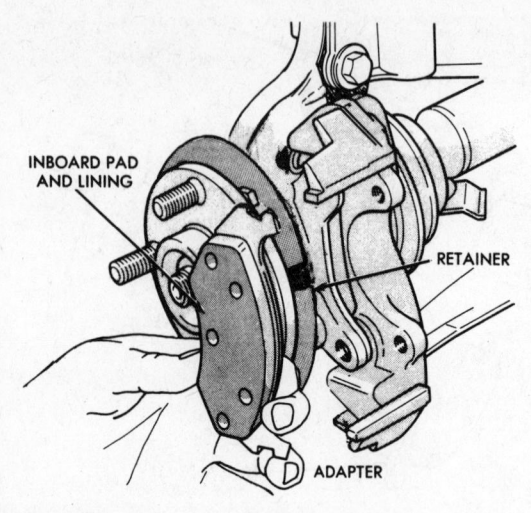

BRAKES

Inner disc pad

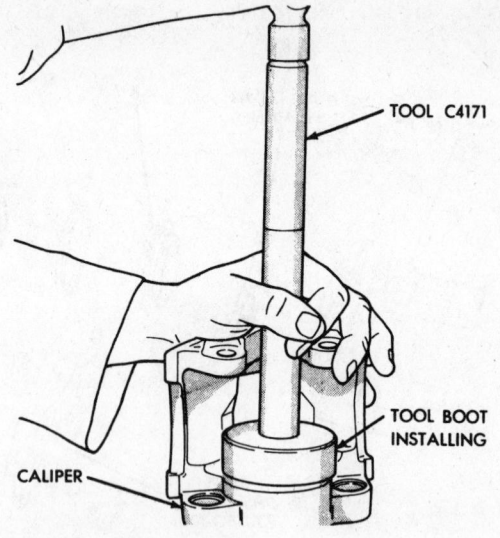

Installing boot in caliper

CALIPER OVERHAUL

1. Remove the caliper as previously outlined leaving the brake line connected.
2. Carefully have your helper depress the brake pedal to hydraulically push the piston out of the bore.

CAUTION: *Under no condition should air pressure be used to remove the piston. Personal injury could result from this practice.*

3. Disconnect the brake line from the caliper.
4. Place the caliper in a vise.

CAUTION: *Excessive vise pressure will cause bore distortion and piston binding.*

5. Remove the dust boot and discard it.
6. Use a plastic rod to work the piston seal out of its groove in the piston bore. Discard the old seal.

NOTE: *Do not use a metal tool for this procedure, because of the possibility of scratching the piston bore, or damaging the edges of the seal.*

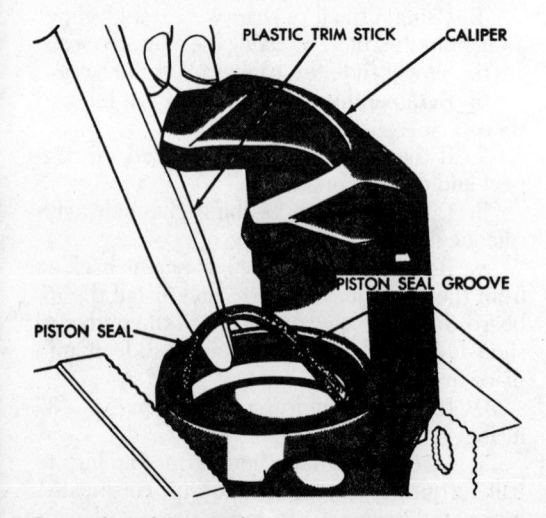

7. Remove the bushings from the caliper by pressing them out, using a suitable tool. Discard the old bushings.
8. Clean all parts using alcohol and blow dry with compressed air.

NOTE: *Whenever a caliper has been disassembled, a new boot and seal must be installed.*

9. Inspect the piston bore for scoring or pitting. Bores with light scratches can be cleaned up. If the bore is scratched beyond repair, the caliper should be replaced.
10. Dip the new piston seal in clean brake fluid and install in the bore groove.

CAUTION: *Never use an old piston seal.*

11. Coat the new piston with clean brake fluid, leaving a generous amount inside the boot.
12. Position the dust boot over the piston.
13. Install the piston into the bore, pushing it past the piston seal until it bottoms in the bore.

CAUTION: *Force must be applied uniformly to avoid cocking the piston.*

14. Position the dust boot in the counterbore.
15. Using tool #C-4689 and C-4171 or their equivalents install the dust boot.
16. Remove the Teflon® sleeves from the guide pin bushings before installing the bushings into the caliper. After the new bushings are installed in the caliper, reinstall the Teflon® sleeves into the bushings.
17. Be sure the flanges extend over the caliper casting evenly on both sides.
18. When reinstalling the calipers use new seal washers.
19. Bleed the brake system.

Removing piston seal

BRAKES 107

Brake Disc

REMOVAL AND INSTALLATION

1. Raise and support the front end on jackstands.
2. Remove the caliper from the rotor, but do not disconnect the brake line.
3. Suspend the caliper out of the way with wire. Do not put stress on the brake hose.
4. On ATE systems, remove the adapter from the knuckle.
5. Remove the rotor from the drive flange studs.
6. Coat both sides of the rotor with alcohol and slide it onto the studs.
7. Install the adapter (ATE systems).
8. Install the caliper.

INSPECTION

Light scoring is acceptable. Heavy scoring or warping will necessitate refinishing or replacement of the disc. The brake disc must be replaced if cracks or burned marks are evident.

Check the thickness of the disc. Measure the thickness at 12 equally spaced points 1 inch from the edge of the disc. If thickness varies more than 0.0005 in. the disc should be refinished, provided equal amounts are out from each side and the thickness does not fall below .882 in.

Check the run-out of the disc. Total runout of the disc installed on the car should not exceed 0.0005 in. The disc can be resurfaced to correct minor variations as long as equal amounts are cut from each side and the thickness is at least .882 in. after resurfacing.

Check the run-out of the hub (disc removed). It should not be more than 0.002 in. If so, the hub should be replaced.

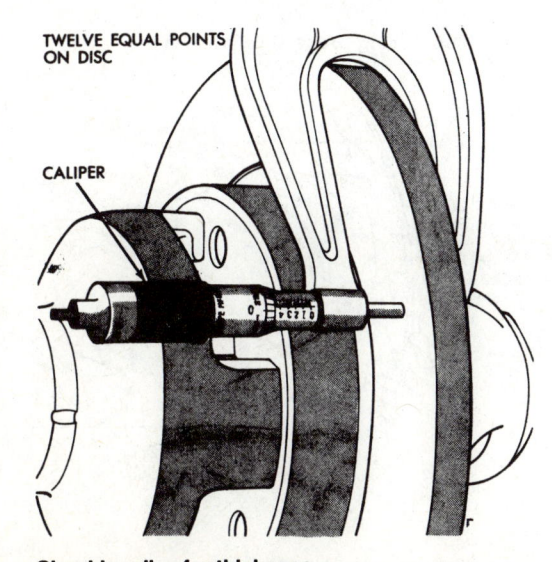

Checking disc for thickness

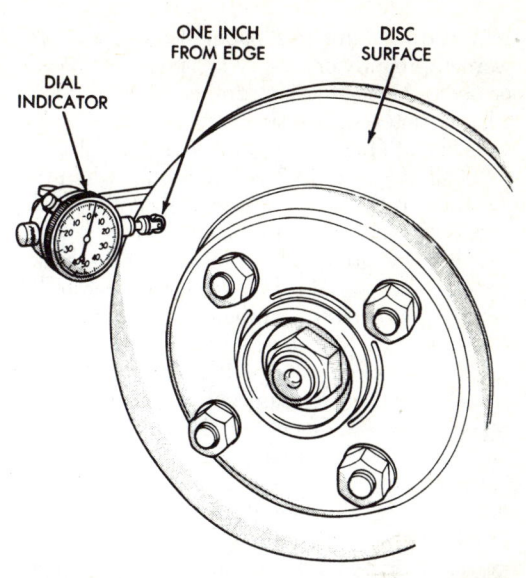

Checking disc for run-out

REAR DRUM BRAKES

Brake Drums

REMOVAL AND INSTALLATION

1. Jack up your car and support it with jack stands.
2. Remove the rear wheels.
3. Insert a brake spoon and release the brake shoe drag by moving up on the left side and down on the right side.
5. Remove the grease cap.
6. Remove the cotter pin, locknut, and washer.
7. Remove the brake drum and bearings.
8. Installation is the reverse of removal. Adjust the wheel bearings.

INSPECTION

Measure drum run-out and diameter. If the drum is not to specifications, have the drum resurfaced. The run-out should not exceed .006 inch. The diameter variation (ovalness) of the drum must not exceed .0025 inch in 30° or .0035 inch in 360°. All brake drums will show markings of the maximum allowable diameter.

Once the drum is off, clean the shoes and springs with a damp rag to remove the accumulated brake dust.

NOTE: *Avoid exposure to brake dust. Brake dust contains asbestos, a known cancer causing agent.*

Grease on the shoes can be removed with alcohol or fine sandpaper.

After cleaning, examine the brake shoes for glazed, oily, loose, cracked or improperly worn linings. Light glazing is common and can be

108 BRAKES

removed with fine sandpaper. Linings that are worn improperly or below 1/16" above rivet heads or brake shoe should be replaced. The NHSTA advises states with inspection programs to fail vehicles with brake linings less than 1/32". A good "eyeball" test is to replace the linings when the thickness is the same as or less than the thickness of the metal backing plate (shoe).

Wheel cylinders are a vital part of the brake system and should be inspected carefully. Gently pull back the rubber boots; if any fluid is visible, it's time to replace or rebuild the wheel cylinders. Boots that are distorted, cracked or otherwise damaged, also point to the need for service. Check the flexible brake lines for cracks, chafing or wear.

Check the brake shoe retracting and hold-down springs; they should not be worn or distorted. Be sure that the adjuster mechanism moves freely. The points on the backing plate where the shoes slide should be shiny and free of rust. Rust in these areas suggests that the brake shoes are not moving properly.

Brake Shoes

REMOVAL AND INSTALLATION

NOTE: *If you are not thoroughly familiar with the procedures involved in brake replacement, disassemble and assemble one side at a time, leaving the other wheel intact, as a reference.*

1. Remove the brake drum. See the procedure earlier in this chapter.
2. Unhook the parking brake cable from the secondary (trailing) shoe.
3. Remove the shoe-to-anchor springs (retracting springs). They can be gripped and unhooked with a pair of pliers.
4. Remove the shoe hold down springs: compress them slightly and slide them off of the hold down pins.

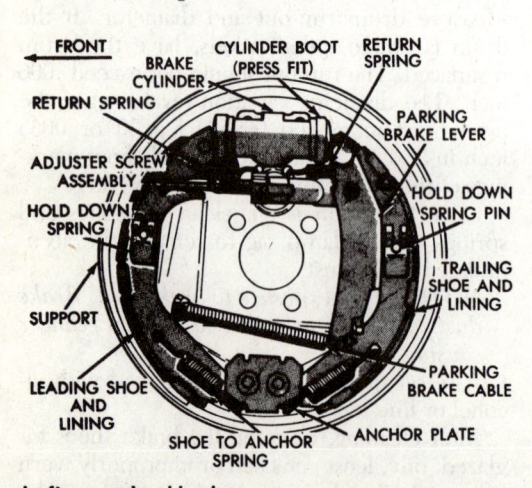

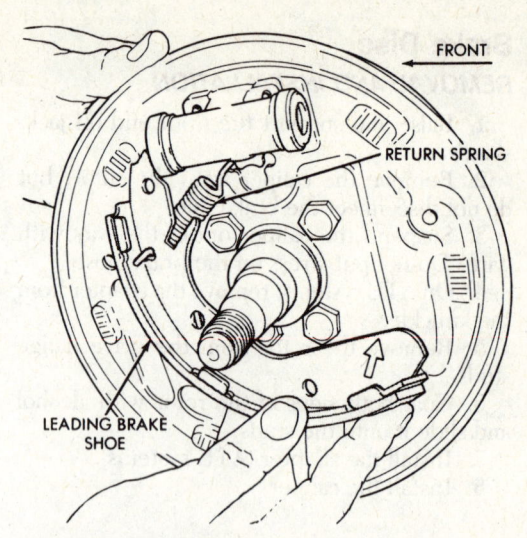

Installing brake drum

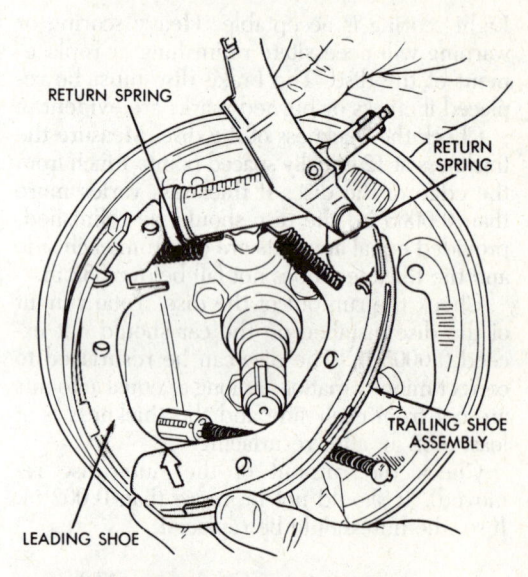

Installing trailing brake shoe and lever

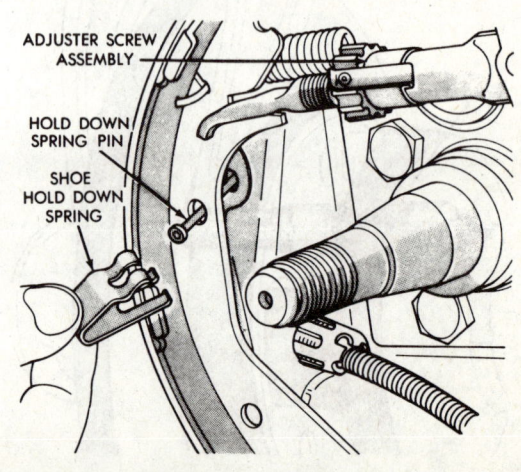

Left rear wheel brake

Installing shoe hold-down spring

BRAKES

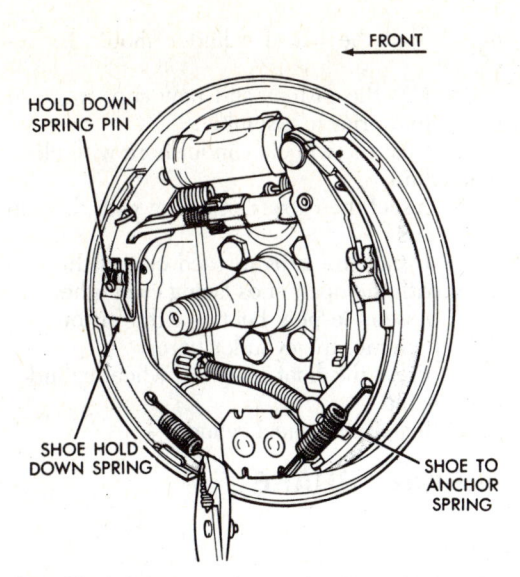

Installing shoe-to-anchor springs

5. Remove the adjuster screw assembly by spreading the shoes apart. The adjuster nut must be fully backed off.
6. Raise the parking brake lever. Pull the secondary (trailing) shoe away from the backing plate so pull-back spring tension is released.
7. Remove the secondary (trailing) shoe and disengage the spring end from the backing plate.
8. Raise the primary (leading) shoe to release spring tension. Remove the shoe and disengage the spring end from the backing plate.
9. Inspect the brakes (see procedures under Brake Drum Inspection).
10. Lubricate the six shoe contact areas on the brake backing plate and the web end of the brake shoe which contacts the anchor plate. Use a multi-purpose lubricant or a high temperature brake grease made for this purpose.
11. Chrysler recommends that the rear wheel bearings be cleaned and repacked whenever the brakes are renewed. Be sure to install a new bearing seal.
12. With the leading shoe return spring in position on the shoe, install the shoe at the same time as you engage the return spring in the end support.
13. Position the end of the shoe under the anchor.
14. With the trailing shoe return spring in position, install the shoe at the same time as you engage the spring in the support (backing plate).
15. Position the end of the shoe under the anchor.
16. Spread the shoes and install the adjuster screw assembly making sure that the forked end that enters the shoe is curved down.
17. Insert the shoe hold down spring pins and install the hold down springs.
18. Install the shoe-to-anchor springs.
19. Install the parking brake cable onto the parking brake lever.
20. Replace the brake drum and tighten the nut to 240–300 in. lbs. while rotating the wheel.
21. Back off the nut enough to release the bearing preload and position the locknut with one pair of slots aligned with the cotter pin hole.
22. Install the cotter pin. The end play should be 0.001–0.003 in.
23. Install the grease cap.

Wheel Cylinders
REMOVAL AND INSTALLATION

1. Jack up your vehicle and support it with jack stands.
2. Remove the brake drums as previously outlined.
3. Visually inspect the wheel cylinder boots for signs of excessive leakage. Replace any boots that are torn or broken.

NOTE: *A slight amount of fluid on the boots*

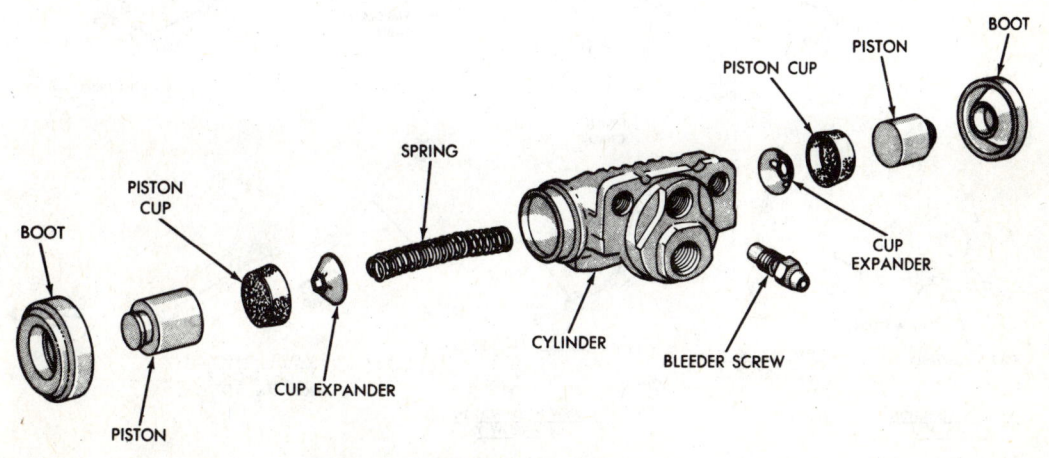

Rear wheel cylinder

110 BRAKES

may not be a leak but may be preservative fluid used at the factory.

4. If a leak has been discovered, remove the brake shoes and check for contamination. Replace the linings if they are soaked with grease or brake fluid.

5. Disconnect the brake line from the wheel cylinder.

6. Remove the wheel cylinder attaching bolts, then pull the wheel cylinder out of its support.

7. Installation is the reverse of removal.

8. Bleed the brake system.

OVERHAUL

1. Pry the boots away from the cylinder and remove the boots and piston as an assembly.

2. Disengage the boot from the piston.

3. Slide the piston into the cylinder bore and press inward to remove the other boot and piston. Also remove the spring with it the cup expanders.

4. Wash all parts (except rubber parts) in clean brake fluid thoroughly. Do not use a rag; lint will adhere to the bore.

5. Inspect the cylinder bores. Light scoring can usually be cleaned up with crocus cloth. Black stains are caused by the piston cups and are no cause of concern. Bad scoring or pitting means that the wheel cylinder should be replaced.

6. Dip the pistons and new cups in clean brake fluid prior to assembly.

7. Coat the wheel cylinder bore with clean brake fluid.

8. Install the expansion spring with the cup expanders.

9. Install the cups in each end of the cylinder with the open ends facing each other.

10. Assemble new boots on the piston and slide them into the cylinder bore.

11. Press the boot over the wheel cylinder until seated.

12. Install the wheel cylinder.

PARKING BRAKE

Cable

ADJUSTMENT

NOTE: *The service brakes must be properly adjusted before adjusting the parking brake.*

1. Release the parking brake lever, then back off the parking brake cable adjuster so there is slack in the cable.

2. Clean and lubricate the adjuster threads.

3. Use a brake spoon to turn the star-wheel adjuster until there is light shoe-to-drum con-

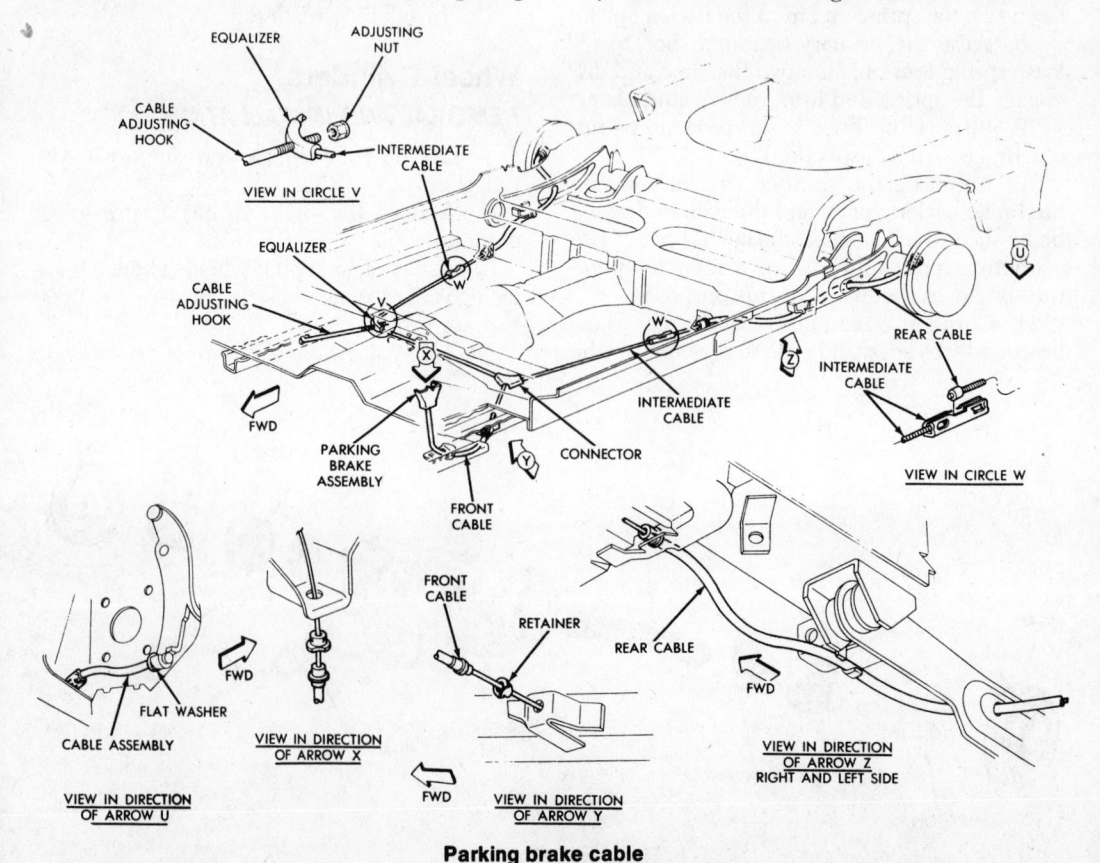

Parking brake cable

BRAKES

Brake Specifications
All measurements given are (in.) unless noted

Model	Lug Nut Torque (ft./lb.)	Master Cylinder Bore	Brake Disc Minimum Thickness	Brake Disc Maximum Run-Out	Brake Drum Diameter	Brake Drum Max. Machine O/S	Brake Drum Max. Wear Limit	Minimum Lining Thickness Front	Minimum Lining Thickness Rear
1981–85	95	.827	.882	.004	7.87 ②	①	①	.300	5/16

① See figure stamped on the drum.
NOTE: Minimum lining thickness is as recommended by the manufacturer. Because of variations in state inspection regulations, the minumum allowable thickness may be different than recommended by the manufacturer.
② Caravelle, 600 and New Yorker: 8.66

tact. Back off the adjuster until the wheel rotates freely with no brake drag.

4. Tighten the parking brake adjuster until a slight drag is felt while rotating the wheels.

5. Loosen the cable adjusting nut until the rear wheels can be rotated freely, then back the cable adjuster nut off 2 full turns.

6. Test the parking brake. The rear wheels should rotate freely without dragging.

REMOVAL AND INSTALLATION
Front Cable

1. Jack up your car and support it with jack stands.
2. Loosen the cable adjusting nut and disengage the cable from the connectors.
3. Lift the floor mat for access to the floor pan.
4. Remove the floor pan seal panel.
5. Pull the cable end forward and disconnect it from the clevis.
6. Pull the cable assembly through the hole.
7. Installation is the reverse of removal.
8. Adjust the service and parking brake.

Rear Cable

1. Jack up your vehicle and support it with jack stands.
2. Remove the rear wheels.
3. Remove the brake drums.
4. Back off the cable adjuster to provide slack in the cable.
5. Compress the retainers on the end of the cable and remove the cable from the chassis mount. A worm gear type hose clamp can be used for this procedure.
6. Disconnect the cable from the brake shoe lever.
7. Use another hose clamp to assist in removing the cable housing from the support clamp. Remove the hose clamp when the cable has been removed.
8. Pull the brake cable from the rear axle.
9. Installation is the reverse of removal.
10. Adjust the service and parking brakes.

Rear Wheel Bearings

The rear wheel bearings should be inspected and relubricated whenever the rear brakes are serviced or at least every 30,000 miles. Repack the bearings with high temperature multi-purpose grease.

Check the lubricant to see if it is contaminated. If it contains dirt or has a milky appearance indicating the presence of water, the bearings should be cleaned and repacked.

Clean the bearings in kerosene, mineral spirits or other suitable cleaning fluid. Do not dry them by spinning the bearings. Allow them to air dry.

1. Raise and support the car with the rear wheels off the floor.
2. Remove the wheel grease cap, cotter pin, nut-lock and bearing adjusting nut.
3. Remove the thrust washer and bearing.
4. Remove the drum from the spindle.
5. Thoroughly clean the old lubricant from the bearings and hub cavity. Inspect the bearing rollers for pitting or other signs of wear. Light discoloration is normal.
6. Repack the bearings with high temperature multi-purpose EP grease and add a small amount of new grease to the hub cavity. Be sure to force the lubricant between all rollers in the bearing.
7. Install the drum on the spindle after coating the polished spindle surfaces with wheel bearing lubricant.
8. Install the outer bearing cone, thrust washer and adjusting nut.
9. Tighten the adjusting nut to 20–25 ft. lbs. while rotating the wheel.
10. Back off the adjusting nut to completely release the preload from the bearing.
11. Tighten the adjusting nut finger-tight.
12. Position the nut-lock with one pair of slots in line with the cotter pin hole. Install the cotter pin.
13. Clean and install the grease cap and wheel.
14. Lower the car.

Troubleshooting 19

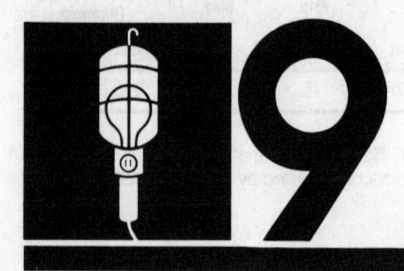

This section is designed to aid in the quick, accurate diagnosis of automotive problems. While automotive repairs can be made by many people, accurate troubleshooting is a rare skill for the amateur and professional alike.

In its simplest state, troubleshooting is an exercise in logic. It is essential to realize that an automobile is really composed of a series of systems. Some of these systems are interrelated; others are not. Automobiles operate within a framework of logical rules and physical laws, and the key to troubleshooting is a good understanding of all the automotive systems.

This section breaks the car or truck down into its component systems, allowing the problem to be isolated. The charts and diagnostic road maps list the most common problems and the most probable causes of trouble. Obviously it would be impossible to list every possible problem that could happen along with every possible cause, but it will locate MOST problems and eliminate a lot of unnecessary guesswork. The systematic format will locate problems within a given system, but, because many automotive systems are interrelated, the solution to your particular problem may be found in a number of systems on the car or truck.

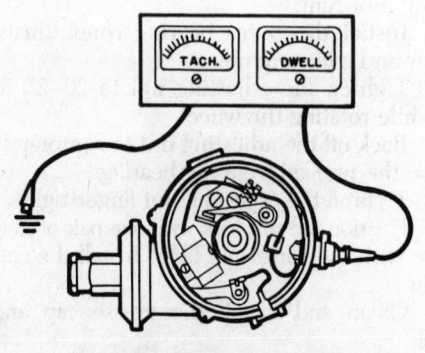

USING THE TROUBLESHOOTING CHARTS

This book contains all of the specific information that the average do-it-yourself mechanic needs to repair and maintain his or her car or truck. The troubleshooting charts are designed to be used in conjunction with the specific procedures and information in the text. For instance, troubleshooting a point-type ignition system is fairly standard for all models, but you may be directed to the text to find procedures for troubleshooting an individual type of electronic ignition. You will also have to refer to the specification charts throughout the book for specifications applicable to your car or truck.

TOOLS AND EQUIPMENT

The tools illustrated in Chapter 1 (plus two more diagnostic pieces) will be adequate to troubleshoot most problems. The two other tools needed are a voltmeter and an ohmmeter. These can be purchased separately or in combination, known as a VOM meter.

In the event that other tools are required, they will be noted in the procedures.

Tach-dwell hooked-up to distributor

TROUBLESHOOTING

Troubleshooting Engine Problems

See Chapters 2, 3, 4 for more information and service procedures.

Index to Systems

System	To Test	Group
Battery	Engine need not be running	1
Starting system	Engine need not be running	2
Primary electrical system	Engine need not be running	3
Secondary electrical system	Engine need not be running	4
Fuel system	Engine need not be running	5
Engine compression	Engine need not be running	6
Engine vacuum	Engine must be running	7
Secondary electrical system	Engine must be running	8
Valve train	Engine must be running	9
Exhaust system	Engine must be running	10
Cooling system	Engine must be running	11
Engine lubrication	Engine must be running	12

Index to Problems

Problem: Symptom	Begin at Specific Diagnosis, Number
Engine Won't Start:	
Starter doesn't turn	1.1, 2.1
Starter turns, engine doesn't	2.1
Starter turns engine very slowly	1.1, 2.4
Starter turns engine normally	3.1, 4.1
Starter turns engine very quickly	6.1
Engine fires intermittently	4.1
Engine fires consistently	5.1, 6.1
Engine Runs Poorly:	
Hard starting	3.1, 4.1, 5.1, 8.1
Rough idle	4.1, 5.1, 8.1
Stalling	3.1, 4.1, 5.1, 8.1
Engine dies at high speeds	4.1, 5.1
Hesitation (on acceleration from standing stop)	5.1, 8.1
Poor pickup	4.1, 5.1, 8.1
Lack of power	3.1, 4.1, 5.1, 8.1
Backfire through the carburetor	4.1, 8.1, 9.1
Backfire through the exhaust	4.1, 8.1, 9.1
Blue exhaust gases	6.1, 7.1
Black exhaust gases	5.1
Running on (after the ignition is shut off)	3.1, 8.1
Susceptible to moisture	4.1
Engine misfires under load	4.1, 7.1, 8.4, 9.1
Engine misfires at speed	4.1, 8.4
Engine misfires at idle	3.1, 4.1, 5.1, 7.1, 8.4

Sample Section

Test and Procedure	Results and Indications	Proceed to
4.1—Check for spark: Hold each spark plug wire approximately ¼" from ground with gloves or a heavy, dry rag. Crank the engine and observe the spark.	If no spark is evident:	4.2
	If spark is good in some cases:	4.3
	If spark is good in all cases:	4.6

114 TROUBLESHOOTING

Specific Diagnosis

This section is arranged so that following each test, instructions are given to proceed to another, until a problem is diagnosed.

Section 1—Battery

Test and Procedure	Results and Indications	Proceed to
1.1—Inspect the battery visually for case condition (corrosion, cracks) and water level.	If case is cracked, replace battery:	1.4
	If the case is intact, remove corrosion with a solution of baking soda and water (**CAUTION:** *do not get the solution into the battery*), and fill with water:	1.2

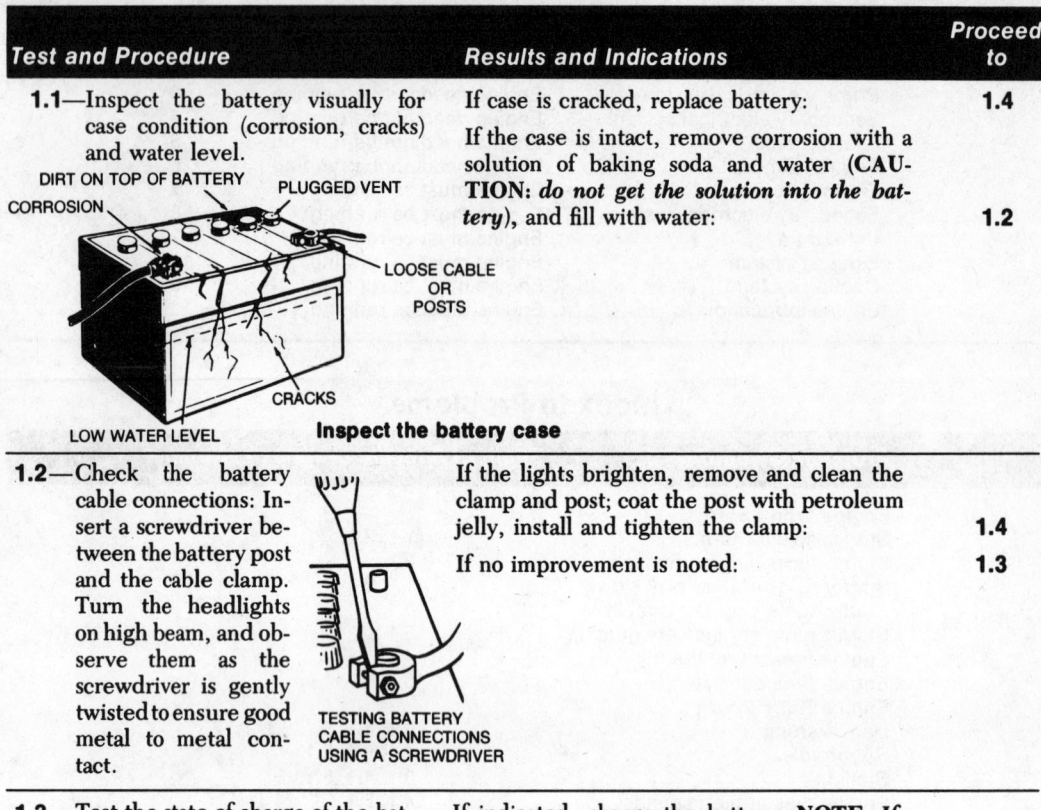

Inspect the battery case

1.2—Check the battery cable connections: Insert a screwdriver between the battery post and the cable clamp. Turn the headlights on high beam, and observe them as the screwdriver is gently twisted to ensure good metal to metal contact.	If the lights brighten, remove and clean the clamp and post; coat the post with petroleum jelly, install and tighten the clamp:	1.4
	If no improvement is noted:	1.3

1.3—Test the state of charge of the battery using an individual cell tester or hydrometer.	If indicated, charge the battery. **NOTE:** *If no obvious reason exists for the low state of charge (i.e., battery age, prolonged storage), proceed to:*	1.4

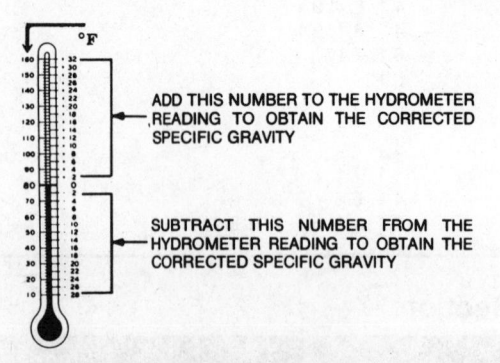

Specific Gravity (@ 80° F.)

Minimum	Battery Charge
1.260	100% Charged
1.230	75% Charged
1.200	50% Charged
1.170	25% Charged
1.140	Very Little Power Left
1.110	Completely Discharged

ADD THIS NUMBER TO THE HYDROMETER READING TO OBTAIN THE CORRECTED SPECIFIC GRAVITY

SUBTRACT THIS NUMBER FROM THE HYDROMETER READING TO OBTAIN THE CORRECTED SPECIFIC GRAVITY

The effects of temperature on battery specific gravity (left) and amount of battery charge in relation to specific gravity (right)

1.4—Visually inspect battery cables for cracking, bad connection to ground, or bad connection to starter.	If necessary, tighten connections or replace the cables:	2.1

Section 2—Starting System
See Chapter 3 for service procedures

Test and Procedure	Results and Indications	Proceed to
Note: Tests in Group 2 are performed with coil high tension lead disconnected to prevent accidental starting.		
2.1—Test the starter motor and solenoid: Connect a jumper from the battery post of the solenoid (or relay) to the starter post of the solenoid (or relay).	If starter turns the engine normally:	2.2
	If the starter buzzes, or turns the engine very slowly:	2.4
	If no response, replace the solenoid (or relay).	3.1
	If the starter turns, but the engine doesn't, ensure that the flywheel ring gear is intact. If the gear is undamaged, replace the starter drive.	3.1
2.2—Determine whether ignition override switches are functioning properly (clutch start switch, neutral safety switch), by connecting a jumper across the switch(es), and turning the ignition switch to "start".	If starter operates, adjust or replace switch:	3.1
	If the starter doesn't operate:	2.3
2.3—Check the ignition switch "start" position: Connect a 12V test lamp or voltmeter between the starter post of the solenoid (or relay) and ground. Turn the ignition switch to the "start" position, and jiggle the key.	If the lamp doesn't light or the meter needle doesn't move when the switch is turned, check the ignition switch for loose connections, cracked insulation, or broken wires. Repair or replace as necessary:	3.1
	If the lamp flickers or needle moves when the key is jiggled, replace the ignition switch.	3.3

Checking the ignition switch "start" position — STARTER RELAY (IF EQUIPPED)

2.4—Remove and bench test the starter, according to specifications in the engine electrical section.	If the starter does not meet specifications, repair or replace as needed:	3.1
	If the starter is operating properly:	2.5
2.5—Determine whether the engine can turn freely: Remove the spark plugs, and check for water in the cylinders. Check for water on the dipstick, or oil in the radiator. Attempt to turn the engine using an 18" flex drive and socket on the crankshaft pulley nut or bolt.	If the engine will turn freely only with the spark plugs out, and hydrostatic lock (water in the cylinders) is ruled out, check valve timing:	9.2
	If engine will not turn freely, and it is known that the clutch and transmission are free, the engine must be disassembled for further evaluation:	Chapter 3

TROUBLESHOOTING

Section 3—Primary Electrical System

Test and Procedure	Results and Indications	Proceed to
3.1—Check the ignition switch "on" position: Connect a jumper wire between the distributor side of the coil and ground, and a 12V test lamp between the switch side of the coil and ground. Remove the high tension lead from the coil. Turn the ignition switch on and jiggle the key.	If the lamp lights:	3.2
	If the lamp flickers when the key is jiggled, replace the ignition switch:	3.3
	If the lamp doesn't light, check for loose or open connections. If none are found, remove the ignition switch and check for continuity. If the switch is faulty, replace it:	3.3

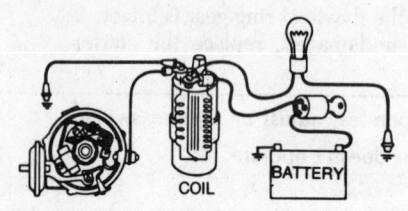

Checking the ignition switch "on" position

3.2—Check the ballast resistor or resistance wire for an open circuit, using an ohmmeter. See Chapter 3 for specific tests.	Replace the resistor or resistance wire if the resistance is zero. NOTE: *Some ignition systems have no ballast resistor.*	3.3

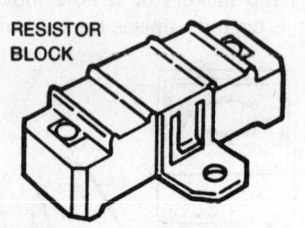

Two types of resistors

3.3—On point-type ignition systems, visually inspect the breaker points for burning, pitting or excessive wear. Gray coloring of the point contact surfaces is normal. Rotate the crankshaft until the contact heel rests on a high point of the distributor cam and adjust the point gap to specifications. On electronic ignition models, remove the distributor cap and visually inspect the armature. Ensure that the armature pin is in place, and that the armature is on tight and rotates when the engine is cranked. Make sure there are no cracks, chips or rounded edges on the armature.	If the breaker points are intact, clean the contact surfaces with fine emery cloth, and adjust the point gap to specifications. If the points are worn, replace them. On electronic systems, replace any parts which appear defective. If condition persists:	3.4

TROUBLESHOOTING 117

Test and Procedure	Results and Indications	Proceed to
3.4—On point-type ignition systems, connect a dwell-meter between the distributor primary lead and ground. Crank the engine and observe the point dwell angle. On electronic ignition systems, conduct a stator (magnetic pickup assembly) test. See Chapter 3.	On point-type systems, adjust the dwell angle if necessary. **NOTE:** *Increasing the point gap decreases the dwell angle and vice-versa.* If the dwell meter shows little or no reading; On electronic ignition systems, if the stator is bad, replace the stator. If the stator is good, proceed to the other tests in Chapter 3.	3.6 3.5

Dwell is a function of point gap

NORMAL DWELL (CLOSE / OPEN)	WIDE GAP — INSUFFICIENT DWELL (SMALL DWELL)	NARROW GAP — EXCESSIVE DWELL (LARGE DWELL)

Test and Procedure	Results and Indications	Proceed to
3.5—On the point-type ignition systems, check the condenser for short: connect an ohmeter across the condenser body and the pigtail lead.	If any reading other than infinite is noted, replace the condenser	3.6

Checking the condenser for short

Test and Procedure	Results and Indications	Proceed to
3.6—Test the coil primary resistance: On point-type ignition systems, connect an ohmmeter across the coil primary terminals, and read the resistance on the low scale. Note whether an external ballast resistor or resistance wire is used. On electronic ignition systems, test the coil primary resistance as in Chapter 3.	Point-type ignition coils utilizing ballast resistors or resistance wires should have approximately 1.0 ohms resistance. Coils with internal resistors should have approximately 4.0 ohms resistance. If values far from the above are noted, replace the coil.	4.1

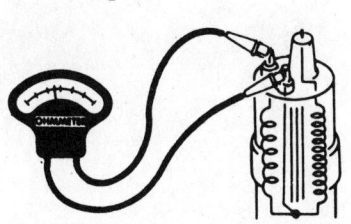

Check the coil primary resistance

118 TROUBLESHOOTING

Section 4—Secondary Electrical System
See Chapters 2–3 for service procedures

Test and Procedure	Results and Indications	Proceed to
4.1—Check for spark: Hold each spark plug wire approximately ¼" from ground with gloves or a heavy, dry rag. Crank the engine, and observe the spark.	If no spark is evident:	4.2
	If spark is good in some cylinders:	4.3
	If spark is good in all cylinders:	4.6

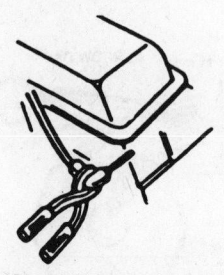

Check for spark at the plugs

4.2—Check for spark at the coil high tension lead: Remove the coil high tension lead from the distributor and position it approximately ¼" from ground. Crank the engine and observe spark. **CAUTION: This test should not be performed on engines equipped with electronic ignition.**	If the spark is good and consistent:	4.3
	If the spark is good but intermittent, test the primary electrical system starting at 3.3:	3.3
	If the spark is weak or non-existent, replace the coil high tension lead, clean and tighten all connections and retest. If no improvement is noted:	4.4
4.3—Visually inspect the distributor cap and rotor for burned or corroded contacts, cracks, carbon tracks, or moisture. Also check the fit of the rotor on the distributor shaft (where applicable).	If moisture is present, dry thoroughly, and retest per 4.1:	4.1
	If burned or excessively corroded contacts, cracks, or carbon tracks are noted, replace the defective part(s) and retest per 4.1:	4.1
	If the rotor and cap appear intact, or are only slightly corroded, clean the contacts thoroughly (including the cap towers and spark plug wire ends) and retest per 4.1:	
	If the spark is good in all cases:	4.6
	If the spark is poor in all cases:	4.5

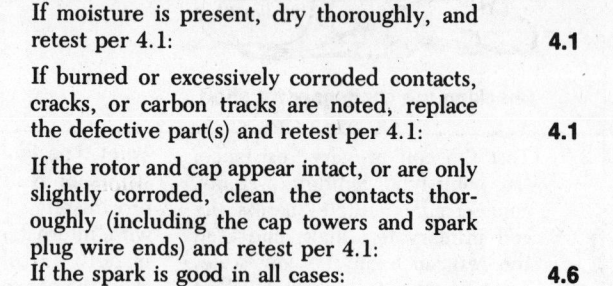

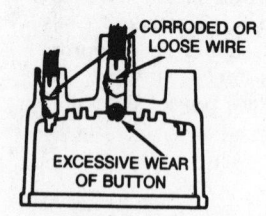

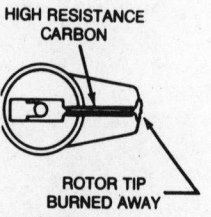

Inspect the distributor cap and rotor

TROUBLESHOOTING

Test and Procedure	Results and Indications	Proceed to
4.4—Check the coil secondary resistance: On point-type systems connect an ohmmeter across the distributor side of the coil and the coil tower. Read the resistance on the high scale of the ohmmeter. On electronic ignition systems, see Chapter 3 for specific tests.	The resistance of a satisfactory coil should be between 4,000 and 10,000 ohms. If resistance is considerably higher (i.e., 40,000 ohms) replace the coil and retest per 4.1. **NOTE:** *This does not apply to high performance coils.*	

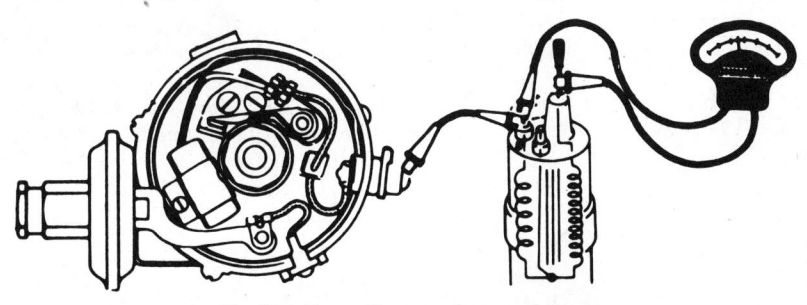

Testing the coil secondary resistance

4.5—Visually inspect the spark plug wires for cracking or brittleness. Ensure that no two wires are positioned so as to cause induction firing (adjacent and parallel). Remove each wire, one by one, and check resistance with an ohmmeter.	Replace any cracked or brittle wires. If any of the wires are defective, replace the entire set. Replace any wires with excessive resistance (over 8000 Ω per foot for suppression wire), and separate any wires that might cause induction firing.	4.6

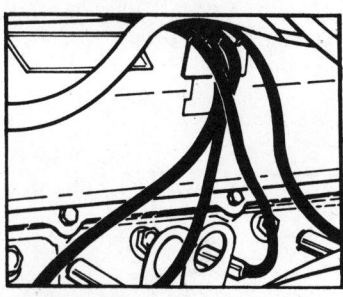

Misfiring can be the result of spark plug leads to adjacent, consecutively firing cylinders running parallel and too close together

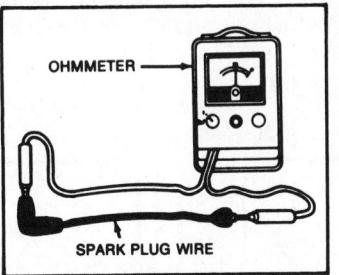

On point-type ignition systems, check the spark plug wires as shown. On electronic ignitions, do not remove the wire from the distributor cap terminal; instead, test through the cap

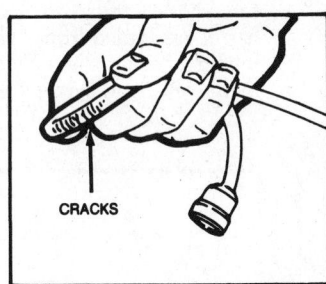

Spark plug wires can be checked visually by bending them in a loop over your finger. This will reveal any cracks, burned or broken insulation. Any wire with cracked insulation should be replaced

4.6—Remove the spark plugs, noting the cylinders from which they were removed, and evaluate according to the color photos in the middle of this book.	See following.	See following.

120 TROUBLESHOOTING

Test and Procedure	Results and Indications	Proceed to
4.7—Examine the location of all the plugs.	The following diagrams illustrate some of the conditions that the location of plugs will reveal.	4.8

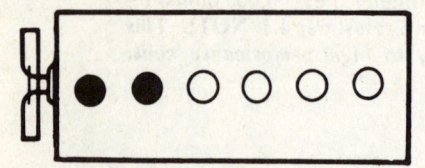

Two adjacent plugs are fouled in a 6-cylinder engine, 4-cylinder engine or either bank of a V-8. This is probably due to a blown head gasket between the two cylinders

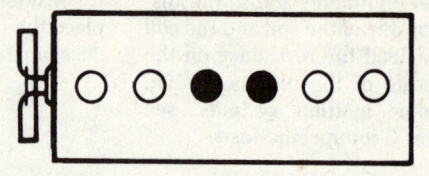

The two center plugs in a 6-cylinder engine are fouled. Raw fuel may be "boiled" out of the carburetor into the intake manifold after the engine is shut-off. Stop-start driving can also foul the center plugs, due to overly rich mixture. Proper float level, a new float needle and seat or use of an insulating spacer may help this problem

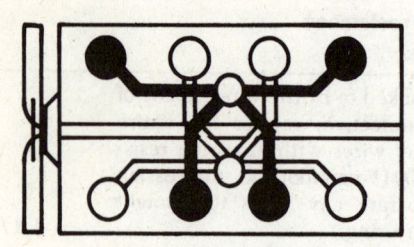

An unbalanced carburetor is indicated. Following the fuel flow on this particular design shows that the cylinders fed by the right-hand barrel are fouled from overly rich mixture, while the cylinders fed by the left-hand barrel are normal

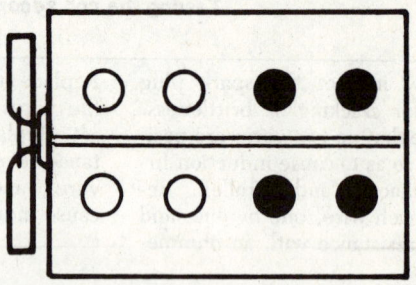

If the four rear plugs are overheated, a cooling system problem is suggested. A thorough cleaning of the cooling system may restore coolant circulation and cure the problem

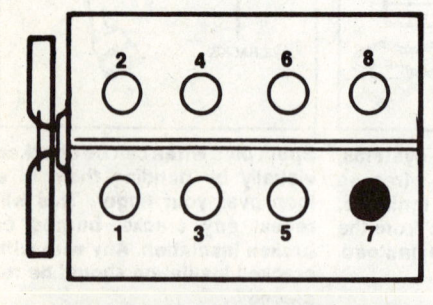

Finding one plug overheated may indicate an intake manifold leak near the affected cylinder. If the overheated plug is the second of two adjacent, consecutively firing plugs, it could be the result of ignition cross-firing. Separating the leads to these two plugs will eliminate cross-fire

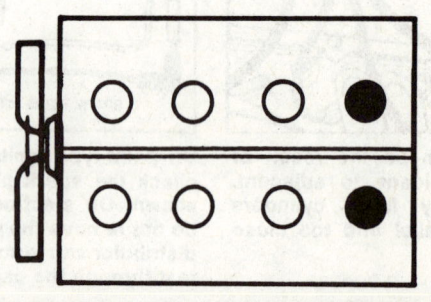

Occasionally, the two rear plugs in large, lightly used V-8's will become oil fouled. High oil consumption and smoky exhaust may also be noticed. It is probably due to plugged oil drain holes in the rear of the cylinder head, causing oil to be sucked in around the valve stems. This usually occurs in the rear cylinders first, because the engine slants that way

TROUBLESHOOTING   121

Test and Procedure	Results and Indications	Proceed to
4.8—Determine the static ignition timing. Using the crankshaft pulley timing marks as a guide, locate top dead center on the compression stroke of the number one cylinder.	The rotor should be pointing toward the No. 1 tower in the distributor cap, and, on electronic ignitions, the armature spoke for that cylinder should be lined up with the stator.	4.8
4.9—Check coil polarity: Connect a voltmeter negative lead to the coil high tension lead, and the positive lead to ground (**NOTE:** *Reverse the hook-up for positive ground systems*). Crank the engine momentarily.	If the voltmeter reads up-scale, the polarity is correct:	5.1
	If the voltmeter reads down-scale, reverse the coil polarity (switch the primary leads):	5.1

Checking coil polarity

Section 5—Fuel System
See Chapter 4 for service procedures

Test and Procedure	Results and Indications	Proceed to
5.1—Determine that the air filter is functioning efficiently: Hold paper elements up to a strong light, and attempt to see light through the filter.	Clean permanent air filters in solvent (or manufacturer's recommendation), and allow to dry. Replace paper elements through which light cannot be seen:	5.2
5.2—Determine whether a flooding condition exists: Flooding is identified by a strong gasoline odor, and excessive gasoline present in the throttle bore(s) of the carburetor.	If flooding is not evident:	5.3
	If flooding is evident, permit the gasoline to dry for a few moments and restart.	
	If flooding doesn't recur:	5.7
	If flooding is persistent:	5.5

If the engine floods repeatedly, check the choke butterfly flap

5.3—Check that fuel is reaching the carburetor: Detach the fuel line at the carburetor inlet. Hold the end of the line in a cup (not styrofoam), and crank the engine.	If fuel flows smoothly:	5.7
	If fuel doesn't flow (**NOTE:** *Make sure that there is fuel in the tank*), or flows erratically:	5.4

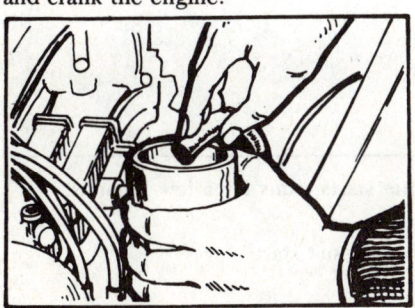

Check the fuel pump by disconnecting the output line (fuel pump-to-carburetor) at the carburetor and operating the starter briefly

122 TROUBLESHOOTING

Test and Procedure	Results and Indications	Proceed to
5.4—Test the fuel pump: Disconnect all fuel lines from the fuel pump. Hold a finger over the input fitting, crank the engine (with electric pump, turn the ignition or pump on); and feel for suction.	If suction is evident, blow out the fuel line to the tank with low pressure compressed air until bubbling is heard from the fuel filler neck. Also blow out the carburetor fuel line (both ends disconnected):	5.7
	If no suction is evident, replace or repair the fuel pump: **NOTE:** *Repeated oil fouling of the spark plugs, or a no-start condition, could be the result of a ruptured vacuum booster pump diaphragm, through which oil or gasoline is being drawn into the intake manifold (where applicable).*	5.7
5.5—Occasionally, small specks of dirt will clog the small jets and orifices in the carburetor. With the engine cold, hold a flat piece of wood or similar material over the carburetor, where possible, and crank the engine.	If the engine starts, but runs roughly the engine is probably not run enough. If the engine won't start:	5.9
5.6—Check the needle and seat: Tap the carburetor in the area of the needle and seat.	If flooding stops, a gasoline additive (e.g., Gumout) will often cure the problem:	5.7
	If flooding continues, check the fuel pump for excessive pressure at the carburetor (according to specifications). If the pressure is normal, the needle and seat must be removed and checked, and/or the float level adjusted:	5.7
5.7—Test the accelerator pump by looking into the throttle bores while operating the throttle.	If the accelerator pump appears to be operating normally:	5.8
	If the accelerator pump is not operating, the pump must be reconditioned. Where possible, service the pump with the carburetor(s) installed on the engine. If necessary, remove the carburetor. Prior to removal:	5.8

Check for gas at the carburetor by looking down the carburetor throat while someone moves the accelerator

5.8—Determine whether the carburetor main fuel system is functioning: Spray a commercial starting fluid into the carburetor while attempting to start the engine.	If the engine starts, runs for a few seconds, and dies:	5.9
	If the engine doesn't start:	6.1

CHILTON'S
AUTO BODY REPAIR TIPS

Tools and Materials • Step-by-Step Illustrated Procedures
How To Repair Dents, Scratches and Rust Holes
Spray Painting and Refinishing Tips

EASY STEP-BY-STEP TIPS FROM PROS

With a little practice, basic body repair procedures can be mastered by any do-it-yourself mechanic. The step-by-step repairs shown here can be applied to almost any type of auto body repair.

TOOLS & MATERIALS

You may already have basic tools, such as hammers and electric drills. Other tools unique to body repair — body hammers, grinding attachments, sanding blocks, dent puller, half-round plastic file and plastic spreaders — are relatively inexpensive and can be obtained wherever auto parts or auto body repair parts are sold. Portable air compressors and paint spray guns can be purchased or rented.

Auto Body Repair Kits

The best and most often used products are available to the do-it-yourselfer in kit form, from major manufacturers of auto body repair products. The same manufacturers also merchandise the individual products for use by pros.

Kits are available to make a wide variety of repairs, including holes, dents and scratches and fiberglass, and offer the advantage of buying the materials you'll need for the job. There is little waste or chance of materials going bad from not being used. Many kits may also contain basic body-working tools such as body files, sanding blocks and spreaders. Check the contents of the kit before buying your tools.

BODY REPAIR TIPS

Safety

Many of the products associated with auto body repair and refinishing contain toxic chemicals. Read all labels before opening containers and store them in a safe place and manner.

• Wear eye protection (safety goggles) when using power tools or when performing any operation that involves the removal of any type of material.

• Wear lung protection (disposable mask or respirator) when grinding, sanding or painting.

Sanding

1 Sand off paint before using a dent puller. When using a non-adhesive sanding disc, cover the back of the disc with an overlapping layer or two of masking tape and trim the edges. The disc will last considerably longer.

2 Use the circular motion of the sanding disc to grind *into* the edge of the repair. Grinding or sanding away from the jagged edge will only tear the sandpaper.

3 Use the palm of your hand flat on the panel to detect high and low spots. Do not use your fingertips. Slide your hand slowly back and forth.

WORKING WITH BODY FILLER

Mixing The Filler

Cleanliness and proper mixing and application are extremely important. Use a clean piece of plastic or glass or a disposable artist's palette to mix body filler.

1 Allow plenty of time and follow directions. No useful purpose will be served by adding more hardener to make it cure (set-up) faster. Less hardener means more curing time, but the mixture dries harder; more hardener means less curing time but a softer mixture.

2 Both the hardener and the filler should be thoroughly kneaded or stirred before mixing. Hardener should be a solid paste and dispense like thin toothpaste. Body filler should be smooth, and free of lumps or thick spots.

Getting the proper amount of hardener in the filler is the trickiest part of preparing the filler. Use the same amount of hardener in cold or warm weather. For contour filler (thick coats), a bead of hardener twice the diameter of the filler is about right. There's about a 15% margin on either side, but, if in doubt use less hardener.

3 Mix the body filler and hardener by wiping across the mixing surface, picking the mixture up and wiping it again. Colder weather requires longer mixing times. Do not mix in a circular motion; this will trap air bubbles which will become holes in the cured filler.

Applying The Filler

1 For best results, filler should not be applied over ¼" thick.

Apply the filler in several coats. Build it up to above the level of the repair surface so that it can be sanded or grated down.

The first coat of filler must be pressed on with a firm wiping motion.

Apply the filler in one direction only. Working the filler back and forth will either pull it off the metal or trap air bubbles.

REPAIRING DENTS

Before you start, take a few minutes to study the damaged area. Try to visualize the shape of the panel before it was damaged. If the damage is on the left fender, look at the right fender and use it as a guide. If there is access to the panel from behind, you can reshape it with a body hammer. If not, you'll have to use a dent puller. Go slowly and work the metal a little at a time. Get the panel as straight as possible before applying filler.

1 This dent is typical of one that can be pulled out or hammered out from behind. Remove the headlight cover, headlight assembly and turn signal housing.

2 Drill a series of holes ½ the size of the end of the dent puller along the stress line. Make some trial pulls and assess the results. If necessary, drill more holes and try again. Do not hurry.

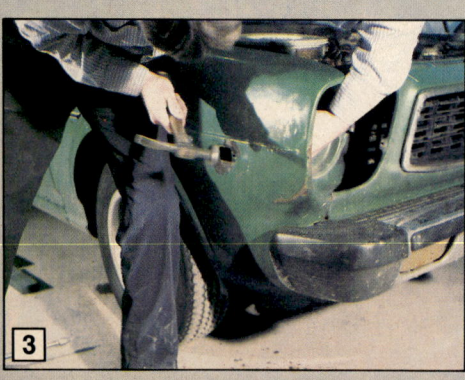

3 If possible, use a body hammer and block to shape the metal back to its original contours. Get the metal back as close to its original shape as possible. Don't depend on body filler to fill dents.

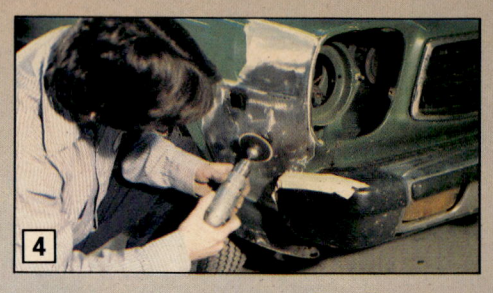

4 Using an 80-grit grinding disc on an electric drill, grind the paint from the surrounding area down to bare metal. Use a new grinding pad to prevent heat buildup that will warp metal.

5 The area should look like this when you're finished grinding. Knock the drill holes in and tape over small openings to keep plastic filler out.

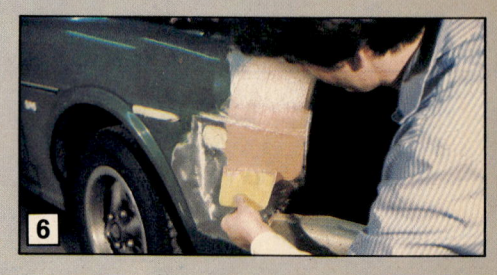

6 Mix the body filler (see Body Repair Tips). Spread the body filler evenly over the entire area (see Body Repair Tips). Be sure to cover the area completely.

7 Let the body filler dry until the surface can just be scratched with your fingernail. Knock the high spots from the body filler with a body file ("Cheesegrater"). Check frequently with the palm of your hand for high and low spots.

8 Check to be sure that trim pieces that will be installed later will fit exactly. Sand the area with 40-grit paper.

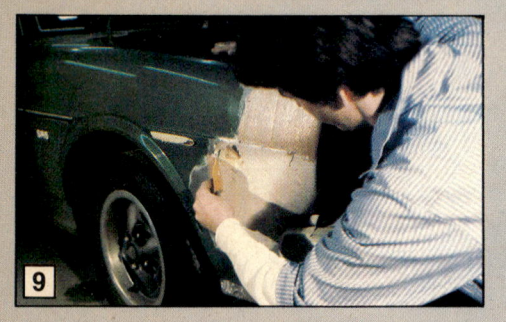

9 If you wind up with low spots, you may have to apply another layer of filler.

10 Knock the high spots off with 40-grit paper. When you are satisfied with the contours of the repair, apply a thin coat of filler to cover pin holes and scratches.

11 Block sand the area with 40-grit paper to a smooth finish. Pay particular attention to body lines and ridges that must be well-defined.

12 Sand the area with 400 paper and then finish with a scuff pad. The finished repair is ready for priming and painting (see Painting Tips).

Materials and photos courtesy of Ritt Jones Auto Body, Prospect Park, PA.

REPAIRING RUST HOLES

There are many ways to repair rust holes. The fiberglass cloth kit shown here is one of the most cost efficient for the owner because it provides a strong repair that resists cracking and moisture and is relatively easy to use. It can be used on large and small holes (with or without backing) and can be applied over contoured areas. Remember, however, that short of replacing an entire panel, no repair is a guarantee that the rust will not return.

1 Remove any trim that will be in the way. Clean away all loose debris. Cut away all the rusted metal. But be sure to leave enough metal to retain the contour or body shape.

2 Grind away all traces of rust with a 24-grit grinding disc. Be sure to grind back 3-4 inches from the edge of the hole down to bare metal and be sure all traces of paint, primer and rust are removed.

3 Block sand the area with 80 or 100 grit sandpaper to get a clear, shiny surface and feathered paint edge. Tap the edges of the hole inward with a ball peen hammer.

4 If you are going to use release film, cut a piece about 2-3" larger than the area you have sanded. Place the film over the repair and mark the sanded area on the film. Avoid any unnecessary wrinkling of the film.

5 Cut 2 pieces of fiberglass matte to match the shape of the repair. One piece should be about 1" smaller than the sanded area and the second piece should be 1" smaller than the first. Mix enough filler and hardener to saturate the fiberglass material (see Body Repair Tips).

6 Lay the release sheet on a flat surface and spread an even layer of filler, large enough to cover the repair. Lay the smaller piece of fiberglass cloth in the center of the sheet and spread another layer of filler over the fiberglass cloth. Repeat the operation for the larger piece of cloth.

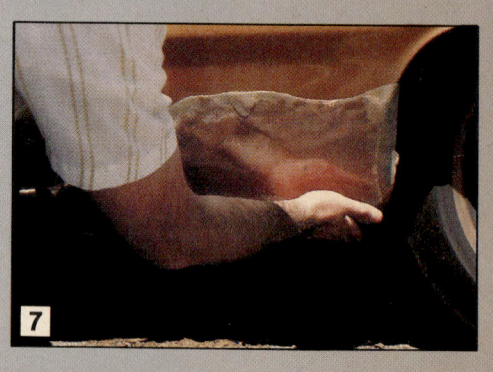

7 Place the repair material over the repair area, with the release film facing outward. Use a spreader and work from the center outward to smooth the material, following the body contours. Be sure to remove all air bubbles.

8 Wait until the repair has dried tack-free and peel off the release sheet. The ideal working temperature is 60°-90° F. Cooler or warmer temperatures or high humidity may require additional curing time. Wait longer, if in doubt.

9 Sand and feather-edge the entire area. The initial sanding can be done with a sanding disc on an electric drill if care is used. Finish the sanding with a block sander. Low spots can be filled with body filler; this may require several applications.

10 When the filler can just be scratched with a fingernail, knock the high spots down with a body file and smooth the entire area with 80-grit. Feather the filled areas into the surrounding areas.

11 When the area is sanded smooth, mix some topcoat and hardener and apply it directly with a spreader. This will give a smooth finish and prevent the glass matte from showing through the paint.

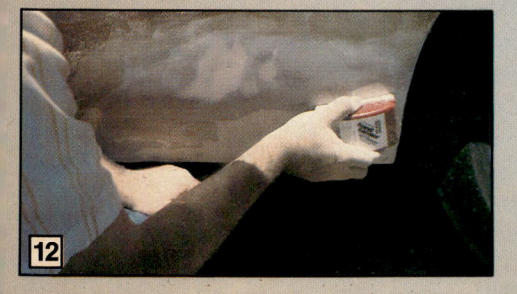

12 Block sand the topcoat smooth with finishing sandpaper (200 grit), and 400 grit. The repair is ready for masking, priming and painting (see Painting Tips).

Materials and photos courtesy Marson Corporation, Chelsea, Massachusetts

PAINTING TIPS

Preparation

1 SANDING — Use a 400 or 600 grit wet or dry sandpaper. Wet-sand the area with a 1/4 sheet of sandpaper soaked in clean water. Keep the paper wet while sanding. Sand the area until the repaired area tapers into the original finish.

2 CLEANING — Wash the area to be painted thoroughly with water and a clean rag. Rinse it thoroughly and wipe the surface dry until you're sure it's completely free of dirt, dust, fingerprints, wax, detergent or other foreign matter.

3 MASKING — Protect any areas you don't want to overspray by covering them with masking tape and newspaper. Be careful not get fingerprints on the area to be painted.

4 PRIMING — All exposed metal should be primed before painting. Primer protects the metal and provides an excellent surface for paint adhesion. When the primer is dry, wet-sand the area again with 600 grit wet-sandpaper. Clean the area again after sanding.

Painting Techniques

Paint applied from either a spray gun or a spray can (for small areas) will provide good results. Experiment on an old piece of metal to get the right combination before you begin painting.

SPRAYING VISCOSITY (SPRAY GUN ONLY) — Paint should be thinned to spraying viscosity according to the directions on the can. Use only the recommended thinner or reducer and the same amount of reduction regardless of temperature.

AIR PRESSURE (SPRAY GUN ONLY) — This is extremely important. Be sure you are using the proper recommended pressure.

TEMPERATURE — The surface to be painted should be approximately the same temperature as the surrounding air. Applying warm paint to a cold surface, or vice versa, will completely upset the paint characteristics.

THICKNESS — Spray with smooth strokes. In general, the thicker the coat of paint, the longer the drying time. Apply several thin coats about 30 seconds apart. The paint should remain wet long enough to flow out and no longer; heavier coats will only produce sags or wrinkles. Spray a light (fog) coat, followed by heavier color coats.

DISTANCE — The ideal spraying distance is 8"-12" from the gun or can to the surface. Shorter distances will produce ripples, while greater distances will result in orange peel, dry film and poor color match and loss of material due to overspray.

OVERLAPPING — The gun or can should be kept at right angles to the surface at all times. Work to a wet edge at an even speed, using a 50% overlap and direct the center of the spray at the lower or nearest edge of the previous stroke.

RUBBING OUT (BLENDING) FRESH PAINT — Let the paint dry thoroughly. Runs or imperfections can be sanded out, primed and repainted.

Don't be in too big a hurry to remove the masking. This only produces paint ridges. When the finish has dried for at least a week, apply a small amount of fine grade rubbing compound with a clean, wet cloth. Use lots of water and blend the new paint with the surrounding area.

WRONG	CORRECT	WRONG
Thin coat. Stroke too fast, not enough overlap, gun too far away.	Medium coat. Proper distance, good stroke, proper overlap.	Heavy coat. Stroke too slow, too much overlap, gun too close.

TROUBLESHOOTING

Test and Procedure	Results and Indications	Proceed to
5.9—Uncommon fuel system malfunctions: See below:	If the problem is solved:	**6.1**
	If the problem remains, remove and recondition the carburetor.	

Condition	Indication	Test	Prevailing Weather Conditions	Remedy
Vapor lock	Engine will not restart shortly after running.	Cool the components of the fuel system until the engine starts. Vapor lock can be cured faster by draping a wet cloth over a mechanical fuel pump.	Hot to very hot	Ensure that the exhaust manifold heat control valve is operating. Check with the vehicle manufacturer for the recommended solution to vapor lock on the model in question.
Carburetor icing	Engine will not idle, stalls at low speeds.	Visually inspect the throttle plate area of the throttle bores for frost.	High humidity, 32–40° F.	Ensure that the exhaust manifold heat control valve is operating, and that the intake manifold heat riser is not blocked.
Water in the fuel	Engine sputters and stalls; may not start.	Pump a small amount of fuel into a glass jar. Allow to stand, and inspect for droplets or a layer of water.	High humidity, extreme temperature changes.	For droplets, use one or two cans of commercial gas line anti-freeze. For a layer of water, the tank must be drained, and the fuel lines blown out with compressed air.

Section 6—Engine Compression
See Chapter 3 for service procedures

6.1—Test engine compression: Remove all spark plugs. Block the throttle wide open. Insert a compression gauge into a spark plug port, crank the engine to obtain the maximum reading, and record.	If compression is within limits on all cylinders:	**7.1**
	If gauge reading is extremely low on all cylinders:	**6.2**
	If gauge reading is low on one or two cylinders: (If gauge readings are identical and low on two or more adjacent cylinders, the head gasket must be replaced.)	**6.2**
	Checking compression	
6.2—Test engine compression (wet): Squirt approximately 30 cc. of engine oil into each cylinder, and retest per 6.1.	If the readings improve, worn or cracked rings or broken pistons are indicated:	**See Chapter 3**
	If the readings do not improve, burned or excessively carboned valves or a jumped timing chain are indicated: NOTE: *A jumped timing chain is often indicated by difficult cranking.*	**7.1**

124 TROUBLESHOOTING

Section 7—Engine Vacuum
See Chapter 3 for service procedures

Test and Procedure	Results and Indications	Proceed to
7.1—Attach a vacuum gauge to the intake manifold beyond the throttle plate. Start the engine, and observe the action of the needle over the range of engine speeds.	See below.	See below

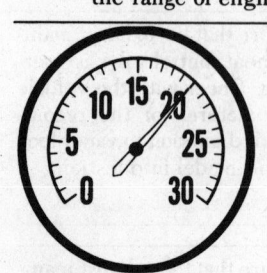

INDICATION: normal engine in good condition

Proceed to: 8.1

Normal engine
Gauge reading: steady, from 17–22 in./Hg.

INDICATION: sticking valves or ignition miss

Proceed to: 9.1, 8.3

Sticking valves
Gauge reading: intermittent fluctuation at idle

INDICATION: late ignition or valve timing, low compression, stuck throttle valve, leaking carburetor or manifold gasket

Proceed to: 6.1

Incorrect valve timing
Gauge reading: low (10–15 in./Hg) but steady

INDICATION: improper carburetor adjustment or minor intake leak.

Proceed to: 7.2

Carburetor requires adjustment
Gauge reading: drifting needle

INDICATION: ignition miss, blown cylinder head gasket, leaking valve or weak valve spring

Proceed to: 8.3, 6.1

Blown head gasket
Gauge reading: needle fluctuates as engine speed increases

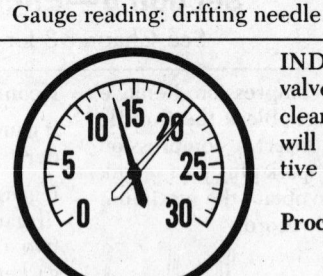

INDICATION: burnt valve or faulty valve clearance. Needle will fall when defective valve operates

Proceed to: 9.1

Burnt or leaking valves
Gauge reading: steady needle, but drops regularly

INDICATION: choked muffler, excessive back pressure in system

Proceed to: 10.1

Clogged exhaust system
Gauge reading: gradual drop in reading at idle

INDICATION: worn valve guides

Proceed to: 9.1

Worn valve guides
Gauge reading: needle vibrates excessively at idle, but steadies as engine speed increases

White pointer = steady gauge hand | Black pointer = fluctuating gauge hand

TROUBLESHOOTING

Test and Procedure	Results and Indications	Proceed to
7.2—Attach a vacuum gauge per 7.1, and test for an intake manifold leak. Squirt a small amount of oil around the intake manifold gaskets, carburetor gaskets, plugs and fittings. Observe the action of the vacuum gauge.	If the reading improves, replace the indicated gasket, or seal the indicated fitting or plug: If the reading remains low:	8.1 7.3
7.3—Test all vacuum hoses and accessories for leaks as described in 7.2. Also check the carburetor body (dashpots, automatic choke mechanism, throttle shafts) for leaks in the same manner.	If the reading improves, service or replace the offending part(s): If the reading remains low:	8.1 6.1

Section 8—Secondary Electrical System
See Chapter 2 for service procedures

Test and Procedure	Results and Indications	Proceed to
8.1—Remove the distributor cap and check to make sure that the rotor turns when the engine is cranked. Visually inspect the distributor components.	Clean, tighten or replace any components which appear defective.	8.2
8.2—Connect a timing light (per manufacturer's recommendation) and check the dynamic ignition timing. Disconnect and plug the vacuum hose(s) to the distributor if specified, start the engine, and observe the timing marks at the specified engine speed.	If the timing is not correct, adjust to specifications by rotating the distributor in the engine: (Advance timing by rotating distributor opposite normal direction of rotor rotation, retard timing by rotating distributor in same direction as rotor rotation.)	8.3
8.3—Check the operation of the distributor advance mechanism(s): To test the mechanical advance, disconnect the vacuum lines from the distributor advance unit and observe the timing marks with a timing light as the engine speed is increased from idle. If the mark moves smoothly, without hesitation, it may be assumed that the mechanical advance is functioning properly. To test vacuum advance and/or retard systems, alternately crimp and release the vacuum line, and observe the timing mark for movement. If movement is noted, the system is operating.	If the systems are functioning: If the systems are not functioning, remove the distributor, and test on a distributor tester:	8.4 8.4
8.4—Locate an ignition miss: With the engine running, remove each spark plug wire, one at a time, until one is found that doesn't cause the engine to roughen and slow down.	When the missing cylinder is identified:	4.1

126 TROUBLESHOOTING

Section 9—Valve Train
See Chapter 3 for service procedures

Test and Procedure	Results and Indications	Proceed to
9.1—Evaluate the valve train: Remove the valve cover, and ensure that the valves are adjusted to specifications. A mechanic's stethoscope may be used to aid in the diagnosis of the valve train. By pushing the probe on or near push rods or rockers, valve noise often can be isolated. A timing light also may be used to diagnose valve problems. Connect the light according to manufacturer's recommendations, and start the engine. Vary the firing moment of the light by increasing the engine speed (and therefore the ignition advance), and moving the trigger from cylinder to cylinder. Observe the movement of each valve.	Sticking valves or erratic valve train motion can be observed with the timing light. The cylinder head must be disassembled for repairs.	**See Chapter 3**
9.2—Check the valve timing: Locate top dead center of the No. 1 piston, and install a degree wheel or tape on the crankshaft pulley or damper with zero corresponding to an index mark on the engine. Rotate the crankshaft in its direction of rotation, and observe the opening of the No. 1 cylinder intake valve. The opening should correspond with the correct mark on the degree wheel according to specifications.	If the timing is not correct, the timing cover must be removed for further investigation.	**See Chapter 3**

Section 10—Exhaust System

Test and Procedure	Results and Indications	Proceed to
10.1—Determine whether the exhaust manifold heat control valve is operating: Operate the valve by hand to determine whether it is free to move. If the valve is free, run the engine to operating temperature and observe the action of the valve, to ensure that it is opening.	If the valve sticks, spray it with a suitable solvent, open and close the valve to free it, and retest. If the valve functions properly: If the valve does not free, or does not operate, replace the valve:	**10.2** **10.2**
10.2—Ensure that there are no exhaust restrictions: Visually inspect the exhaust system for kinks, dents, or crushing. Also note that gases are flowing freely from the tailpipe at all engine speeds, indicating no restriction in the muffler or resonator.	Replace any damaged portion of the system:	**11.1**

TROUBLESHOOTING

Section 11—Cooling System
See Chapter 3 for service procedures

Test and Procedure	Results and Indications	Proceed to
11.1—Visually inspect the fan belt for glazing, cracks, and fraying, and replace if necessary. Tighten the belt so that the longest span has approximately ½″ play at its midpoint under thumb pressure (see Chapter 1).	Replace or tighten the fan belt as necessary:	11.2

Checking belt tension

11.2—Check the fluid level of the cooling system.	If full or slightly low, fill as necessary:	11.5
	If extremely low:	11.3
11.3—Visually inspect the external portions of the cooling system (radiator, radiator hoses, thermostat elbow, water pump seals, heater hoses, etc.) for leaks. If none are found, pressurize the cooling system to 14–15 psi.	If cooling system holds the pressure:	11.5
	If cooling system loses pressure rapidly, reinspect external parts of the system for leaks under pressure. If none are found, check dipstick for coolant in crankcase. If no coolant is present, but pressure loss continues:	11.4
	If coolant is evident in crankcase, remove cylinder head(s), and check gasket(s). If gaskets are intact, block and cylinder head(s) should be checked for cracks or holes. If the gasket(s) is blown, replace, and purge the crankcase of coolant:	12.6
	NOTE: *Occasionally, due to atmospheric and driving conditions, condensation of water can occur in the crankcase. This causes the oil to appear milky white. To remedy, run the engine until hot, and change the oil and oil filter.*	
11.4—Check for combustion leaks into the cooling system: Pressurize the cooling system as above. Start the engine, and observe the pressure gauge. If the needle fluctuates, remove each spark plug wire, one at a time, noting which cylinder(s) reduce or eliminate the fluctuation.	Cylinders which reduce or eliminate the fluctuation, when the spark plug wire is removed, are leaking into the cooling system. Replace the head gasket on the affected cylinder bank(s).	

Pressurizing the cooling system

128 TROUBLESHOOTING

Test and Procedure	Results and Indications	Proceed to
11.5—Check the radiator pressure cap: Attach a radiator pressure tester to the radiator cap (wet the seal prior to installation). Quickly pump up the pressure, noting the point at which the cap releases.	If the cap releases within ± 1 psi of the specified rating, it is operating properly:	11.6
	If the cap releases at more than ± 1 psi of the specified rating, it should be replaced:	11.6

Checking radiator pressure cap

Test and Procedure	Results and Indications	Proceed to
11.6—Test the thermostat: Start the engine cold, remove the radiator cap, and insert a thermometer into the radiator. Allow the engine to idle. After a short while, there will be a sudden, rapid increase in coolant temperature. The temperature at which this sharp rise stops is the thermostat opening temperature.	If the thermostat opens at or about the specified temperature:	11.7
	If the temperature doesn't increase: (If the temperature increases slowly and gradually, replace the thermostat.)	11.7
11.7—Check the water pump: Remove the thermostat elbow and the thermostat, disconnect the coil high tension lead (to prevent starting), and crank the engine momentarily.	If coolant flows, replace the thermostat and retest per 11.6:	11.6
	If coolant doesn't flow, reverse flush the cooling system to alleviate any blockage that might exist. If system is not blocked, and coolant will not flow, replace the water pump.	

Section 12—Lubrication
See Chapter 3 for service procedures

Test and Procedure	Results and Indications	Proceed to
12.1—Check the oil pressure gauge or warning light: If the gauge shows low pressure, or the light is on for no obvious reason, remove the oil pressure sender. Install an accurate oil pressure gauge and run the engine momentarily.	If oil pressure builds normally, run engine for a few moments to determine that it is functioning normally, and replace the sender.	—
	If the pressure remains low:	12.2
	If the pressure surges:	12.3
	If the oil pressure is zero:	12.3
12.2—Visually inspect the oil: If the oil is watery or very thin, milky, or foamy, replace the oil and oil filter.	If the oil is normal:	12.3
	If after replacing oil the pressure remains low:	12.3
	If after replacing oil the pressure becomes normal:	—

TROUBLESHOOTING

Test and Procedure	Results and Indications	Proceed to
12.3—Inspect the oil pressure relief valve and spring, to ensure that it is not sticking or stuck. Remove and thoroughly clean the valve, spring, and the valve body.	If the oil pressure improves: If no improvement is noted:	— 12.4
12.4—Check to ensure that the oil pump is not cavitating (sucking air instead of oil): See that the crankcase is neither over nor underfull, and that the pickup in the sump is in the proper position and free from sludge.	Fill or drain the crankcase to the proper capacity, and clean the pickup screen in solvent if necessary. If no improvement is noted:	12.5
12.5—Inspect the oil pump drive and the oil pump:	If the pump drive or the oil pump appear to be defective, service as necessary and retest per 12.1:	12.1
	If the pump drive and pump appear to be operating normally, the engine should be disassembled to determine where blockage exists:	See Chapter 3
12.6—Purge the engine of ethylene glycol coolant: Completely drain the crankcase and the oil filter. Obtain a commercial butyl cellosolve base solvent, designated for this purpose, and follow the instructions precisely. Following this, install a new oil filter and refill the crankcase with the proper weight oil. The next oil and filter change should follow shortly thereafter (1000 miles).		

TROUBLESHOOTING EMISSION CONTROL SYSTEMS

See Chapter 4 for procedures applicable to individual emission control systems used on specific combinations of engine/transmission/model.

TROUBLESHOOTING THE CARBURETOR
See Chapter 4 for service procedures

Carburetor problems cannot be effectively isolated unless all other engine systems (particularly ignition and emission) are functioning properly and the engine is properly tuned.

TROUBLESHOOTING

Condition	Possible Cause
Engine cranks, but does not start	1. Improper starting procedure 2. No fuel in tank 3. Clogged fuel line or filter 4. Defective fuel pump 5. Choke valve not closing properly 6. Engine flooded 7. Choke valve not unloading 8. Throttle linkage not making full travel 9. Stuck needle or float 10. Leaking float needle or seat 11. Improper float adjustment
Engine stalls	1. Improperly adjusted idle speed or mixture **Engine hot** 2. Improperly adjusted dashpot 3. Defective or improperly adjusted solenoid 4. Incorrect fuel level in fuel bowl 5. Fuel pump pressure too high 6. Leaking float needle seat 7. Secondary throttle valve stuck open 8. Air or fuel leaks 9. Idle air bleeds plugged or missing 10. Idle passages plugged **Engine Cold** 11. Incorrectly adjusted choke 12. Improperly adjusted fast idle speed 13. Air leaks 14. Plugged idle or idle air passages 15. Stuck choke valve or binding linkage 16. Stuck secondary throttle valves 17. Engine flooding—high fuel level 18. Leaking or misaligned float
Engine hesitates on acceleration	1. Clogged fuel filter 2. Leaking fuel pump diaphragm 3. Low fuel pump pressure 4. Secondary throttle valves stuck, bent or misadjusted 5. Sticking or binding air valve 6. Defective accelerator pump 7. Vacuum leaks 8. Clogged air filter 9. Incorrect choke adjustment (engine cold)
Engine feels sluggish or flat on acceleration	1. Improperly adjusted idle speed or mixture 2. Clogged fuel filter 3. Defective accelerator pump 4. Dirty, plugged or incorrect main metering jets 5. Bent or sticking main metering rods 6. Sticking throttle valves 7. Stuck heat riser 8. Binding or stuck air valve 9. Dirty, plugged or incorrect secondary jets 10. Bent or sticking secondary metering rods. 11. Throttle body or manifold heat passages plugged 12. Improperly adjusted choke or choke vacuum break.
Carburetor floods	1. Defective fuel pump. Pressure too high. 2. Stuck choke valve 3. Dirty, worn or damaged float or needle valve/seat 4. Incorrect float/fuel level 5. Leaking float bowl

TROUBLESHOOTING

Condition	Possible Cause
Engine idles roughly and stalls	1. Incorrect idle speed 2. Clogged fuel filter 3. Dirt in fuel system or carburetor 4. Loose carburetor screws or attaching bolts 5. Broken carburetor gaskets 6. Air leaks 7. Dirty carburetor 8. Worn idle mixture needles 9. Throttle valves stuck open 10. Incorrectly adjusted float or fuel level 11. Clogged air filter
Engine runs unevenly or surges	1. Defective fuel pump 2. Dirty or clogged fuel filter 3. Plugged, loose or incorrect main metering jets or rods 4. Air leaks 5. Bent or sticking main metering rods 6. Stuck power piston 7. Incorrect float adjustment 8. Incorrect idle speed or mixture 9. Dirty or plugged idle system passages 10. Hard, brittle or broken gaskets 11. Loose attaching or mounting screws 12. Stuck or misaligned secondary throttle valves
Poor fuel economy	1. Poor driving habits 2. Stuck choke valve 3. Binding choke linkage 4. Stuck heat riser 5. Incorrect idle mixture 6. Defective accelerator pump 7. Air leaks 8. Plugged, loose or incorrect main metering jets 9. Improperly adjusted float or fuel level 10. Bent, misaligned or fuel-clogged float 11. Leaking float needle seat 12. Fuel leak 13. Accelerator pump discharge ball not seating properly 14. Incorrect main jets
Engine lacks high speed performance or power	1. Incorrect throttle linkage adjustment 2. Stuck or binding power piston 3. Defective accelerator pump 4. Air leaks 5. Incorrect float setting or fuel level 6. Dirty, plugged, worn or incorrect main metering jets or rods 7. Binding or sticking air valve 8. Brittle or cracked gaskets 9. Bent, incorrect or improperly adjusted secondary metering rods 10. Clogged fuel filter 11. Clogged air filter 12. Defective fuel pump

TROUBLESHOOTING FUEL INJECTION PROBLEMS

Each fuel injection system has its own unique components and test procedures, for which it is impossible to generalize. Refer to Chapter 4 of this Repair & Tune-Up Guide for specific test and repair procedures, if the vehicle is equipped with fuel injection.

TROUBLESHOOTING ELECTRICAL PROBLEMS
See Chapter 5 for service procedures

For any electrical system to operate, it must make a complete circuit. This simply means that the power flow from the battery must make a complete circle. When an electrical component is operating, power flows from the battery to the component, passes through the component causing it to perform its function (lighting a light bulb), and then returns to the battery through the ground of the circuit. This ground is usually (but not always) the metal part of the car or truck on which the electrical component is mounted.

Perhaps the easiest way to visualize this is to think of connecting a light bulb with two wires attached to it to the battery. If one of the two wires attached to the light bulb were attached to the negative post of the battery and the other were attached to the positive post of the battery, you would have a complete circuit. Current from the battery would flow to the light bulb, causing it to light, and return to the negative post of the battery.

The normal automotive circuit differs from this simple example in two ways. First, instead of having a return wire from the bulb to the battery, the light bulb returns the current to the battery through the chassis of the vehicle. Since the negative battery cable is attached to the chassis and the chassis is made of electrically conductive metal, the chassis of the vehicle can serve as a ground wire to complete the circuit. Secondly, most automotive circuits contain switches to turn components on and off as required.

Every complete circuit from a power source must include a component which is using the power from the power source. If you were to disconnect the light bulb from the wires and touch the two wires together (don't do this) the power supply wire to the component would be grounded before the normal ground connection for the circuit.

Because grounding a wire from a power source makes a complete circuit—less the required component to use the power—this phenomenon is called a short circuit. Common causes are: broken insulation (exposing the metal wire to a metal part of the car or truck), or a shorted switch.

Some electrical components which require a large amount of current to operate also have a relay in their circuit. Since these circuits carry a large amount of current, the thickness of the wire in the circuit (gauge size) is also greater. If this large wire were connected from the component to the control switch on the instrument panel, and then back to the component, a voltage drop would occur in the circuit. To prevent this potential drop in voltage, an electromagnetic switch (relay) is used. The large wires in the circuit are connected from the battery to one side of the relay, and from the opposite side of the relay to the component. The relay is normally open, preventing current from passing through the circuit. An additional, smaller, wire is connected from the relay to the control switch for the circuit. When the control switch is turned on, it grounds the smaller wire from the relay and completes the circuit. This closes the relay and allows current to flow from the battery to the component. The horn, headlight, and starter circuits are three which use relays.

It is possible for larger surges of current to pass through the electrical system of your car or truck. If this surge of current were to reach an electrical component, it could burn it out. To prevent this, fuses, circuit breakers or fusible links are connected into the current supply wires of most of the major electrical systems. When an electrical current of excessive power passes through the component's fuse, the fuse blows out and breaks the circuit, saving the component from destruction.

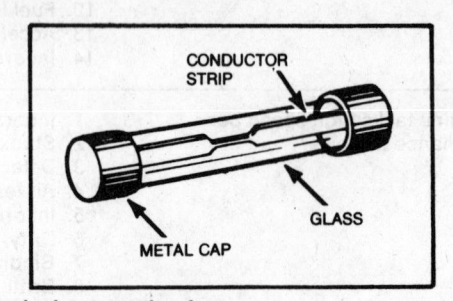

Typical automotive fuse

A circuit breaker is basically a self-repairing fuse. The circuit breaker opens the circuit the same way a fuse does. However, when either the short is removed from the circuit or the surge subsides, the circuit breaker resets itself and does not have to be replaced as a fuse does.

A fuse link is a wire that acts as a fuse. It is normally connected between the starter relay and the main wiring harness. This connection is usually under the hood. The fuse link (if installed) protects all the

TROUBLESHOOTING

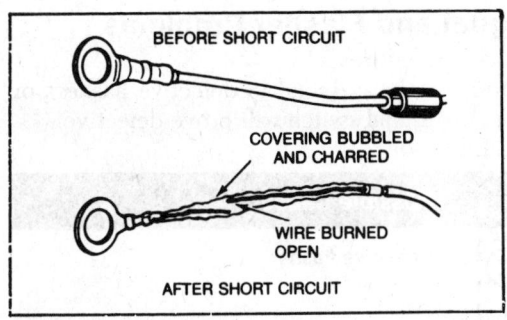

Most fusible links show a charred, melted insulation when they burn out

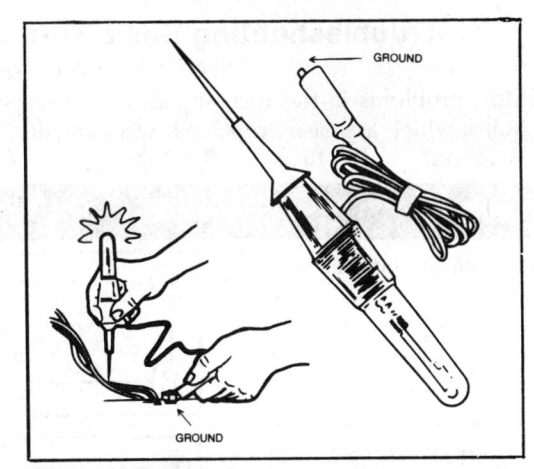

The test light will show the presence of current when touched to a hot wire and grounded at the other end

chassis electrical components, and is the probable cause of trouble when none of the electrical components function, unless the battery is disconnected or dead.

Electrical problems generally fall into one of three areas:

1. The component that is not functioning is not receiving current.
2. The component itself is not functioning.
3. The component is not properly grounded.

The electrical system can be checked with a test light and a jumper wire. A test light is a device that looks like a pointed screwdriver with a wire attached to it and has a light bulb in its handle. A jumper wire is a piece of insulated wire with an alligator clip attached to each end.

If a component is not working, you must follow a systematic plan to determine which of the three causes is the villain.

1. Turn on the switch that controls the inoperable component.
2. Disconnect the power supply wire from the component.
3. Attach the ground wire on the test light to a good metal ground.
4. Touch the probe end of the test light to the end of the power supply wire that was disconnected from the component. If the component is receiving current, the test light will go on.

NOTE: *Some components work only when the ignition switch is turned on.*

If the test light does not go on, then the problem is in the circuit between the battery and the component. This includes all the switches, fuses, and relays in the system. Follow the wire that runs back to the battery. The problem is an open circuit between the battery and the component. If the fuse is blown and, when replaced, immediately blows again, there is a short circuit in the system which must be located and repaired. If there is a switch in the system, bypass it with a jumper wire. This is done by connecting one end of the jumper wire to the power supply wire into the switch and the other end of the jumper wire to the wire coming out of the switch. If the test light lights with the jumper wire installed, the switch or whatever was bypassed is defective.

NOTE: *Never substitute the jumper wire for the component, since it is required to use the power from the power source.*

5. If the bulb in the test light goes on, then the current is getting to the component that is not working. This eliminates the first of the three possible causes. Connect the power supply wire and connect a jumper wire from the component to a good metal ground. Do this with the switch which controls the component turned on, and also the ignition switch turned on if it is required for the component to work. If the component works with the jumper wire installed, then it has a bad ground. This is usually caused by the metal area on which the component mounts to the chassis being coated with some type of foreign matter.

6. If neither test located the source of the trouble, then the component itself is defective. Remember that for any electrical system to work, all connections must be clean and tight.

134 TROUBLESHOOTING

Troubleshooting Basic Turn Signal and Flasher Problems
See Chapter 5 for service procedures

Most problems in the turn signals or flasher system can be reduced to defective flashers or bulbs, which are easily replaced. Occasionally, the turn signal switch will prove defective.

F = Front   R = Rear   ● = Lights off   ○ = Lights on

Condition		Possible Cause
Turn signals light, but do not flash	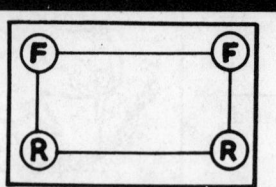	Defective flasher
No turn signals light on either side	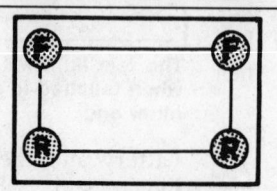	Blown fuse. Replace if defective. Defective flasher. Check by substitution. Open circuit, short circuit or poor ground.
Both turn signals on one side don't work	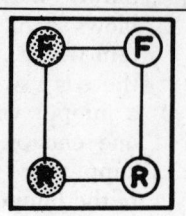	Bad bulbs. Bad ground in both (or either) housings.
One turn signal light on one side doesn't work	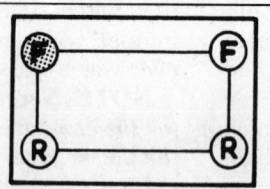	Defective bulb. Corrosion in socket. Clean contacts. Poor ground at socket.
Turn signal flashes too fast or too slowly	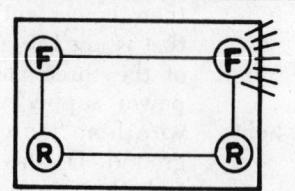	Check any bulb on the side flashing too fast. A heavy-duty bulb is probably installed in place of a regular bulb. Check the bulb flashing too slowly. A standard bulb was probably installed in place of a heavy-duty bulb. Loose connections or corrosion at the bulb socket.
Indicator lights don't work in either direction		Check if the turn signals are working. Check the dash indicator lights. Check the flasher by substitution.
One indicator light doesn't light		On systems with one dash indicator: See if the lights work on the same side. Often the filaments have been reversed in systems combining stoplights with taillights and turn signals. Check the flasher by substitution. On systems with two indicators: Check the bulbs on the same side. Check the indicator light bulb. Check the flasher by substitution.

TROUBLESHOOTING 135

Troubleshooting Lighting Problems
See Chapter 5 for service procedures

Condition	Possible Cause
One or more lights don't work, but others do	1. Defective bulb(s) 2. Blown fuse(s) 3. Dirty fuse clips or light sockets 4. Poor ground circuit
Lights burn out quickly	1. Incorrect voltage regulator setting or defective regulator 2. Poor battery/alternator connections
Lights go dim	1. Low/discharged battery 2. Alternator not charging 3. Corroded sockets or connections 4. Low voltage output
Lights flicker	1. Loose connection 2. Poor ground. (Run ground wire from light housing to frame) 3. Circuit breaker operating (short circuit)
Lights "flare"—Some flare is normal on acceleration—If excessive, see "Lights Burn Out Quickly"	High voltage setting
Lights glare—approaching drivers are blinded	1. Lights adjusted too high 2. Rear springs or shocks sagging 3. Rear tires soft

Troubleshooting Dash Gauge Problems

Most problems can be traced to a defective sending unit or faulty wiring. Occasionally, the gauge itself is at fault. See Chapter 5 for service procedures.

Condition	Possible Cause

COOLANT TEMPERATURE GAUGE

Condition	Possible Cause
Gauge reads erratically or not at all	1. Loose or dirty connections 2. Defective sending unit. 3. Defective gauge. To test a bi-metal gauge, remove the wire from the sending unit. Ground the wire for an instant. If the gauge registers, replace the sending unit. To test a magnetic gauge, disconnect the wire at the sending unit. With ignition ON gauge should register COLD. Ground the wire; gauge should register HOT.

AMMETER GAUGE—TURN HEADLIGHTS ON (DO NOT START ENGINE). NOTE REACTION

Condition	Possible Cause
Ammeter shows charge Ammeter shows discharge Ammeter does not move	1. Connections reversed on gauge 2. Ammeter is OK 3. Loose connections or faulty wiring 4. Defective gauge

136 TROUBLESHOOTING

Condition	Possible Cause

OIL PRESSURE GAUGE

Gauge does not register or is inaccurate	1. On mechanical gauge, Bourdon tube may be bent or kinked. 2. Low oil pressure. Remove sending unit. Idle the engine briefly. If no oil flows from sending unit hole, problem is in engine. 3. Defective gauge. Remove the wire from the sending unit and ground it for an instant with the ignition ON. A good gauge will go to the top of the scale. 4. Defective wiring. Check the wiring to the gauge. If it's OK and the gauge doesn't register when grounded, replace the gauge. 5. Defective sending unit.

ALL GAUGES

All gauges do not operate All gauges read low or erratically All gauges pegged	1. Blown fuse 2. Defective instrument regulator 3. Defective or dirty instrument voltage regulator 4. Loss of ground between instrument voltage regulator and frame 5. Defective instrument regulator

WARNING LIGHTS

Light(s) do not come on when ignition is ON, but engine is not started	1. Defective bulb 2. Defective wire 3. Defective sending unit. Disconnect the wire from the sending unit and ground it. Replace the sending unit if the light comes on with the ignition ON.
Light comes on with engine running	4. Problem in individual system 5. Defective sending unit

Troubleshooting Clutch Problems

It is false economy to replace individual clutch components. The pressure plate, clutch plate and throwout bearing should be replaced as a set, and the flywheel face inspected, whenever the clutch is overhauled. See Chapter 6 for service procedures.

Condition	Possible Cause
Clutch chatter	1. Grease on driven plate (disc) facing 2. Binding clutch linkage or cable 3. Loose, damaged facings on driven plate (disc) 4. Engine mounts loose 5. Incorrect height adjustment of pressure plate release levers 6. Clutch housing or housing to transmission adapter misalignment 7. Loose driven plate hub
Clutch grabbing	1. Oil, grease on driven plate (disc) facing 2. Broken pressure plate 3. Warped or binding driven plate. Driven plate binding on clutch shaft
Clutch slips	1. Lack of lubrication in clutch linkage or cable (linkage or cable binds, causes incomplete engagement) 2. Incorrect pedal, or linkage adjustment 3. Broken pressure plate springs 4. Weak pressure plate springs 5. Grease on driven plate facings (disc)

Troubleshooting Clutch Problems (cont.)

Condition	Possible Cause
Incomplete clutch release	1. Incorrect pedal or linkage adjustment or linkage or cable binding 2. Incorrect height adjustment on pressure plate release levers 3. Loose, broken facings on driven plate (disc) 4. Bent, dished, warped driven plate caused by overheating
Grinding, whirring grating noise when pedal is depressed	1. Worn or defective throwout bearing 2. Starter drive teeth contacting flywheel ring gear teeth. Look for milled or polished teeth on ring gear.
Squeal, howl, trumpeting noise when pedal is being released (occurs during first inch to inch and one-half of pedal travel)	Pilot bushing worn or lack of lubricant. If bushing appears OK, polish bushing with emery cloth, soak lube wick in oil, lube bushing with oil, apply film of chassis grease to clutch shaft pilot hub, reassemble. NOTE: Bushing wear may be due to misalignment of clutch housing or housing to transmission adapter
Vibration or clutch pedal pulsation with clutch disengaged (pedal fully depressed)	1. Worn or defective engine transmission mounts 2. Flywheel run out. (Flywheel run out at face not to exceed 0.005") 3. Damaged or defective clutch components

Troubleshooting Manual Transmission Problems
See Chapter 6 for service procedures

Condition	Possible Cause
Transmission jumps out of gear	1. Misalignment of transmission case or clutch housing. 2. Worn pilot bearing in crankshaft. 3. Bent transmission shaft. 4. Worn high speed sliding gear. 5. Worn teeth or end-play in clutch shaft. 6. Insufficient spring tension on shifter rail plunger. 7. Bent or loose shifter fork. 8. Gears not engaging completely. 9. Loose or worn bearings on clutch shaft or mainshaft. 10. Worn gear teeth. 11. Worn or damaged detent balls.
Transmission sticks in gear	1. Clutch not releasing fully. 2. Burred or battered teeth on clutch shaft, or sliding sleeve. 3. Burred or battered transmission mainshaft. 4. Frozen synchronizing clutch. 5. Stuck shifter rail plunger. 6. Gearshift lever twisting and binding shifter rail. 7. Battered teeth on high speed sliding gear or on sleeve. 8. Improper lubrication, or lack of lubrication. 9. Corroded transmission parts. 10. Defective mainshaft pilot bearing. 11. Locked gear bearings will give same effect as stuck in gear.
Transmission gears will not synchronize	1. Binding pilot bearing on mainshaft, will synchronize in high gear only. 2. Clutch not releasing fully. 3. Detent spring weak or broken. 4. Weak or broken springs under balls in sliding gear sleeve. 5. Binding bearing on clutch shaft, or binding countershaft. 6. Binding pilot bearing in crankshaft. 7. Badly worn gear teeth. 8. Improper lubrication. 9. Constant mesh gear not turning freely on transmission mainshaft. Will synchronize in that gear only.

TROUBLESHOOTING

Condition	Possible Cause
Gears spinning when shifting into gear from neutral	1. Clutch not releasing fully. 2. In some cases an extremely light lubricant in transmission will cause gears to continue to spin for a short time after clutch is released. 3. Binding pilot bearing in crankshaft.
Transmission noisy in all gears	1. Insufficient lubricant, or improper lubricant. 2. Worn countergear bearings. 3. Worn or damaged main drive gear or countergear. 4. Damaged main drive gear or mainshaft bearings. 5. Worn or damaged countergear anti-lash plate.
Transmission noisy in neutral only	1. Damaged main drive gear bearing. 2. Damaged or loose mainshaft pilot bearing. 3. Worn or damaged countergear anti-lash plate. 4. Worn countergear bearings.
Transmission noisy in one gear only	1. Damaged or worn constant mesh gears. 2. Worn or damaged countergear bearings. 3. Damaged or worn synchronizer.
Transmission noisy in reverse only	1. Worn or damaged reverse idler gear or idler bushing. 2. Worn or damaged mainshaft reverse gear. 3. Worn or damaged reverse countergear. 4. Damaged shift mechanism.

TROUBLESHOOTING AUTOMATIC TRANSMISSION PROBLEMS

Keeping alert to changes in the operating characteristics of the transmission (changing shift points, noises, etc.) can prevent small problems from becoming large ones. If the problem cannot be traced to loose bolts, fluid level, misadjusted linkage, clogged filters or similar problems, you should probably seek professional service.

Transmission Fluid Indications

The appearance and odor of the transmission fluid can give valuable clues to the overall condition of the transmission. Always note the appearance of the fluid when you check the fluid level or change the fluid. Rub a small amount of fluid between your fingers to feel for grit and smell the fluid on the dipstick.

If the fluid appears:	It indicates:
Clear and red colored	Normal operation
Discolored (extremely dark red or brownish) or smells burned	Band or clutch pack failure, usually caused by an overheated transmission. Hauling very heavy loads with insufficient power or failure to change the fluid often result in overheating. Do not confuse this appearance with newer fluids that have a darker red color and a strong odor (though not a burned odor).
Foamy or aerated (light in color and full of bubbles)	1. The level is too high (gear train is churning oil) 2. An internal air leak (air is mixing with the fluid). Have the transmission checked professionally.
Solid residue in the fluid	Defective bands, clutch pack or bearings. Bits of band material or metal abrasives are clinging to the dipstick. Have the transmission checked professionally.
Varnish coating on the dipstick	The transmission fluid is overheating

TROUBLESHOOTING DRIVE AXLE PROBLEMS

First, determine when the noise is most noticeable.

Drive Noise: Produced under vehicle acceleration.

Coast Noise: Produced while coasting with a closed throttle.

Float Noise: Occurs while maintaining constant speed (just enough to keep speed constant) on a level road.

External Noise Elimination

It is advisable to make a thorough road test to determine whether the noise originates in the rear axle or whether it originates from the tires, engine, transmission, wheel bearings or road surface. Noise originating from other places cannot be corrected by servicing the rear axle.

ROAD NOISE

Brick or rough surfaced concrete roads produce noises that seem to come from the rear axle. Road noise is usually identical in Drive or Coast and driving on a different type of road will tell whether the road is the problem.

TIRE NOISE

Tire noise can be mistaken as rear axle noise, even though the tires on the front are at fault. Snow tread and mud tread tires or tires worn unevenly will frequently cause vibrations which seem to originate elsewhere; *temporarily, and for test purposes only,* inflate the tires to 40–50 lbs. This will significantly alter the noise produced by the tires, but will not alter noise from the rear axle. Noises from the rear axle will normally cease at speeds below 30 mph on coast, while tire noise will continue at lower tone as speed is decreased. The rear axle noise will usually change from drive conditions to coast conditions, while tire noise will not. Do not forget to lower the tire pressure to normal after the test is complete.

ENGINE/TRANSMISSION NOISE

Determine at what speed the noise is most pronounced, then stop in a quiet place. With the transmission in Neutral, run the engine through speeds corresponding to road speeds where the noise was noticed. Noises produced with the vehicle standing still are coming from the engine or transmission.

FRONT WHEEL BEARINGS

Front wheel bearing noises, sometimes confused with rear axle noises, will not change when comparing drive and coast conditions. While holding the speed steady, lightly apply the footbrake. This will often cause wheel bearing noise to lessen, as some of the weight is taken off the bearing. Front wheel bearings are easily checked by jacking up the wheels and spinning the wheels. Shaking the wheels will also determine if the wheel bearings are excessively loose.

REAR AXLE NOISES

Eliminating other possible sources can narrow the cause to the rear axle, which normally produces noise from worn gears or bearings. Gear noises tend to peak in a narrow speed range, while bearing noises will usually vary in pitch with engine speeds.

Noise Diagnosis

The Noise Is:	Most Probably Produced By:
1. Identical under Drive or Coast	Road surface, tires or front wheel bearings
2. Different depending on road surface	Road surface or tires
3. Lower as speed is lowered	Tires
4. Similar when standing or moving	Engine or transmission
5. A vibration	Unbalanced tires, rear wheel bearing, unbalanced driveshaft or worn U-joint
6. A knock or click about every two tire revolutions	Rear wheel bearing
7. Most pronounced on turns	Damaged differential gears
8. A steady low-pitched whirring or scraping, starting at low speeds	Damaged or worn pinion bearing
9. A chattering vibration on turns	Wrong differential lubricant or worn clutch plates (limited slip rear axle)
10. Noticed only in Drive, Coast or Float conditions	Worn ring gear and/or pinion gear

140 TROUBLESHOOTING

Troubleshooting Steering & Suspension Problems

Condition	Possible Cause
Hard steering (wheel is hard to turn)	1. Improper tire pressure 2. Loose or glazed pump drive belt 3. Low or incorrect fluid 4. Loose, bent or poorly lubricated front end parts 5. Improper front end alignment (excessive caster) 6. Bind in steering column or linkage 7. Kinked hydraulic hose 8. Air in hydraulic system 9. Low pump output or leaks in system 10. Obstruction in lines 11. Pump valves sticking or out of adjustment 12. Incorrect wheel alignment
Loose steering (too much play in steering wheel)	1. Loose wheel bearings 2. Faulty shocks 3. Worn linkage or suspension components 4. Loose steering gear mounting or linkage points 5. Steering mechanism worn or improperly adjusted 6. Valve spool improperly adjusted 7. Worn ball joints, tie-rod ends, etc.
Veers or wanders (pulls to one side with hands off steering wheel)	1. Improper tire pressure 2. Improper front end alignment 3. Dragging or improperly adjusted brakes 4. Bent frame 5. Improper rear end alignment 6. Faulty shocks or springs 7. Loose or bent front end components 8. Play in Pitman arm 9. Steering gear mountings loose 10. Loose wheel bearings 11. Binding Pitman arm 12. Spool valve sticking or improperly adjusted 13. Worn ball joints
Wheel oscillation or vibration transmitted through steering wheel	1. Low or uneven tire pressure 2. Loose wheel bearings 3. Improper front end alignment 4. Bent spindle 5. Worn, bent or broken front end components 6. Tires out of round or out of balance 7. Excessive lateral runout in disc brake rotor 8. Loose or bent shock absorber or strut
Noises (see also "Troubleshooting Drive Axle Problems")	1. Loose belts 2. Low fluid, air in system 3. Foreign matter in system 4. Improper lubrication 5. Interference or chafing in linkage 6. Steering gear mountings loose 7. Incorrect adjustment or wear in gear box 8. Faulty valves or wear in pump 9. Kinked hydraulic lines 10. Worn wheel bearings
Poor return of steering	1. Over-inflated tires 2. Improperly aligned front end (excessive caster) 3. Binding in steering column 4. No lubrication in front end 5. Steering gear adjusted too tight
Uneven tire wear (see "How To Read Tire Wear")	1. Incorrect tire pressure 2. Improperly aligned front end 3. Tires out-of-balance 4. Bent or worn suspension parts

TROUBLESHOOTING

HOW TO READ TIRE WEAR

The way your tires wear is a good indicator of other parts of the suspension. Abnormal wear patterns are often caused by the need for simple tire maintenance, or for front end alignment.

Excessive wear at the center of the tread indicates that the air pressure in the tire is consistently too high. The tire is riding on the center of the tread and wearing it prematurely. Occasionally, this wear pattern can result from outrageously wide tires on narrow rims. The cure for this is to replace either the tires or the wheels.

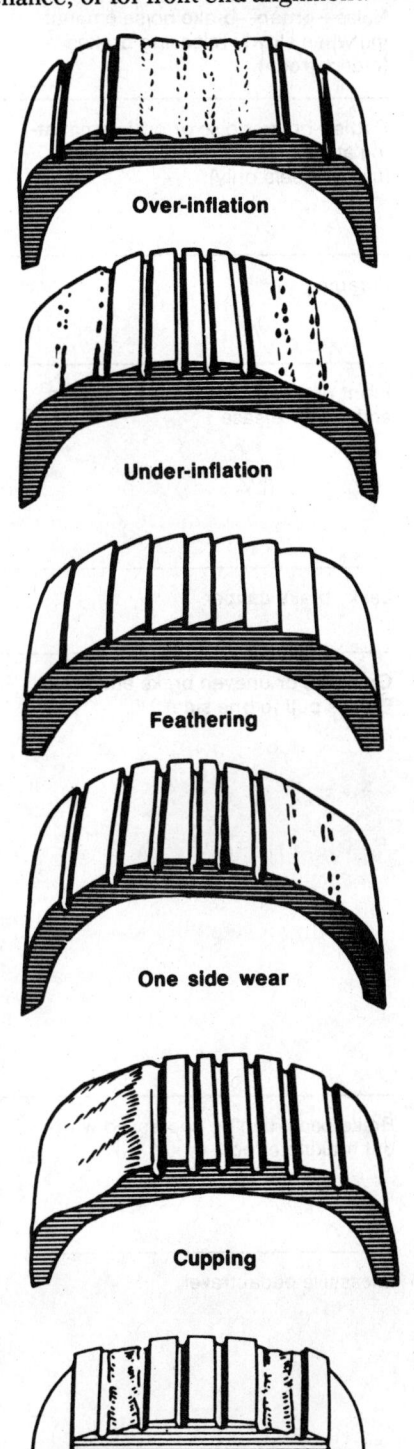

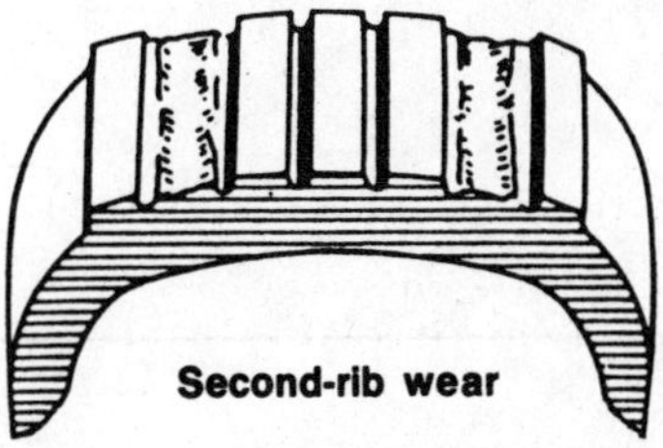

Over-inflation

This type of wear usually results from consistent under-inflation. When a tire is under-inflated, there is too much contact with the road by the outer treads, which wear prematurely. When this type of wear occurs, and the tire pressure is known to be consistently correct, a bent or worn steering component or the need for wheel alignment could be indicated.

Under-inflation

Feathering is a condition when the edge of each tread rib develops a slightly rounded edge on one side and a sharp edge on the other. By running your hand over the tire, you can usually feel the sharper edges before you'll be able to see them. The most common causes of feathering are incorrect toe-in setting or deteriorated bushings in the front suspension.

Feathering

When an inner or outer rib wears faster than the rest of the tire, the need for wheel alignment is indicated. There is excessive camber in the front suspension, causing the wheel to lean too much putting excessive load on one side of the tire. Misalignment could also be due to sagging springs, worn ball joints, or worn control arm bushings. Be sure the vehicle is loaded the way it's normally driven when you have the wheels aligned.

One side wear

Cups or scalloped dips appearing around the edge of the tread almost always indicate worn (sometimes bent) suspension parts. Adjustment of wheel alignment alone will seldom cure the problem. Any worn component that connects the wheel to the suspension can cause this type of wear. Occasionally, wheels that are out of balance will wear like this, but wheel imbalance usually shows up as bald spots between the outside edges and center of the tread.

Cupping

Second-rib wear is usually found only in radial tires, and appears where the steel belts end in relation to the tread. It can be kept to a minimum by paying careful attention to tire pressure and frequently rotating the tires. This is often considered normal wear but excessive amounts indicate that the tires are too wide for the wheels.

Second-rib wear

TROUBLESHOOTING

Troubleshooting Disc Brake Problems

Condition	Possible Cause
Noise—groan—brake noise emanating when slowly releasing brakes (creep-groan)	Not detrimental to function of disc brakes—no corrective action required. (This noise may be eliminated by slightly increasing or decreasing brake pedal efforts.)
Rattle—brake noise or rattle emanating at low speeds on rough roads, (front wheels only).	1. Shoe anti-rattle spring missing or not properly positioned. 2. Excessive clearance between shoe and caliper. 3. Soft or broken caliper seals. 4. Deformed or misaligned disc. 5. Loose caliper.
Scraping	1. Mounting bolts too long. 2. Loose wheel bearings. 3. Bent, loose, or misaligned splash shield.
Front brakes heat up during driving and fail to release	1. Operator riding brake pedal. 2. Stop light switch improperly adjusted. 3. Sticking pedal linkage. 4. Frozen or seized piston. 5. Residual pressure valve in master cylinder. 6. Power brake malfunction. 7. Proportioning valve malfunction.
Leaky brake caliper	1. Damaged or worn caliper piston seal. 2. Scores or corrosion on surface of cylinder bore.
Grabbing or uneven brake action—Brakes pull to one side	1. Causes listed under "Brakes Pull". 2. Power brake malfunction. 3. Low fluid level in master cylinder. 4. Air in hydraulic system. 5. Brake fluid, oil or grease on linings. 6. Unmatched linings. 7. Distorted brake pads. 8. Frozen or seized pistons. 9. Incorrect tire pressure. 10. Front end out of alignment. 11. Broken rear spring. 12. Brake caliper pistons sticking. 13. Restricted hose or line. 14. Caliper not in proper alignment to braking disc. 15. Stuck or malfunctioning metering valve. 16. Soft or broken caliper seals. 17. Loose caliper.
Brake pedal can be depressed without braking effect	1. Air in hydraulic system or improper bleeding procedure. 2. Leak past primary cup in master cylinder. 3. Leak in system. 4. Rear brakes out of adjustment. 5. Bleeder screw open.
Excessive pedal travel	1. Air, leak, or insufficient fluid in system or caliper. 2. Warped or excessively tapered shoe and lining assembly. 3. Excessive disc runout. 4. Rear brake adjustment required. 5. Loose wheel bearing adjustment. 6. Damaged caliper piston seal. 7. Improper brake fluid (boil). 8. Power brake malfunction. 9. Weak or soft hoses.

Troubleshooting Disc Brake Problems (cont.)

Condition	Possible Cause
Brake roughness or chatter (pedal pumping)	1. Excessive thickness variation of braking disc. 2. Excessive lateral runout of braking disc. 3. Rear brake drums out-of-round. 4. Excessive front bearing clearance.
Excessive pedal effort	1. Brake fluid, oil or grease on linings. 2. Incorrect lining. 3. Frozen or seized pistons. 4. Power brake malfunction. 5. Kinked or collapsed hose or line. 6. Stuck metering valve. 7. Scored caliper or master cylinder bore. 8. Seized caliper pistons.
Brake pedal fades (pedal travel increases with foot on brake)	1. Rough master cylinder or caliper bore. 2. Loose or broken hydraulic lines/connections. 3. Air in hydraulic system. 4. Fluid level low. 5. Weak or soft hoses. 6. Inferior quality brake shoes or fluid. 7. Worn master cylinder piston cups or seals.

Troubleshooting Drum Brakes

Condition	Possible Cause
Pedal goes to floor	1. Fluid low in reservoir. 2. Air in hydraulic system. 3. Improperly adjusted brake. 4. Leaking wheel cylinders. 5. Loose or broken brake lines. 6. Leaking or worn master cylinder. 7. Excessively worn brake lining.
Spongy brake pedal	1. Air in hydraulic system. 2. Improper brake fluid (low boiling point). 3. Excessively worn or cracked brake drums. 4. Broken pedal pivot bushing.
Brakes pulling	1. Contaminated lining. 2. Front end out of alignment. 3. Incorrect brake adjustment. 4. Unmatched brake lining. 5. Brake drums out of round. 6. Brake shoes distorted. 7. Restricted brake hose or line. 8. Broken rear spring. 9. Worn brake linings. 10. Uneven lining wear. 11. Glazed brake lining. 12. Excessive brake lining dust. 13. Heat spotted brake drums. 14. Weak brake return springs. 15. Faulty automatic adjusters. 16. Low or incorrect tire pressure.

144 TROUBLESHOOTING

Condition	Possible Cause
Squealing brakes	1. Glazed brake lining. 2. Saturated brake lining. 3. Weak or broken brake shoe retaining spring. 4. Broken or weak brake shoe return spring. 5. Incorrect brake lining. 6. Distorted brake shoes. 7. Bent support plate. 8. Dust in brakes or scored brake drums. 9. Linings worn below limit. 10. Uneven brake lining wear. 11. Heat spotted brake drums.
Chirping brakes	1. Out of round drum or eccentric axle flange pilot.
Dragging brakes	1. Incorrect wheel or parking brake adjustment. 2. Parking brakes engaged or improperly adjusted. 3. Weak or broken brake shoe return spring. 4. Brake pedal binding. 5. Master cylinder cup sticking. 6. Obstructed master cylinder relief port. 7. Saturated brake lining. 8. Bent or out of round brake drum. 9. Contaminated or improper brake fluid. 10. Sticking wheel cylinder pistons. 11. Driver riding brake pedal. 12. Defective proportioning valve. 13. Insufficient brake shoe lubricant.
Hard pedal	1. Brake booster inoperative. 2. Incorrect brake lining. 3. Restricted brake line or hose. 4. Frozen brake pedal linkage. 5. Stuck wheel cylinder. 6. Binding pedal linkage. 7. Faulty proportioning valve.
Wheel locks	1. Contaminated brake lining. 2. Loose or torn brake lining. 3. Wheel cylinder cups sticking. 4. Incorrect wheel bearing adjustment. 5. Faulty proportioning valve.
Brakes fade (high speed)	1. Incorrect lining. 2. Overheated brake drums. 3. Incorrect brake fluid (low boiling temperature). 4. Saturated brake lining. 5. Leak in hydraulic system. 6. Faulty automatic adjusters.
Pedal pulsates	1. Bent or out of round brake drum.
Brake chatter and shoe knock	1. Out of round brake drum. 2. Loose support plate. 3. Bent support plate. 4. Distorted brake shoes. 5. Machine grooves in contact face of brake drum (Shoe Knock). 6. Contaminated brake lining. 7. Missing or loose components. 8. Incorrect lining material. 9. Out-of-round brake drums. 10. Heat spotted or scored brake drums. 11. Out-of-balance wheels.

Troubleshooting Drum Brakes (cont.)

Condition	Possible Cause
Brakes do not self adjust	1. Adjuster screw frozen in thread. 2. Adjuster screw corroded at thrust washer. 3. Adjuster lever does not engage star wheel. 4. Adjuster installed on wrong wheel.
Brake light glows	1. Leak in the hydraulic system. 2. Air in the system. 3. Improperly adjusted master cylinder pushrod. 4. Uneven lining wear. 5. Failure to center combination valve or proportioning valve.

Mechanic's Data

General Conversion Table

Multiply By	To Convert	To	
LENGTH			
2.54	Inches	Centimeters	.3937
25.4	Inches	Millimeters	.03937
30.48	Feet	Centimeters	.0328
.304	Feet	Meters	3.28
.914	Yards	Meters	1.094
1.609	Miles	Kilometers	.621
VOLUME			
.473	Pints	Liters	2.11
.946	Quarts	Liters	1.06
3.785	Gallons	Liters	.264
.016	Cubic inches	Liters	61.02
16.39	Cubic inches	Cubic cms.	.061
28.3	Cubic feet	Liters	.0353
MASS (Weight)			
28.35	Ounces	Grams	.035
.4536	Pounds	Kilograms	2.20
—	To obtain	From	Multiply by

Multiply By	To Convert	To	
AREA			
.645	Square inches	Square cms.	.155
.836	Square yds.	Square meters	1.196
FORCE			
4.448	Pounds	Newtons	.225
.138	Ft./lbs.	Kilogram/meters	7.23
1.36	Ft./lbs.	Newton-meters	.737
.112	In./lbs.	Newton-meters	8.844
PRESSURE			
.068	Psi	Atmospheres	14.7
6.89	Psi	Kilopascals	.145
OTHER			
1.104	Horsepower (DIN)	Horsepower (SAE)	.9861
.746	Horsepower (SAE)	Kilowatts (KW)	1.34
1.60	Mph	Km/h	.625
.425	Mpg	Km/1	2.35
—	To obtain	From	Multiply by

Tap Drill Sizes

National Coarse or U.S.S.

Screw & Tap Size	Threads Per Inch	Use Drill Number
No. 5	40	39
No. 6	32	36
No. 8	32	29
No. 10	24	25
No. 12	24	17
1/4	20	8
5/16	18	F
3/8	16	5/16
7/16	14	U
1/2	13	27/64
9/16	12	31/64
5/8	11	17/32
3/4	10	21/32
7/8	9	49/64

National Coarse or U.S.S.

Screw & Tap Size	Threads Per Inch	Use Drill Number
1	8	7/8
1 1/8	7	63/64
1 1/4	7	1 7/64
1 1/2	6	1 11/32

National Fine or S.A.E.

Screw & Tap Size	Threads Per Inch	Use Drill Number
No. 5	44	37
No. 6	40	33
No. 8	36	29
No. 10	32	21

National Fine or S.A.E.

Screw & Tap Size	Threads Per Inch	Use Drill Number
No. 12	28	15
1/4	28	3
6/16	24	1
3/8	24	Q
7/16	20	W
1/2	20	29/64
9/16	18	33/64
5/8	18	37/64
3/4	16	11/16
7/8	14	13/16
1 1/8	12	1 3/64
1 1/4	12	1 11/64
1 1/2	12	1 27/64

MECHANIC'S DATA

Drill Sizes In Decimal Equivalents

Inch	Decimal	Wire	mm	Inch	Decimal	Wire	mm	Inch	Decimal	Wire & Letter	mm	Inch	Decimal	Letter	mm	Inch	Decimal	mm
1/64	.0156		.39		.0730	49			.1614		4.1		.2717		6.9		.4331	11.0
	.0157		.4		.0748		1.9		.1654		4.2		.2720	I		7/16	.4375	11.11
	.0160	78			.0760	48			.1660	19			.2756		7.0		.4528	11.5
	.0165		.42		.0768		1.95		.1673		4.25		.2770	J		29/64	.4531	11.51
	.0173		.44	5/64	.0781		1.98		.1693		4.3		.2795		7.1	15/32	.4688	11.90
	.0177		.45		.0785	47			.1695	18			.2810	K			.4724	12.0
	.0180	77			.0787		2.0	11/64	.1719		4.36	9/32	.2812		7.14	31/64	.4844	12.30
	.0181		.46		.0807		2.05		.1730	17			.2835		7.2		.4921	12.5
	.0189		.48		.0810	46			.1732		4.4		.2854		7.25	1/2	.5000	12.70
	.0197		.5		.0820	45			.1770	16			.2874		7.3		.5118	13.0
	.0200	76			.0827		2.1		.1772		4.5		.2900	L		33/64	.5156	13.09
	.0210	75			.0846		2.15		.1800	15			.2913		7.4	17/32	.5312	13.49
	.0217		.55		.0860	44			.1811		4.6		.2950	M			.5315	13.5
	.0225	74			.0866		2.2		.1820	14			.2953		7.5	35/64	.5469	13.89
	.0236		.6		.0886		2.25		.1850	13			.2969		7.54		.5512	14.0
	.0240	73			.0890	43			.1850		4.7	19/64	.2992		7.6	9/16	.5625	14.28
	.0250	72			.0906		2.3		.1870		4.75		.3020	N			.5709	14.5
	.0256		.65		.0925		2.35	3/16	.1875		4.76		.3031		7.7	37/64	.5781	14.68
	.0260	71			.0935	42			.1890		4.8		.3051		7.75		.5906	15.0
	.0276		.7	3/32	.0938		2.38		.1890	12			.3071		7.8	19/32	.5938	15.08
	.0280	70			.0945		2.4		.1910	11			.3110		7.9	39/64	.6094	15.47
	.0292	69			.0960	41			.1929		4.9		.3125		7.93		.6102	15.5
	.0295		.75		.0965		2.45		.1935	10		5/16	.3150		8.0	5/8	.6250	15.87
	.0310	68			.0980	40			.1960	9			.3160	O			.6299	16.0
1/32	.0312		.79		.0981		2.5		.1969		5.0		.3189		8.1	41/64	.6406	16.27
	.0315		.8		.0995	39			.1990	8			.3228		8.2		.6496	16.5
	.0320	67			.1015	38			.2008		5.1		.3230	P		21/32	.6562	16.66
	.0330	66			.1024		2.6		.2010	7			.3248		8.25		.6693	17.0
	.0335		.85		.1040	37		13/64	.2031		5.16		.3268		8.3	43/64	.6719	17.06
	.0350	65			.1063		2.7		.2040	6		21/64	.3281		8.33	11/16	.6875	17.46
	.0354		.9		.1065	36			.2047		5.2		.3307		8.4		.6890	17.5
	.0360	64			.1083		2.75		.2055	5			.3320	Q		45/64	.7031	17.85
	.0370	63		7/64	.1094		2.77		.2067		5.25		.3346		8.5		.7087	18.0
	.0374		.95		.1100	35			.2087		5.3		.3386		8.6	23/32	.7188	18.25
	.0380	62			.1102		2.8		.2090	4			.3390	R			.7283	18.5
	.0390	61			.1110	34			.2126		5.4		.3425		8.7	47/64	.7344	18.65
	.0394		1.0		.1130	33			.2130	3		11/32	.3438		8.73		.7480	19.0
	.0400	60			.1142		2.9		.2165		5.5		.3445		8.75	3/4	.7500	19.05
	.0410	59			.1160	32		7/32	.2188		5.55		.3465		8.8	49/64	.7656	19.44
	.0413		1.05		.1181		3.0		.2205		5.6		.3480	S			.7677	19.5
	.0420	58			.1200	31			.2210	2			.3504		8.9	25/32	.7812	19.84
	.0430	57			.1220		3.1		.2244		5.7		.3543		9.0		.7874	20.0
	.0433		1.1	1/8	.1250		3.17		.2264		5.75		.3580	T		51/64	.7969	20.24
	.0453		1.15		.1260		3.2		.2280	1			.3583		9.1		.8071	20.5
	.0465	56			.1280		3.25		.2283		5.8	23/64	.3594		9.12	13/16	.8125	20.63
3/64	.0469		1.19		.1285	30			.2323		5.9		.3622		9.2		.8268	21.0
	.0472		1.2		.1299		3.3		.2340	A			.3642		9.25	53/64	.8281	21.03
	.0492		1.25		.1339		3.4	15/64	.2344		5.95		.3661		9.3	27/32	.8438	21.43
	.0512		1.3		.1360	29			.2362		6.0		.3680	U			.8465	21.5
	.0520	55			.1378		3.5		.2380	B			.3701		9.4	55/64	.8594	21.82
	.0531		1.35		.1405	28			.2402		6.1		.3740		9.5		.8661	22.0
	.0550	54		9/64	.1406		3.57		.2420	C		3/8	.3750		9.52	7/8	.8750	22.22
	.0551		1.4		.1417		3.6		.2441		6.2		.3770	V			.8858	22.5
	.0571		1.45		.1440	27			.2460	D			.3780		9.6	57/64	.8906	22.62
	.0591		1.5		.1457		3.7		.2461		6.25		.3819		9.7		.9055	23.0
	.0595	53			.1470	26			.2480		6.3		.3839		9.75	29/32	.9062	23.01
	.0610		1.55		.1476		3.75	1/4	.2500	E	6.35		.3858		9.8	59/64	.9219	23.41
1/16	.0625		1.59		.1495	25			.2520		6.		.3860	W			.9252	23.5
	.0630		1.6		.1496		3.8		.2559		6.5		.3898		9.9	15/16	.9375	23.81
	.0635	52			.1520	24			.2570	F		25/64	.3906		9.92		.9449	24.0
	.0650		1.65		.1535		3.9		.2598		6.6		.3937		10.0	61/64	.9531	24.2
	.0669		1.7		.1540	23			.2610	G			.3970	X			.9646	24.5
	.0670	51		5/32	.1562		3.96		.2638		6.7		.4040	Y		31/64	.9688	24.6
	.0689		1.75		.1570	22		17/64	.2656		6.74	13/32	.4062		10.31		.9843	25.0
	.0700	50			.1575		4.0		.2657		6.75		.4130	Z		63/64	.9844	25.0
	.0709		1.8		.1590	21			.2660	H			.4134		10.5	1	1.0000	25.4
	.0728		1.85		.1610	20			.2677		6.8	27/64	.4219		10.71			

Index

A

Air cleaner, 6
Air conditioning
   Sight glass inspection, 11
Alternator, 32
Automatic transmission
   Adjustment, 89
   Filter change, 18, 88
   Removal and installation, 91

B

Ball joints, 92
Battery
   Jump starting, 19
   Maintenance, 14, 33
Belt tension adjustment, 8
Brakes
   Bleeding, 102, 103
   Caliper, 104
   Fluid level, 13
   Fluid recommendations, 13
   Front brakes, 104
   Master cylinder, 101
   Parking brake, 110
   Power booster, 103
   Rear brakes, 107

C

Camber, 95
Camshaft and bearings, 51
Capacities, 15
Carburetor
   Adjustment, 31, 68-69
   Overhaul, 69
   Replacement, 67
Catalytic converter, 61
Chassis lubrication, 18
Clutch
   Adjustment, 87
   Replacement, 87
Compression, 40
Connecting rod and bearings, 52
Control arm, 94
Cooling system, 13
Crankcase ventilation (PCV), 7
Crankshaft, 56
Cylinder head
   Removal and installation, 41
   Torque sequence, 42

D

Differential
   Fluid change, 18
Distributor
   Removal and installation, 32

E

Electrical
   Chassis, 76
   Engine, 32
Electronic ignition, 26
Emission controls, 61
Engine
   Camshaft, 51
   Cylinder head torque sequence, 42
   Design, 34
   Exhaust maniforld, 45
   Identification, 3
   Intake manifold, 45
   Oil recommendations, 11
   Pistons and rings, 52
   Rebuilding, 37
   Removal and installation, 35
   Rocker arm (or shaft), 45
   Specifications, 34
   Timing belt, chain (or gears), 46-47, 48
   Tune-up, 24
   Valves, 43
Evaporative canister, 7
Exhaust manifold, 45
Exhaust system, 60

F

Fan belt adjustment, 8
Firing order, 32
Fluid level checks
   Battery, 14
   Coolant, 13
   Engine oil, 11
   Master cylinder, 13
   Power steering pump, 14
   Steering gear, 14
   Transmission, 12, 13
Fluid recommendations, 11
Front suspension
   Ball joints, 92
   Lower control arm, 94
   Wheel alignment, 95
Front wheel bearing, 18
Fuel injection, 71
Fuel filter, 15
Fuel pump, 66
Fuel system, 66
Fuel tank, 75
Fusible links, 82

G

Gearshift linkage adjustment
   Automatic, 89
   Manual, 86

H

Halfshaft, 83
Hand brake, 110
Headlights, 82
Heater, 76
Hoses, 10

… INDEX 149

I

Identification
  Vehicle, 3
  Engine, 3
  Transmission, 3
Idle speed and mixture, 31
Ignition switch, 98
Instrument cluster, 81
Intake manifold, 45

J

Jacking points, 20
Jump starting, 19

L

Lower control arm, 94
Lubrication
  Chassis, 18
  Differential, 18
  Engine, 17
  Transmission, 18

M

Manifolds
  Intake, 45
  Exhaust, 45
Manual transmission, 83
Master cylinder, 101
Model identification, 3

N

Neutral safety switch, 89

O

Oil and fuel recommendations, 16
Oil change, 17
Oil filter (engine), 17
Oil pan, 58
Oil pump, 58

P

Parking brake, 110
Pistons and rings, 52
PCV valve, 7
Power brakes, 103
Power steering pump, 14

R

Radiator, 59
Radio, 79
Rear axle, 96
Rear suspension, 95
Regulator, 33
Rear main oil seal, 58
Rings, 53
Routine maintenance, 6

S

Safety notice, ii
Serial number location, 3
Shock absorbers, 95
Spark plugs, 24
Specifications
  Brakes, 111
  Capacities, 15
  Carburetor, 72
  Crankshaft and connecting rod, 35
  General engine, 34
  Piston and ring, 34, 36
  Torque, 36
  Tune-up, 27
  Valve, 35
  Wheel alignment, 95
Speedometer cable, 82
Springs
  Front, 92
  Rear, 95
Starter, 33
Steering wheel, 98
Stripped threads, 38
Struts, 92

T

Thermostat, 60
Tie-rod, 99
Timing (ignition), 26
Tires, 14
Tools, 1
Towing, 18
Transmission
  Automatic, 88
  Manual, 83
  Fluid change, 17, 18
Troubleshooting, 112
Tune-up
  Procedures, 24
  Specifications, 27
Turbocharger, 45
Turn signal switch, 98

V

Valves
  Adjustment, 29
  Service, 43
  Specifications, 35
Vehicle identification, 3

W

Water pump, 59
Wheel alignment, 95
Wheel bearings, 18, 111
Wheel cylinders, 109
Windshield wipers
  Arm, 80
  Linkage, 80
  Motor, 79

Chilton's Repair & Tune-Up Guides

The Complete line covers domestic cars, imports, trucks, vans, RV's and 4-wheel drive vehicles.

RTUG Title	Part No.
AMC 1975-82	7199
Covers all U.S. and Canadian models	
Aspen/Volare 1976-80	6637
Covers all U.S. and Canadian models	
Audi 1970-73	5902
Covers all U.S. and Canadian models.	
Audi 4000/5000 1978-81	7028
Covers all U.S. and Canadian models including turbocharged and diesel engines	
Barracuda/Challenger 1965-72	5807
Covers all U.S. and Canadian models	
Blazer/Jimmy 1969-82	6931
Covers all U.S. and Canadian 2- and 4-wheel drive models, including diesel engines	
BMW 1970-82	6844
Covers U.S. and Canadian models	
Buick/Olds/Pontiac 1975-85	7308
Covers U.S. and Canadian full size rear wheel drive models	
Cadillac 1967-84	7462
Covers all U.S. and Canadian rear wheel drive models	
Camaro 1967-81	6735
Covers all U.S. and Canadian models	
Camaro 1982-85	7317
Covers all U.S. and Canadian models	
Capri 1970-77	6695
Covers all U.S. and Canadian models	
Caravan/Voyager 1984-85	7482
Covers all U.S. and Canadian models	
Century/Regal 1975-85	7307
Covers all U.S. and Canadian rear wheel drive models, including turbocharged engines	
Champ/Arrow/Sapporo 1978-83	7041
Covers all U.S. and Canadian models	
Chevette/1000 1976-86	6836
Covers all U.S. and Canadian models	
Chevrolet 1968-85	7135
Covers all U.S. and Canadian models	
Chevrolet 1968-79 Spanish	7082
Chevrolet/GMC Pick-Ups 1970-82 Spanish	7468
Chevrolet/GMC Pick-Ups and Suburban 1970-86	6936
Covers all U.S. and Canadian $1/2$, $3/4$ and 1 ton models, including 4-wheel drive and diesel engines	
Chevrolet LUV 1972-81	6815
Covers all U.S. and Canadian models	
Chevrolet Mid-Size 1964-86	6840
Covers all U.S. and Canadian models of 1964-77 Chevelle, Malibu & Malibu SS; 1974-77 Laguna; 1978-85 Malibu; 1970-86 Monte Carlo; 1964-84 El Camino, including diesel engines	
Chevrolet Nova 1986	7658
Covers all U.S. and Canadian models	
Chevy/GMC Vans 1967-84	6930
Covers all U.S. and Canadian models of $1/2$, $3/4$, and 1 ton vans, cutaways, and motor home chassis, including diesel engines	
Chevy S-10 Blazer/GMC S-15 Jimmy 1982-85	7383
Covers all U.S. and Canadian models	
Chevy S-10/GMC S-15 Pick-Ups 1982-85	7310
Covers all U.S. and Canadian models	
Chevy II/Nova 1962-79	6841
Covers all U.S. and Canadian models	
Chrysler K- and E-Car 1981-85	7163
Covers all U.S. and Canadian front wheel drive models	
Colt/Challenger/Vista/Conquest 1971-85	7037
Covers all U.S. and Canadian models	
Corolla/Carina/Tercel/Starlet 1970-85	7036
Covers all U.S. and Canadian models	
Corona/Cressida/Crown/Mk.II/Camry/Van 1970-84	7044
Covers all U.S. and Canadian models	

RTUG Title	Part No.
Corvair 1960-69	6691
Covers all U.S. and Canadian models	
Corvette 1953-62	6576
Covers all U.S. and Canadian models	
Corvette 1963-84	6843
Covers all U.S. and Canadian models	
Cutlass 1970-85	6933
Covers all U.S. and Canadian models	
Dart/Demon 1968-76	6324
Covers all U.S. and Canadian models	
Datsun 1961-72	5790
Covers all U.S. and Canadian models of Nissan Patrol; 1500, 1600 and 2000 sports cars; Pick-Ups; 410, 411, 510, 1200 and 240Z	
Datsun 1973-80 Spanish	7083
Datsun/Nissan F-10, 310, Stanza, Pulsar 1977-86	7196
Covers all U.S. and Canadian models	
Datsun/Nissan Pick-Ups 1970-84	6816
Covers all U.S and Canadian models	
Datsun/Nissan Z & ZX 1970-86	6932
Covers all U.S. and Canadian models	
Datsun/Nissan 1200, 210, Sentra 1973-86	7197
Covers all U.S. and Canadian models	
Datsun/Nissan 200SX, 510, 610, 710, 810, Maxima 1973-84	7170
Covers all U.S. and Canadian models	
Dodge 1968-77	6554
Covers all U.S. and Canadian models	
Dodge Charger 1967-70	6486
Covers all U.S. and Canadian models	
Dodge/Plymouth Trucks 1967-84	7459
Covers all $1/2$, $3/4$, and 1 ton 2- and 4-wheel drive U.S. and Canadian models, including diesel engines	
Dodge/Plymouth Vans 1967-84	6934
Covers all $1/2$, $3/4$, and 1 ton U.S. and Canadian models of vans, cutaways and motor home chassis	
D-50/Arrow Pick-Up 1979-81	7032
Covers all U.S. and Canadian models	
Fairlane/Torino 1962-75	6320
Covers all U.S. and Canadian models	
Fairmont/Zephyr 1978-83	6965
Covers all U.S. and Canadian models	
Fiat 1969-81	7042
Covers all U.S. and Canadian models	
Fiesta 1978-80	6846
Covers all U.S. and Canadian models	
Firebird 1967-81	5996
Covers all U.S. and Canadian models	
Firebird 1982-85	7345
Covers all U.S. and Canadian models	
Ford 1968-79 Spanish	7084
Ford Bronco 1966-83	7140
Covers all U.S. and Canadian models	
Ford Bronco II 1984	7408
Covers all U.S. and Canadian models	
Ford Courier 1972-82	6983
Covers all U.S. and Canadian models	
Ford/Mercury Front Wheel Drive 1981-85	7055
Covers all U.S. and Canadian models Escort, EXP, Tempo, Lynx, LN-7 and Topaz	
Ford/Mercury/Lincoln 1968-85	6842
Covers all U.S. and Canadian models of FORD Country Sedan, Country Squire, Crown Victoria, Custom, Custom 500, Galaxie 500, LTD through 1982, Ranch Wagon, and XL; MERCURY Colony Park, Commuter, Marquis through 1982, Gran Marquis, Monterey and Park Lane; LINCOLN Continental and Towne Car	
Ford/Mercury/Lincoln Mid-Size 1971-85	6696
Covers all U.S. and Canadian models of FORD Elite, 1983-85 LTD, 1977-79 LTD II, Ranchero, Torino, Gran Torino, 1977-85 Thunderbird; MERCURY 1972-85 Cougar,	

continued on next page

RTUG Title	Part No.
1983-85 Marquis, Montego, 1980-85 XR-7; LINCOLN 1982-85 Continental, 1984-85 Mark VII, 1978-80 Versailles	
Ford Pick-Ups 1965-86	6913
Covers all 1/2, 3/4 and 1 ton, 2- and 4-wheel drive U.S. and Canadian pick-up, chassis cab and camper models, including diesel engines	
Ford Pick-Ups 1965-82 Spanish	7469
Ford Ranger 1983-84	7338
Covers all U.S. and Canadian models	
Ford Vans 1961-86	6849
Covers all U.S. and Canadian 1/2, 3/4 and 1 ton van and cutaway chassis models, including diesel engines	
GM A-Body 1982-85	7309
Covers all front wheel drive U.S. and Canadian models of BUICK Century, CHEVROLET Celebrity, OLDSMOBILE Cutlass Ciera and PONTIAC 6000	
GM C-Body 1985	7587
Covers all front wheel drive U.S. and Canadian models of BUICK Electra Park Avenue and Electra T-Type, CADILLAC Fleetwood and deVille, OLDSMOBILE 98 Regency and Regency Brougham	
GM J-Car 1982-85	7059
Covers all U.S. and Canadian models of BUICK Skyhawk, CHEVROLET Cavalier, CADILLAC Cimarron, OLDSMOBILE Firenza and PONTIAC 2000 and Sunbird	
GM N-Body 1985-86	7657
Covers all U.S. and Canadian models of front wheel drive BUICK Somerset and Skylark, OLDSMOBILE Calais, and PONTIAC Grand Am	
GM X-Body 1980-85	7049
Covers all U.S. and Canadian models of BUICK Skylark, CHEVROLET Citation, OLDSMOBILE Omega and PONTIAC Phoenix	
GM Subcompact 1971-80	6935
Covers all U.S. and Canadian models of BUICK Skyhawk (1975-80), CHEVROLET Vega and Monza, OLDSMOBILE Starfire, and PONTIAC Astre and 1975-80 Sunbird	
Granada/Monarch 1975-82	6937
Covers all U.S. and Canadian models	
Honda 1973-84	6980
Covers all U.S. and Canadian models	
International Scout 1967-73	5912
Covers all U.S. and Canadian models	
Jeep 1945-87	6817
Covers all U.S. and Canadian CJ-2A, CJ-3A, CJ-3B, CJ-5, CJ-6, CJ-7, Scrambler and Wrangler models	
Jeep Wagoneer, Commando, Cherokee, Truck 1957-86	6739
Covers all U.S. and Canadian models of Wagoneer, Cherokee, Grand Wagoneer, Jeepster, Jeepster Commando, J-100, J-200, J-300, J-10, J20, FC-150 and FC-170	
Laser/Daytona 1984-85	7563
Covers all U.S. and Canadian models	
Maverick/Comet 1970-77	6634
Covers all U.S. and Canadian models	
Mazda 1971-84	6981
Covers all U.S. and Canadian models of RX-2, RX-3, RX-4, 808, 1300, 1600, Cosmo, GLC and 626	
Mazda Pick-Ups 1972-86	7659
Covers all U.S. and Canadian models	
Mercedes-Benz 1959-70	6065
Covers all U.S. and Canadian models	
Mereceds-Benz 1968-73	5907
Covers all U.S. and Canadian models	

RTUG Title	Part No.
Mercedes-Benz 1974-84	6809
Covers all U.S. and Canadian models	
Mitsubishi, Cordia, Tredia, Starion, Galant 1983-85	7583
Covers all U.S. and Canadian models	
MG 1961-81	6780
Covers all U.S. and Canadian models	
Mustang/Capri/Merkur 1979-85	6963
Covers all U.S. and Canadian models	
Mustang/Cougar 1965-73	6542
Covers all U.S. and Canadian models	
Mustang II 1974-78	6812
Covers all U.S. and Canadian models	
Omni/Horizon/Rampage 1978-84	6845
Covers all U.S. and Canadian models of DODGE omni, Miser, 024, Charger 2.2; PLYMOUTH Horizon, Miser, TC3, TC3 Tourismo; Rampage	
Opel 1971-75	6575
Covers all U.S. and Canadian models	
Peugeot 1970-74	5982
Covers all U.S. and Canadian models	
Pinto/Bobcat 1971-80	7027
Covers all U.S. and Canadian models	
Plymouth 1968-76	6552
Covers all U.S. and Canadian models	
Pontiac Fiero 1984-85	7571
Covers all U.S. and Canadian models	
Pontiac Mid-Size 1974-83	7346
Covers all U.S. and Canadian models of Ventura, Grand Am, LeMans, Grand LeMans, GTO, Phoenix, and Grand Prix	
Porsche 924/928 1976-81	7048
Covers all U.S. and Canadian models	
Renault 1975-85	7165
Covers all U.S. and Canadian models	
Roadrunner/Satellite/Belvedere/GTX 1968-73	5821
Covers all U.S. and Canadian models	
RX-7 1979-81	7031
Covers all U.S. and Canadian models	
SAAB 99 1969-75	5988
Covers all U.S. and Canadian models	
SAAB 900 1979-85	7572
Covers all U.S. and Canadian models	
Snowmobiles 1976-80	6978
Covers Arctic Cat, John Deere, Kawasaki, Polaris, Ski-Doo and Yamaha	
Subaru 1970-84	6982
Covers all U.S. and Canadian models	
Tempest/GTO/LeMans 1968-73	5905
Covers all U.S. and Canadian models	
Toyota 1966-70	5795
Covers all U.S. and Canadian models of Corona, MkII, Corolla, Crown, Land Cruiser, Stout and Hi-Lux	
Toyota 1970-79 Spanish	7467
Toyota Celica/Supra 1971-85	7043
Covers all U.S. and Canadian models	
Toyota Trucks 1970-85	7035
Covers all U.S. and Canadian models of pick-ups, Land Cruiser and 4Runner	
Valiant/Duster 1968-76	6326
Covers all U.S. and Canadian models	
Volvo 1956-69	6529
Covers all U.S. and Canadian models	
Volvo 1970-83	7040
Covers all U.S. and Canadian models	
VW Front Wheel Drive 1974-85	6962
Covers all U.S. and Canadian models	
VW 1949-71	5796
Covers all U.S. and Canadian models	
VW 1970-79 Spanish	7081
VW 1970-81	6837
Covers all U.S. and Canadian Beetles, Karmann Ghia, Fastback, Squareback, Vans, 411 and 412	

Chilton's Repair & Tune-Up Guides are available at your local retailer or by mailing a check or money order for **$13.50** plus **$2.50** to cover postage and handling to:

Chilton Book Company
Dept. DM
Radnor, PA 19089

NOTE: When ordering be sure to include your name & address, book part No. & title.